MEN  MONEY & POLICY

essays
in honor of
KARL R. BOPP

EDITED BY DAVID P. EASTBURN

FEDERAL RESERVE BANK OF PHILADELPHIA

TABLE OF CONTENTS

PAGE

FOREWORD 1

ABOUT KARL R. BOPP

 Joseph A. Livingston 6

 Thomas B. McCabe 14

 Alfred H. Williams 15

 Robert N. Hilkert 17

 David P. Eastburn 27

INTRODUCTION

 William McC. Martin, Jr. 35

IMPACTS OF THEORY ON POLICY:
THE EARLY YEARS OF THE FEDERAL RESERVE

 Lester V. Chandler 41

SOME CHANGES IN IDEAS ON CENTRAL BANKING

 Elmer Wood 55

POLICY NORMS AND CENTRAL BANKING

 Allan Sproul 67

REAPPRAISING THE FEDERAL RESERVE
DISCOUNT MECHANISM

 Robert C. Holland 79

THE 1966 CREDIT CRUNCH

 Alfred Hayes 91

NEW STANDARDS FOR CREDIT AND MONETARY POLICY

 George W. Mitchell 105

BANK COMPETITION AND MONETARY POLICY

 Guy E. Noyes 117

COMMERCIAL BANKING AND THE FEDERAL RESERVE:
A RECORD OF MISUNDERSTANDING

 Willis W. Alexander 125

TABLE OF CONTENTS—Continued

PAGE

NEW TOOLS OF MONETARY CONTROL ABROAD
George Garvy 131

MAKING PEACE WITH GOLD
Ralph A. Young 151

CAPITAL MOVEMENTS AND BALANCE-OF-PAYMENTS
ADJUSTMENT
Robert V. Roosa 171

CURRENCY CRISES: THE RECORD AND THE REMEDY
Frederick L. Deming 195

ECONOMISTS AND PUBLIC POLICY
Charls E. Walker 213

CENTRAL BANK LEADERS AND CENTRAL
BANK CREDIBILITY
C. R. Whittlesey 219

CENTRAL BANKERS: THEIR ATTRIBUTES
AND DEVELOPMENT
C. Canby Balderston 233

THE ROLE OF THE DIRECTOR:
THE IDEAL AND THE REAL
Willis J. Winn 241

THE FEDERAL RESERVE AS A LIVING INSTITUTION:
A PRESCRIPTION FOR THE FUTURE
David P. Eastburn 253

FOREWORD

HAVING HEARD from time to time of the tribulations of editors of books of essays, I launched this enterprise early in 1969 with full expectation of many delays and complications—especially given the fact that the authors of the essays are busy and important men. That the expectation was not realized is testimony to the respect and affection all of us have for Karl Bopp. This volume is clearly a labor of love.

The contributors were selected because of their close association with Karl in various stages of his career, principally as teaching or Federal Reserve colleagues, and/or as students. A complete biography of the authors would be much too voluminous to include here. But at the risk of omitting important chunks of many illustrious careers, I have listed below the primary relationships between the contributors and Karl Bopp.

Joseph A. Livingston—Economic Columnist, *Philadelphia Evening Bulletin,* and syndicated columnist.

Thomas B. McCabe—Member, 1937-1948, Deputy Chairman, 1938, Chairman, 1939-1948, Board of Directors of Federal Reserve Bank of Philadelphia; Chairman, Board of Governors of the Federal Reserve System, 1948-1951.

Alfred H. Williams—President, Federal Reserve Bank of Philadelphia, 1941-1958.

Robert N. Hilkert—Staff, 1942-1958, First Vice President, 1958-1970, Federal Reserve Bank of Philadelphia.

David P. Eastburn—Student of Karl R. Bopp, University of Pennsylvania; Staff, 1942-1970, President, 1970—, Federal Reserve Bank of Philadelphia.

William McC. Martin—Chairman, Board of Governors of the Federal Reserve System, 1951-1970.

Lester V. Chandler—Student with Karl R. Bopp, University of Missouri; Professor, Princeton University, 1950-1969; Member, 1954-1959, Deputy Chairman, 1958-1959, Board of Directors of Federal Reserve Bank of Philadelphia.

Elmer Wood—Professor, 1930-1962, Professor Emeritus, 1962—, University of Missouri.

Allan Sproul—President, Federal Reserve Bank of New York, 1941-1956.

George W. Mitchell—Staff, Federal Reserve Bank of Chicago, 1944-1948, 1951-1961; Member, Board of Governors of the Federal Reserve System, 1961—.

Alfred Hayes—President, Federal Reserve Bank of New York, 1956—.

Robert C. Holland—Student of Karl R. Bopp, University of Pennsylvania; Staff, Federal Reserve Bank of Chicago, 1949-1961; Staff, Board of Governors of the Federal Reserve System, 1961—.

Guy E. Noyes—Student of Karl R. Bopp, University of Missouri; Staff, Board of Governors of the Federal Reserve System, 1948-1965.

Willis W. Alexander—Student of Karl R. Bopp, University of Missouri; President, 1968-1969, Executive Vice President, 1969—, The American Bankers Association.

George Garvy—Staff, Federal Reserve Bank of New York, 1943—.

Ralph A. Young—Staff, Board of Governors of the Federal Reserve System, 1946-1967.

Robert V. Roosa—Staff, Federal Reserve Bank of New York, 1946-1960; Under Secretary of the Treasury for Monetary Affairs, 1961-1964.

Frederick L. Deming—Staff, 1941-1953, First Vice President, 1953-1957, Federal Reserve Bank of St. Louis; President, Federal Reserve Bank of Minneapolis, 1957-1965; Under Secretary of the Treasury for Monetary Affairs, 1965-1969.

Charls E. Walker—Student of Karl R. Bopp, University of Pennsylvania; Staff, Federal Reserve Bank of Philadelphia, 1953; Staff, Federal Reserve Bank of Dallas, 1954-1961; Assistant to Secretary of the Treasury, 1959-1961; Executive Vice President, The American Bankers Association, 1961-1969; Under Secretary of the Treasury, 1969—.

Charles R. Whittlesey—Professor, 1940-1967, Professor Emeritus, 1967—, University of Pennsylvania.

C. Canby Balderston—Member, 1942-1953, Deputy Chairman, 1949-1953, Board of Directors of Federal Reserve Bank of Philadelphia; Member, 1954-1966, Vice Chairman, 1955-1966, Board of Governors of the Federal Reserve System.

Willis J. Winn—Member, 1962——, Deputy Chairman, 1965-1966, Chairman, 1966——, Board of Directors of Federal Reserve Bank of Philadelphia.

I am greatly indebted to the contributors for their cooperation and consideration.

Thanks are due also to many others for help in various respects, especially to Robert N. Hilkert, Lester V. Chandler, and George W. Mitchell for assistance in planning the volume; Charles J. Mustoe and Dorothy Bowen for considerable editorial help; and James A. Crawford for being a patient and understanding printer.

D.P.E.

February, 1970

ABOUT KARL R. BOPP

"Let the Proceedings Begin," commanded the Red Queen. "Knave, read!"

The Knave of Hearts faced the assemblage, unrolled a scroll and read:

"For his 29 years of diligence, devotion, and distinction in the Federal Reserve System, for his dedication to research, teaching, and learning, for his commitment to excellence and originality, for the freedom he granted to others, for his integrity and modesty, and for never wearing his Phi Beta Kappa key in public . . . ."

"Stop, Knave, stop," intervened the Lord High Privy Councilor. "This is a fiction of a demented imagination, a hoax on the Queen, a weird jest: Who can measure to such qualifications?"

Alice jumped to her feet. "If it please your majesty, the Lord Councilor has the object where the subject should be. In this case the qualifications fit the man, not the man the qualifications."

The Red Queen paid heed neither to Alice nor the Lord Councilor. She declared: "This is a courtroom, not a commencement, a hearing, not a ceremony. I came to listen to a petition, not a citation. Proceed!"

"The petitioner should be permitted to speak for himself," answered Alice.

"Can he do that?" demanded the March Hare. "His dossier says he's a constant husband, married to the same wife—Ruth—for 38 years. How can he speak for himself?"

"As his counsel in this proceeding," responded Alice, "I assure you he does. He believes in the freedom of speech, the division of labor, the law of diminishing returns, the marginal utility of excess verbiage, and, as a modern economist, he's familiar with the Phillips curve."

"What's that?" the Carpenter asked hopefully, putting aside his copy of Playboy.

"What's what?" replied Alice.

"The Phillips curve," answered the Carpenter.

"Not what you're thinking of," said the Privy

Councilor. "It's a statistical model for unemployment, not in the least related to a Powers model."

"But let me go on," pleaded Alice. "Early in his married life, the petitioner made his choice: To live tolerantly in preference to Ruthlessly."

The Red Queen shuffled some papers, whispered to the White Queen who sat next to her, and said: "Where is this petitioner?"

The Knave of Hearts brought in a man of medium height, gray-white hair, and erect mien.

"Your last name, please," said the Red Queen. "Spell it for the record."

"B O P P."

"Pronounce it," said the Queen.

"Bopp to rhyme with pope."

"Very interesting," said the Walrus. "Can you think of a few more rhymes?"

"Mope, rope, lope."

"Excellent, excellent," said the Red Queen, who was catching on to the Walrus's purpose. "How about some more rhymes?"

The petitioner, without hesitating, answered: "Of course, if it please your royal highness—slope, nope, cope."

"Fine," said the Walrus. "Can you continue?"

"If it please the Queen."

The Queen nodded.

"Well, then, there's grope and . . ."

Alice was on her feet again. "Don't you think, your majesty, that gives the idea. It's Bopp to rhyme with soap and hope, not sop and hop."

The Red Queen yielded, and said: "Does he have given names?"

"Karl Richard," the petitioner replied.

"And what is your petition?" the Red Queen asked.

"I plan to retire. I would like your permission."

"What do you intend to do in retirement?"

"Nothing."

"I shouldn't think that would take planning," interjected the Mad Hatter.

"Oh, but it does," interceded Alice. "It's easy to do what you have to do. You have to plan to do what you want to do."

"Substantiate that!" demanded the Lord High Councilor.

"My client," said Alice, "is 64. He has served his time!"

"That's not the question," declared the Walrus. "Has time served him?"

"Very well," said Alice. "So well that he's asking for early retirement. He saved a year."

"How does one learn to do that?" asked the Red Queen.

"From parents," answered Alice. "His father was a carpenter, who worked hard and lived according to Benjamin Franklin. A penny saved is a penny earned and time is money. The petitioner used his time well. Let me show you."

Alice unfurled on a huge chart a *curriculum vitae* of Karl Richard Bopp, born February 2, 1906, in Kirkwood, Missouri.

"So, he's from Missouri," said the March Hare.

"Very much so," said Alice. "He went to school in Missouri and was the first member of his family ever to go to college. He entered the University of Missouri in 1924. He got his A.B. in 1928, his M.A. in 1929, and in 1931 married Ruth Callies, also a Missouri graduate. And as a reward for his good judgment, Missouri granted him a Ph.D. and made him an assistant professor!"

"So Missouri is in the blood stream," said the Lord High Privy Councilor. "But where is it?"

"At Columbia," answered the petitioner.

"And where's that?" persisted the Privy Councilor.

"Midway between St. Louis and Kansas City," replied Bopp.

"In other words neither here, nor there," asserted the Mock Turtle.

"You mean not anywhere?" asked the Mad Hatter.

"It's everywhere," protested Alice. "Everywhere that men gather to communicate ideas, reflect on the nature of the universe, study the behavior of men—everywhere that men devote their minds to understanding. Education has no locale. It's ubiquitous, irrepressible, omnipresent, and eternal."

"Nevertheless," decided the Red Queen, "Columbia, Missouri, is a strange place. Where I come from you have to run twice as fast to stay in the same place, but this man Bopp progressed by staying in the same place."

Alice beamed. "You're so perceptive, your royal highness. He won a Social Science Research Council grant to study the central banking system in Germany, he taught summer school at the University of Seattle, and was advanced to an associate professorship at Missouri in 1937."

The Walrus began counting on his tusks—aloud: "One, two, three . . ." Finally, he exclaimed: "Utterly unbelievable. Bopp must have the patience of Job. In 1937, he had been at Missouri 13 years."

"Yes," said Alice, "that's right. And he remained in academic limbo until 1941, but in between he won a Guggenheim fellowship to study central banking in the United States and Great Britain."

The Red Queen summoned the Executioner. "Stand by," she commanded. "I think you'll have work to do."

Alice was alarmed. "Why do you say that?" she asked.

"Why do I say that, why do I say that?" shouted the Red Queen. "I can read, can't I? I see what's in the newspapers. I know the shape of the pound and the dollar and the Bank of England and the Federal Reserve System. If this is the result of Bopp's study, he ought to do another study. But if the first study got us where we are,

I hardly think we can afford another. I'm considering: Can we afford Bopp?"

"Maybe he studied too much," suggested the March Hare. "According to the chart, he became successively director of research at the Federal Reserve Bank of Philadelphia, then vice president in charge of research, and in 1958, president."

"Fancy that," exclaimed the Mock Turtle. "An economist—president of a Federal Reserve Bank!"

"That was a depression year. The country was in bad shape," said the Lord High Privy Councilor, as if that explained everything and anything. The Red Queen nodded and bade the Executioner to relax.

Hastily Alice continued. "Bopp is not here as a defendant. He's a petitioner, expecting his due."

"I think we're making too much ado about his due," said the Lord High Privy Councilor.

"Let him get up early in the morning," said the irrepressible Mad Hatter. "An early riser gets the dew. Besides, if he has done all Alice says he's done, I should think he has gathered more dew than most men in a lifetime."

"If it please your majesty," persisted Alice, "I'd like to go on. Dr. Bopp did what had to be done. He was technical secretary of the Bretton Woods Monetary Conference. He did one of the first papers on Hjalmar Schacht, head of the German Reichsbank, and he was special assistant to Thomas B. McCabe, when President Truman appointed McCabe chairman of the Federal Reserve Board. Later Bopp became chairman of meetings of the Sunday Breakfast Club in Philadelphia, he . . ."

"Hmph," hmphed the Walrus. "When a man becomes chairman of something, it means he hasn't enough to do."

"On the contrary," said Alice, "the busier a man is, the more he's in demand. And these are such strange meetings. The Sunday Breakfast Club convenes Wednesday evenings for dinner at the Midday Club. Dr. Bopp had to find speakers who had something to say and at the same time hold the attention of Philadelphia's leading businessmen. That's a major achievement!"

"An achievement! What's so hard about that?" argued the Walrus.

"Have you ever tried to keep a Philadelphia businessman awake after dinner?" asked Alice.

The White Queen broke her silence: "If Bopp did that, we can't afford to let him retire. Such talent, wisdom, and experience must not go to waste."

"It won't," promised Alice.

"How can you promise that, when he plans to do nothing?" asked the Red Queen. "Do you plan to upset his plan?"

"I won't have to," said Alice. "I'll leave that to others. Dr. Bopp has lectured at the Stonier School of Banking, the School of Banking of the South, University of Pennsylvania, Princeton, Columbia, Wisconsin. He has made commencement speeches, has been granted honorary degrees, is a trustee of Temple University. Dr. Bopp knows what time is for—to use it in behalf of others."

"I get it, I get it," chortled the March Hare. "Then, in retirement, he'll have the other half for himself!"

"That's not what I wanted to say," responded Alice. "In modern society, a man saves up time by working. He produces more than he consumes. His underconsumption—his pension and his stocks and bonds—gives him time to be his own taskmaster. Then a man does what he has to do."

"I could have told you that," said the Mock Turtle. "Retirement is a continuation. A man's past is his future compulsion."

"I quite agree," said Alice. "Dr. Bopp began his working career during the Great Depression. He helped piece together the post-World War II monetary system at Bretton Woods . . . ."

"God is merciful, he'll forgive him for that!" said the March Hare. "But can we?"

Alice paid no attention, but went right on: "He was active in the Federal Reserve System when it supported President Truman's bond market before the 1951 Accord. He was a policy-maker at the Federal Reserve during the 1960-1969 Kennedy-Johnson prosperity."

"Hmph, hmph," hmphed the Walrus, who was especialy skilled at hmphing. "And now look at the state of the world! Inflation, inflation every-where. I don't see how Dr. Bopp can afford to retire."

"Well, Dr. Bopp is following the Federal Re-serve's too-early formula. The Open Market Com-mittee used to act after the fact. It didn't make credit easy until it could see the whites of a re-cession's eyes. Then, when it was accused of tardi-ness, it followed the other course. It decided to act before a recession was evident. It didn't wait for a trend, it anticipated turning points."

"That explains everything," said the Mad Hat-ter. "Retire early before it's too late."

The Red Queen began tapping her mace. "Enough of this prattle," she shouted. "Let's get to the question. What will a man do who plans to do nothing?"

"If you'll forgive me," said Alice, "there's a better question. That is, what won't Dr. Bopp do? He'll have a problem.

"He has lectured in so many places, made so many speeches, been consulted by so many busi-nessmen and bankers, that he'll be hard put to find time to do nothing. He'll be asked to lecture here, lecture there, serve on this board, chair that panel, speak here and there and everywhere."

"Well, we can now come to a decision," said the Red Queen with finality. "Can we grant a retirement petition to a man who won't be allowed to retire?"

She conferred briefly with the White Queen. Finally, she pronounced: "The petition is granted. Karl Richard Bopp has our consent to do what is beyond his nature to do—nothing. He has his freedom to stop one career—and to begin another."

At the pronouncement, Alice, the Walrus, the Mad Hatter, the March Hare, and the Knave of Hearts rushed up to the petitioner. "Congratulations, congratulations," they shouted in unison and separately.

"But is a man who intends to do nothing to be congratulated?" asked Dr. Bopp.

"No," replied the Lord High Privy Councilor, "and I speak for the Queens when I say this. You are to be congratulated because freedom to a man like you is a license to do what you have always done—serve others. But if you overdo it, you'll be penalized. You'll lose your Social Security!"

"So," advised the White Queen, "you must try to say 'no' more often than 'yes.' The secret of doing nothing is doing what you want to do."

"Please, your majesty, may we adjourn on that?" asked Alice.

The Red Queen looked at the White Queen, the White Queen looked at the Red Queen, and both pronounced in unison: "Adjournment is our prerogative. Besides, this is a beginning not an ending."

"But that is what adjournment means," said Alice. "An ending for a new beginning."

Even the Red Queen was pleased. She said: "If that be so, the proceeding is adjourned."

J. A. LIVINGSTON

KARL R. BOPP is one of the most competent students of the functions and problems of central banking that we have in the Federal Reserve System. His extraordinary talents came to my attention in the summers of 1940 and 1941, when he participated in the special studies on executive development in the Federal Reserve Banks as conducted by C. Canby Balderston, Dean of the Wharton School of Finance and Commerce of the University of Pennsylvania.

At the time, I was Chairman of the Federal Reserve Bank of Philadelphia and I had been delegated by the Chairmen's Conference of the Federal Reserve Banks to serve with General Robert Wood, Chairman of the Federal Reserve Bank of Chicago, and Owen D. Young, Chairman of the Federal Reserve Bank of New York, to make a comprehensive study of one of the most controversial issues between the Federal Reserve Banks and the Board of Governors in Washington—executive development and compensation in the Federal Reserve Banks.

In making this study, Karl Bopp made such an impression on me that I tried to persuade him to leave the academic world and join the Federal Reserve System. I found that the Governors and staff of the System in Washington were as deeply impressed with him as I was, and they offered him a position in Washington at the same time that we offered him one with the Philadelphia Reserve Bank. Karl finally decided to accept the Philadelphia offer and was made Director of Research of the Bank in 1941. His work was so outstanding that he was made Vice President of Research in 1947 and became President of the Bank in 1958.

When I went to Washington as Chairman of the Board of Governors of the System in 1948, Karl became a special assistant to me in the summer of that year. During my three years' service as Chairman of the Board of Governors, he and Alfred H. Williams, Karl's predecessor as president of the Philadelphia Bank, were among the few of my closest advisors on the innumerable problems which faced the System in that critical period, 1948-1951.

I recall an incident during Karl's early service with the Federal Reserve when Chief Justice Biggs of the United States Court in Philadelphia asked me who could make the best presentation to him on the subject of gold. I told him that I thought Karl Bopp was well-qualified on the subject and that if he would come to lunch at the Bank with Karl and me, I would have Karl give him an illustrated lecture on the subject. Judge Biggs then asked if he could bring his associates on the bench. I gladly acquiesced, and Karl made the presentation to the entire court. When he had finished, the Chief Justice told him it was one of the most comprehensive presentations he had ever listened to in or out of court.

Since my service with the Federal Reserve System, Karl has been of inestimable value to me over the years as an advisor on innumerable economic questions. My affection and admiration for him have grown deeper with the passage of time.

THOMAS B. McCABE

For All of Us who write in this volume, the occasion offers an opportunity to reexamine some of our basic philosophies. Accordingly, I have found it illuminating to think of Karl Bopp in terms of a simple formula which has proved itself many times, at least to my satisfaction, as a prescription for a fruitful life. This formula has four components.

First is technical competence—the understanding and mastery of a special field. This knowledge gives its possessor great opportunity to serve his fellow man and, by the same token, brings rich rewards to the possessor. Karl has been fortunate in this regard. Possessed of a brilliant mind, an endowment for which he can take no credit, he has applied his mind rigorously and imaginatively so that he has become one of the leading authorities in the field of central banking. During my stint as president of the Philadelphia Reserve Bank, I was a beneficiary of Karl's expertise; and for that I am grateful.

Second is a broad intellectual outlook. For example, a knowledge of history gives one a comprehension of social change. It gives one a tie to the past and a sense of continuity. This attribute Karl has in abundance. He takes an intellectual approach in solving problems by drawing on a vast background of knowledge and experience. Such breadth and depth adds stability and perspective—characteristics which have served Karl well.

Third is social intelligence. This may be roughly defined as capacity to understand and deal with men, especially men in groups—for mass action is increasingly a characteristic of human behavior. A dozen years ago, when I sat in the chair which Karl is now relinquishing, I was greatly impressed by the fact that the human family was on the move; it was experiencing a social flux, worldwide. Today this momentum is so rapid that few of us can keep up with it. Karl has both observed the changes and has been part of the action, doing "his thing" with skill and insight, and keeping his antennae always alert to the tempo of social change.

Finally, a fourth element is a well-knit set of ethical, moral, and spiritual values. These values set up a central drive, within the leader, of interest in and respect for the other fellow—his personality and worth as an individual. In this Karl has few peers. He has carried on and developed in his own distinctive style what has been for many years a tradition at the Philadelphia Bank—a concern for people. It is this concern which will enable us to overcome the almost overwhelming problems confronting us. If I may be permitted to plagiarize myself, I should like to quote from a talk given many years ago: "To those of you who would become leaders I say, if you have a spark of interest in your fellow man, fan it into a flame. If you succeed, there follows an integration of your many loyalties, some of which hitherto, no doubt, have been conflicting. If you are entirely successful you will achieve the inner poise and strength so necessary in these days of economic doubt, social tension, personal frustration, and seeming defeat." In the case of Karl the evidence speaks for itself.

ALFRED H. WILLIAMS

IN A LECTURE at one of the schools of banking, I said that a man might do a better job of solving personnel problems by first asking himself, "How should I *as a gentleman* handle this situation?" Called upon to explain the term, not commonly used today, I said:

I think of a gentleman as one who is a kind person, who is considerate, who would not willingly hurt another person, a man who retains his personal dignity even when under pressure, and who respects the dignity of others even when it seems not to be deserved. I think of a gentleman as one who commands respect but does not demand it. I think of him as a man exercising inner strength which is so much more effective than the outward flexing of one's physical or managerial muscles.

That is a fairly good description of Karl Bopp, and I am sure I had him in mind when I made the statement. For many years he has influenced almost everything I have said and done so that I am never quite sure whether I am expressing my own thought or his. At best it's a mix.

Of course, I know why I was invited to write in *personal* vein about Karl. No man knows him as I do, and no man knows me as he does. For more than a quarter of a century we have had almost daily association. We have shared our thoughts and feelings on every conceivable subject from Federal Reserve to family. We have dealt with each other with complete honesty and full candor. Ours is a deep and abiding friendship. Ours has been a managerial partnership, but with never a question as to whose word was final. Our simultaneous retirement won't change the quality of our friendship and I don't think it will change the basic nature of the partnership. It is because of my love and respect for him that he will always be the senior partner.

In the light of this it must be clear that I accepted this invitation with grateful enthusiasm, and yet not without a twinge of reluctance. Karl would not want me to write about his virtues and neglect to say anything about his faults. It is one thing for us to discuss our limitations with each other, as we have done. It is quite another thing to air them in public. Karl has always insisted upon honesty of presentation, and I must abide by that demand.

Fortunately, what appears to be a fault, looked upon short-run, turns out in most instances to be a virtue when viewed long-run. We are dealing with a very complex person, one whose thoughts and actions are never off-the-cuff, even though they often appear to be. With Karl each judgment is weighed in the light of the past, the present, and the future. Those who evaluate his decisions occasionally lose sight of the time perspective. Karl has no use for judgments which are merely expedient or opportunistic. His thought-processes and his methodology, just to give this a pragmatic touch, enable him to avoid that which he abhors. This point has not always been fully understood by some of the day-to-day administrators. Even I occasionally lost sight of this, and I should have known better. One of Karl's lasting gifts to his colleagues is the sharpening of abilities to see things in perspective.

We must consider carefully Karl's modesty. Of course, it is a virtue, but on many occasions I looked upon it as a fault. I often told him so and, curiously, he agreed. However, modesty is such a part of him that he can do little about it. One can overcome false modesty, but genuine modesty is quite intractable. There isn't anything about Karl that is false. His faults, if faults they are, are as genuine as his virtues.

Let me illustrate the complexity of Karl's modesty. On the agenda of each meeting of our Board of Directors is the item called "Opening Statement of the President." It was only on infrequent occasions that Karl made such a statement, but it was carefully prepared, often worked on for many days, and usually tried out on me. And when he made the statement at the meeting, we saw Karl at his very best. I know of no such occasion when at least one board member didn't say, "I wish we had a tape of that." One would think that with the enthusiastic response he invariably received he would have done it with greater frequency. I urged him many times, but to no avail. What was the reason?

Karl felt that even as president he should not always occupy the center of the stage. In the development of men he believed that others should have that opportunity. He felt that there was always the possibility that by making the opening statement he would take the edge off presentations about to be made by other economists. This was fully in character. Karl set the climate and the stage which enabled others to grow and to demonstrate their abilities.

And yet I feel sure in my own mind that his motivation was not totally managerial, even though he genuinely believed it. Underneath it all was that old business of personal modesty and innate humility. At this point in time I have convinced myself that Karl was right as he thought in terms of the continuing institution. Had he, however, been less modest we would have had more gems, and I think the directors would have liked it better. On the other hand, it would have reduced the opportunities of men coming along. Everybody judges the trade-off from where he sits. Karl saw it all in realistic perspective. Modesty— virtue or fault? Or both?

Similarly, Karl made few speeches, fewer than the office certainly permitted. But when he made a speech, it drew attention. He had something to say and he said it well. He had an intuitive sense of timing. He understood that there were times to talk and times to remain silent, times to be an individual president and times to be, first of all, a member of the System. No one knows as I do that he had many speeches that he never made, and I am sure that the reasons for not making them were sound. I speak with understandable bias, however, when I say that the banking world would have gained much by hearing more from Karl. I always wanted others to share the inspiration and stimulation which I received from him. I know that he was fully convinced of the correctness of his forbearance as a matter of policy, but I am equally convinced that that old modesty greatly influenced the policy. Karl simply is not a showman and he felt that others might misinterpret his motives were he to make too many speeches, a risk he was unwilling to take. But again, he was thinking more of the institution than of himself. Others took on high-level speaking assignments and were, of course, greatly influenced by Karl's thinking. It was all part of Karl's planned development of the coming generation.

To be sure, there were times when Karl occupied the center of the stage, and on each of these occasions he turned in a stellar performance. I remember so vividly the time he was called upon to speak on the Federal Reserve to a large group of businessmen from Germany. State Department technicians began to set up headphones and other apparatus to permit simultaneous translation. This seemed to bother Karl so he said, "If you will bear with me, I'll try to do this in German." For nearly an hour he held forth, and at the end the group rose as one man and gave him a resounding and long-lasting round of applause. I had never heard Karl speak German before, so I knew he had to be out of practice. He has the kind of mind that doesn't need it.

Most people know that Karl is verbal-minded. He has an unusual command of the language, and this time I mean the English language. Those of us who have worked closely with him know that he is also figure-minded. He has a sixth sense about numbers. On numerous occasions I have sat with him as he perused a report from a subordinate, saying, "These numbers can't be right, at least not all of them." He has a quick eye for a sour number, but also an intuitive sense of internal consistency. Anyone who turns in a table of figures to Karl had better double check his numbers. He's sure to be caught if there is an error.

I have often thought that Karl would have made a good judge on the bench. On the one hand, he can be about as objective as any man can be; at least he keeps his biases under complete control. On the other hand, he knows when to inject just the right amount of subjectivity, especially when dealing with the destiny of human beings. Over the years I have admired the quality of mercy which characterized his decisions. He never failed to take into account what seemed best for the man as well as best for the institution. More than once he explained his decision to me by saying, "The institution can survive this, but

the man can't. We must save the man." On some
of these decisions he lost sleep even though he
knew that his is a thoroughly reliable conscience.

Everyone knows of Karl's firmness. I am one
of the few who knows that it goes further than
that. Karl can be plain stubborn. Few of his positions have been absolutely rigid and inflexible, but
there has been an occasional one. Although to
others his firmness was displayed with outward
calm, his tensions were shown when we were
alone, in his office or mine. I've seen him set his
jaw, dig his heel into the rug, press down on the
arms of the chair, and just let go. He would admit his sheer stubbornness, usually adding that the
issue required it. These occasions were few and
far between, and always carefully considered, but
they were electric. Somehow I usually managed
to make some remark that relieved the tension.
After all, what's a first vice president for?

It was always a great event when Karl took on
single-handed a group of academic economists,
especially when one knew in advance that some
would use the occasion to voice their strong criticism of Federal Reserve policy. Having been an
academic economist Karl understood fully the
difference between having the responsibility for
policy and not having it. Those who don't have
the responsibility typically create the impression of
being braver men. I remember only one occasion
when he answered a barrage with just a bit of pique.
His comment was:

> When I was a professor of money and banking
> I used to wonder how Federal Reserve officials
> could be so stupid. Now that I've had some
> years as a central banker with responsibility, I
> often wonder how professors of money and
> banking can be so naive.

He may have overstated the case, but it cleared
the atmosphere. One must not infer from this that
Karl ever tried to cover up Federal Reserve mis-

takes. He did, however, feel it important for people to know why the Fed can't play errorless ball.
He felt it important, too, that we learn from our
mistakes.

So many of Karl's attributes and skills testify
to his qualifications as an ideal teacher. One
learns from him in the ivory tower, in the marketplace, or at the other end of his log which seems
always to be close by. He avoids producing answers because he has faith in his ability to ask
the right questions. His object is to get the rest of
us to think, to come up with our own answers.
He has a sly way of pressing so that one is soon
transported from the shallow to the deeper water.
He never tries to trap his learner, but the learner
often traps himself by not recognizing the errors
in his thinking. A lesson learned *from* Karl stays
learned. So does a lesson learned *by* him. It may
be that he is an ideal teacher because he is an
ideal student.

Men from other Federal Reserve Banks have
often said that they don't quite understand how
the Philadelphia Bank operates. They have characterized the management as democratic and informal. Even the word loose has been used. It has
been none of these. The management, under Karl's
direction—and I mean direction—has been as
democratic as could be tolerated at any given time.
Karl has never believed in management by committee or by town meeting. Functions were assigned,
responsibilities allocated, and accountabilities fixed.
There was never anything informal or loose about
Karl's belief in the principle of delegation. He never
lost sight of the fact that no matter how effectively
duties and powers might be distributed, it was he,
the president, who had to bear the final responsibility for the results achieved by the institution.
While not one to throw his weight around, Karl
never lost sight of the fact that the president is
chief executive officer.

It was this specific assignment of powers and

accountabilities which enabled men to have a strong sense of operational freedom. It was this, as well as the setting of the climate and managerial tone, that enabled men to cooperate, to consult one another, to work together, to form their own temporary *ad hoc* groupings in finding solutions to problems. Each man knew the decisions he was expected to make. When an officer called in other officers for consultation, a common occurrence, it might have looked as though a group decision were being made. Not so, the officer was using the talents of others to help him make the decision which he alone had to make, and which all the others knew was his to make. The president was available for consultation, but he carefully avoided making the decision which had been delegated. This is not to say that he didn't influence the decision, but it never came as an order. Karl tried very hard to be just another member of the group seeking the appropriate solution to the problem. In this situation the cynical person might say that, after all, it really was the president who made that decision. In saying this he failed to appreciate Karl's great skill in group discussion. Karl made the decisions he was supposed to make, not the ones somebody else was supposed to make. He saw to it that we understood this.

Karl knew how to use a first vice president. He never believed that the office called for him to be a chief *operating* officer. His job was to be chief *administrative* officer, and there is a difference. He took his cue from the Federal Reserve Act which says that the first vice president is to act in the absence or disability of the president. This means he has to think more like a president than like an officer in charge of operations. Being a chief operating officer is such a vast assignment that it can't be given to the first vice president if he is to be the continuous understudy of the president. He has to be in continuous association with the president, working on the problems with which the president is constantly occupied. It is because of Karl's behavior toward me that as junior partner with him I have never had the slightest urge to be a senior partner elsewhere. He saw to it that there could be no more rewarding job anywhere in the System than mine. He did it by just being himself.

Karl's job has in some ways been a lonely one, especially in social relationships. This was deliberate. Rightly or wrongly, and I think rightly, Karl has not fraternized or engaged in social activities to any appreciable extent with commercial bankers. He has always been friendly with them and they have all respected him. He did his socializing in groups, seldom with individuals. He had a kind of inner feeling that with his responsibilities as a central banker his behavior might just possibly be misconstrued were he to become too closely attached socially to the heads of large commercial banks. I sometimes thought he overdid this obsession, but he again was thinking of the institution, and appearances can often be as damaging as the realities.

It was about for the same reason that both he and I have done very little socializing with our officers. We knew that we had responsibilities for promotions and salaries and we knew the possibilities of misinterpretations of our decisions if made against a background of excessive fraternization. We believe that the officers have understood this and appreciated it. They have looked upon our behavior, I hope, as something of a sacrifice because they must all know how much we would have enjoyed seeing them extracurricularly more than we have. No doubt all this has had something to do with our social dependence upon each other, but, of course, it is not the whole story.

During his entire presidency one of Karl's chief concerns has been the Board of Directors. He has fully understood the chafings of the directors over restrictions on the scope of their powers of decision, particularly in the various authorizations which must be obtained from the Board of Governors. Karl made it clear to them, however, that no president would want to manage a Federal Reserve Bank without the invaluable help given by the directors. Without them, a live and virile institution could soon become just another old line agency. Over the years the Philadelphia Fed has been fortunate in having on its Board first-class men, men of tremendous experience, devoted men with unusual talents. Much of this has been due to Karl himself. A president needs a good board, but a board needs a good president.

It is a temptation to say that Karl's retirement will mark the end of an era. But that would be a half-truth. When he walks out he will be leaving behind him a great tradition, some of which he inherited from his predecessor. Others will carry on where he left off. New men will place their own stamp on the institution but they will adhere to the Karl Bopp demands for integrity, competence, and respect for human dignity. The spirit is here to stay.

Karl will retire a happy man because in the minds of all who know him will be the thought, "Well done, thou good and faithful servant." And Karl will remember this Markham quotation which he knows I have used many times:

> *There is a destiny that makes us brothers,*
> *None goes his way alone.*
> *All that we send into the lives of others,*
> *Comes back into our own.*

He also knows that our simultaneous retirement will not dissolve the Bopp-Hilkert mutual admiration society.

ROBERT N. HILKERT

THERE IS A STORY about Mark Twain to the effect that his wife once tried to break him of profanity by swearing in his presence at every opportunity. Twain's reaction was simply that "she knew the words but didn't quite have the tune." An attempt to summarize Karl Bopp's beliefs as an economist and central banker is certain to produce the same results. I have been a student of Karl Bopp's for over a quarter of a century—for a short time in the University of Pennsylvania classroom and the rest at 925 Chestnut Street. During the same period, I have also been, if I can make the distinction, a student of Karl Bopp. The subject has been at once the most fascinating and most difficult I have ever tackled; the results have been the most inconclusive.

One reason is that Karl is many persons, some of whom Bob Hilkert has already described. As an economist and central banker, Karl has sometimes been an observer, sometimes a participant, and it is as hard for a biographer to keep the two roles straight as it often must have been for him. Early training inculcated in Karl a lifelong fascination for central banking. At Missouri he probed deeply into official records to come up with an insightful view of the agencies of Federal Reserve policy. In subsequent years he has kept detailed notes on index cards of the day-to-day unfolding of momentous events in Federal Reserve history, all the while participating in important policymaking decisions. The combination of the two personalities —one recording and analyzing with great objectivity, the other debating, deciding, defending, and rationalizing with considerable subjectivity—has made Karl a much more complex person than many of his colleagues. Most of the time it has made for strength, as I intend to demonstrate; but when the two motivations were at war, it could be divisive.

Similarly, Karl Bopp has been both a deeply emotional and an intensely intellectual man; the two characteristics cannot be disentangled. It is as an intellectual that Karl has had his greatest impact, however, and, I suspect, as he would wish to be judged. All of us who have worked with him have had reason to be awed by—indeed, have on occasion been impaled by—Karl's brilliantly logical mind. It is a mind intolerant of, although through self-discipline patient with, sloppy thinking. It is a cultivated mind, quite as likely to produce an argument from Aristotle or a verse by T. S. Eliot as a subtlety of Wicksell. Of all his associations, I suspect Karl values most highly his membership in the American Philosophical Society.

And it is a scholarly mind. Karl has never felt comfortable with a ghost writer. The list of his own publications, however, is not long; a number of studies emerged in the Missouri days, several more in the 1940's and 1950's during the period in research at Philadelphia, practically none during his presidency of the Bank. But all are the product of deep and careful thought, many of back-breaking research. Perhaps there is, somewhere, a student of central banking who has pored over as many reports, minutes, hearings, and memoranda involving as many central banks as has Karl; but if so I am not aware of his existence; and certainly he has not been a practicing central banker.

This is the unique combination—scholarly research of the major central banks in critical periods, and day-to-day confrontation with current problems of Federal Reserve policy—which has shaped Karl Bopp's philosophy. It has, above all, given him a strong sense of history. By habit, almost compulsion, Karl tends to approach any problem from the direction of historical experience. The result is a curious blend of assurance and skepticism, confidence and humility.

Let me illustrate. In the course of his career, Karl has seen a severe depression, several recessions of varying intensity, and some periods of inflation. From all this he has emerged, so far as I can tell, with no fixed view about the future course of the American economy. True, he has observed many times that something very different happened after World War II than after earlier major wars: the economy has not experienced a decline in prices, and this does signify a basic change in the economy and in public policy. But to say that depressions are ruled out henceforth or that the major problem of the future is chronic inflation is to go too far. History demonstrates that nothing—prosperity, inflation, chronic stagnation, dollar scarcity, or dollar glut—is inevitable. This can be a hopeful view; the problems of the moment can't last forever. Or it can be a pessimistic view; despite all we have learned about how the economy works and how to shape it to our ends, things can happen which we don't anticipate.

Above all it is a humble view. Humility is much in evidence in Karl's most revealing "Confessions of a Central Banker." "The simple truth," he says, "is that no one comprehends enough to be an expert in central banking."[1] This confession of ignorance apparently reflects an evolution from Karl's days in academia when, as he describes himself, he was an intellectual grandson of Irving Fisher. Through Fisher's students, James Harvey Rogers and Harry Gunnison Brown, he learned of the importance of money as a determinant of economic activity. But in the course of time, exposure to the realities of policymaking and recognition of the chaotic state of monetary theory have led him to distrust (although not, he says, without a twinge of conscience) the monetarists' explanations of

---

[1] Karl R. Bopp, "Confessions of a Central Banker," *Essays in Monetary Policy in Honor of Elmer Wood,* Edited by Pinkney C. Walker (Columbia, Mo.: University of Missouri Press, 1965), p. 12.

economic behavior and their mechanistic approaches to policy. It is clear from his "Confessions," however, that his view of the unsatisfactory state of knowledge is not a counsel of despair, but of patience. It is a challenge to research, an invitation to be tolerant of the ideas of others.

And despite what appears to be a thoroughgoing agnosticism about the monetary process, Karl is not without foundations on which to build his view of monetary policy. One of the firmest of the foundations is a strong sense of the role of markets. As he has come to distrust rules of thumb and formulae, he has become impressed by the complex workings of markets. This has led him, on the one hand, to advocate a great deal of discretion in the execution of policy. For example, he has always shrunk from quantifying instructions to the Manager of the Open Market Account. Close observation of the money market has convinced him that the best person to determine the *tactics* of policy is the man on the scene, in the thick of the market. As a participant in determining the *strategy* of policy, Karl has tended to be brief and concise in presentations before the Open Market Committee and has avoided the semantic exercises that sometimes characterize Committee discussions.

On the other hand, his view of markets has convinced him of the fallibility of money managers who attempt to usurp markets' functions. Selective credit controls have always been distasteful, both on philosophical and practical grounds. Voluntary credit restraint has smacked of the real-bills fallacy. As Reserve Bank president, Karl has resisted pressures to lecture commercial bankers about credit restraint, not only because his natural modesty has made it difficult to do this but also because he has not been willing to superimpose his judgments as a central banker on theirs as commercial bankers. He has preferred to let monetary policy speak for itself through the marketplace.

As a non-interventionist, Karl has been pretty much in the mainstream of Federal Reserve tradition. But in a number of other respects he has been an individualist. Three examples come to mind, one having to do with objectives of policy, a second with instruments, and a third with agencies. All are illustrative of his broad, historical approach to policy problems.

Some years ago, as Karl examined the various objectives of monetary policy over time, he saw clearly the conflicts that often exist.[2] This was before the term "trade-off" became commonly used to describe the problem. More recently he has taken exception to the conventional wisdom of including economic growth as an objective of monetary policy. His position has been that monetary policy has relatively little to do with the germinal elements of growth; that an appropriate policy will produce maximum sustainable use of available resources and this, in itself, is a large contribution to growth.

As to the instruments of policy, his views have been influenced strongly by an intensive analysis of operations of the German Reichsbank from its foundation until World War I.[3] Despite the facts that the Reichsbank had no information on the volume of reserves, could not achieve a given level of reserves, and dealt with a banking system whose reserve ratio varied considerably over time, it nevertheless achieved its basic objective. While he has not advocated that the Federal Reserve System actually try to do without reserve requirements as an instrument of policy, still Karl has concluded that the ultimate power of the central

---

[2] Karl R. Bopp, "Central Banking Objectives, Guides, and Measures," *The Journal of Finance,* Vol. IX, No. 1, March 1954, pp. 12-22.

[3] Karl R. Bopp, "Die Tatigkeit der Reichsbank von 1876 bis 1914," published in Germany only, *Weltwirtschaftliches Archiv,* 1954.

bank lies in its ability to create and destroy money and reserves, at times supplying more liquidity and at other times less liquidity than commercial banks wish to hold. A fixed reserve ratio is not an essential ingredient of monetary policy.

Finally, Karl for years has been puzzling over the proper relationship of the Federal Reserve and Government. And although he is still rather tentative in his conclusions, he has arrived at a general position that may seem heretical to staunch defenders of "independence." Because he has become convinced that monetary policy must be part of a coordinated economic policy of Government, he believes that in the rare event of an irreconcilable conflict, the central bank must give way, the central banker must resign. Furthermore, in such a situation the Government, perhaps by joint resolution of Congress, should give clear directions to the central bank as to how to proceed. Karl has arrived at this view not only because such an arrangement is an orderly way to fix responsibility, but also because "independence," carried to its logical extreme, is undemocratic. And while such a position runs the risk that the people may be "wrong," this is likely only in the short run; we must have faith that the democratic process will work in the long run. Finally, his position means that the central bank must earn its "independence." Only by demonstrating that it is right most of the time can it build the public support which enables it to persuade Government to its way of thinking. With that support, the central banker's power of resignation becomes a potent instrument indeed.

*   *   *   *   *   *   *

How to evaluate the contribution of a man? In some cases it may be primarily by written works, in others by policy actions. In the case of Karl Bopp, neither criterion is determining. His contribution, I believe, lies primarily in the impact of these ideas and his personality on people with whom he has worked. In the policy area, he has not been one to dominate deliberations. But he has spoken up at crucial times with an authority that has brought fresh insight to the discussion. Above all, his influence on staff—and here I speak with particular knowledge and feeling—has been profound. He has transmitted a philosophy of freedom in the pursuit of ideas to all of us who have worked with him. And he has made us all aware that monetary policy—as well as everything else of any importance, for that matter—is a human process.

Perhaps the most fitting way to summarize is to relate part of a conversation between us not long before Karl's retirement. In a reflective mood, he wondered whether, after all, perhaps he should have remained in teaching. My reply was that he has never left it.

DAVID P. EASTBURN

INTRODUCTION

WILLIAM McCHESNEY MARTIN, JR.

ANYONE READING the five foregoing appreciations of Karl Bopp will, I think, be struck by one underlying theme. It's a common idea that runs through five different views of a many-sided man and a distinguished career spanning four decades. It is summed up in the phrase: "the cultivated mind."

As those of us who know Karl Bopp—students, colleagues, above all friends—can happily attest, as rare a quality as it is, it is one which he has exemplified in everything he does. But it is more than a rare quality. It is a subtle one that combines several mutually critical components. It implies professional competence, disciplined curiosity, a sense of perspective, a reasonableness tempered (perhaps enriched is a better verb) by the gifts of humility and humanity.

I would like to suggest that it is possible for the men who have contributed to this collection of essays to turn their thoughts constructively toward a wide array of issues confronting our nation today because of the example set by Karl Bopp. And I would add further that his example is a criterion of fundamental importance to central banking at this point in American financial evolution.

Karl Bopp, who is both a student and practitioner of monetary policy, stated the ever-present challenge himself some 20 years ago when he observed that "the history of money demonstrates the difficulty which men have to distinguish the permanent from the temporary." I can affirm from personal experience over much of the same 40 years Karl Bopp has been teaching and serving the Federal Reserve, that making this distinction is a constant imperative.

Ordering our minds to winnow the significant from the transitory, the perceptive from the doctrinaire, and the judicious from the merely expedient is never simple. But for men and women in our central banking profession grappling with the events of our time, it is particularly essential—at least to the best of our individual abilities.

One of the most extraordinary events of this epoch is the explosion of information with which men in public life must endeavor to work. The statistics of this growth, stimulated by the development of the computer and the full flowering of the communications arts, are so familiar there is no need to itemize them. What does deserve mention is the too-often forgotten truth that information is only a human tool and its uses ultimately depend on the cultivated mind to give it meaning and direction. We must search for the place of value in our world of facts.

The business process, which is the concern of most of the contributors in this volume, is a rational process, not a mystical or magic one. And those of us in positions of public trust can function only in the faith that men can master and improve it by the exercise of reason, sharpened and clarified by the discipline of objective study.

The need for rational economic thought is one of the most important of our time. But rationality alone is not enough. The catch is that in economics as in most other public affairs we are dealing with human nature and human beings, and no one has yet devised any system of levers or any formulas or devices by which you can infallibly anticipate or regulate human nature or human beings.

Economists at the Board of Governors and many others working independently are laboring continuously—aided considerably by the advances in communication and computer technology—to isolate and measure more exactly the impact of changes in policy at various stages of this process so we may think and speak with more precision about the ultimate effects of policy changes. But so far, and for some time in the foreseeable future, we must recognize that the precise timing and magnitude of these effects are not subject to exact scientific, proof-positive determination. And so the meaning and direction of facts remain matters of judgment, and matters on which judgments may differ.

I stress these limits on our knowledge in order to suggest why central banking remains an art rather than a science. And as an art, it is an art of moderation, of the balanced way. At all times, we must be aware of the risk that the economy might be undermined by either inflation or deflation. And this is a risk that involves human side effects, side effects which impinge on our polity as well as our economy. Economics involves moral decisions as well as abstract technical ones.

Only a couple of centuries ago the business civilization, or, more precisely, the market system that would furnish its cornerstone, was just coming into recognition as a new way of life that offered a promise of material advancement and individual freedom such as men had never known before.

The market system lifted men's hearts when they first saw in its development an alternative to the other two systems around which society had been organized from time immemorial.

One of these systems, prevailing in the Orient until recent years, employed the forces of tradition to ensure the execution of the count-less jobs that had to be done to keep society going—disagreeable jobs as well as pleasant ones. By custom and usage, jobs were assigned from father to son for generation after generation, and men did the work deemed appropriate to their caste.

The other system antedating the market system was that of authori-tarian rule, in which the whip of centralized power drives workers to the necessary tasks. It was used in ancient Egypt to build the pyramids. It is used in modern Russia to execute the Soviet's five-year plans.

Against these age-old systems of social control, the market system must have appeared to men of vision as a magnificent achievement in social engineering, for it provided a mechanism for sustaining and maintaining an entire society by the free and voluntary activity of its individual members. It constituted a way of life affording to the indi-vidual a dignity unknown under the older social systems. In the market system, each man would be guided to his work by the hope of reward rather than the lash of authority or the chains of caste. Yet, though each might freely go wherever he thought his fortune lay, the interplay of one man in competition with another would result in accomplish-ment of all the tasks society needed done.

The transformation of this country from a wilderness to a highly developed business civilization in less than two centuries demonstrates the results that can be obtained through a system which is directed toward releasing rather than shackling the energies and abilities of the individual.

The advantages of a system where supply capacities and demand wants and needs are matched in open markets cannot be measured in economic terms alone. In addition to the advantages of efficiency in the use of economic resources, there are vast gains in terms of personal liberty. Powers of decision are dispersed among the millions affected, instead of being centralized in a few persons in authority.

The basic concept of the market system has remained with us since the founding of the nation. It has remained the keystone of our society down to this day, although we have done some extensive remodeling of the structure as a whole from time to time.

Some of the remodeling we have done in the past has been for the admirable purpose of correcting structural defects and distortions that were warping the system. Competitive, freely functioning markets are one thing, and rigged markets another. Rules and regulations to prevent manipulation are necessary and essential to a sound structure.

Other remodeling has come about because the American people

have refused to accept economic goals as their sole objective. That was true in older generations, as well as our own. Let it be said, to our credit, that American economic action has often been determined by balancing material advance against other human objectives.

Over the years, the American people, working under their free enterprise system, have produced and are producing material abundance as no people in history. Yet, great as are the wonders of production that have been achieved in the American system, still greater are the wonders of distribution. There would be little gain in convenience, comfort or luxury for Louis XIV or Charles II, or for Anthony and Cleopatra, in living today. Our mass production and distribution system could not do much for them. It can and does provide abundance for the mass of people. It is a system for the many rather than for the few. It has provided greater equality in worldly possessions than any socialist or communist society has done, or showed the slightest prospect of doing.

Most noteworthy of all, perhaps, the American people and the American system of free enterprise have come a bit closer to abolishing poverty and its attendant evils than anyone has ever come before. This is an unfinished task, however, and one that requires the use of our minds and the gift of our hearts—both.

A suggestion is often made these days that if only the Federal Reserve's monetary policy were changed, in some way or another, we could have more new homes, more rapid construction of vitally needed schools, hospitals, and other community facilities, more new automobiles, and more new highways to relieve the traffic jams we have already.

Well, it would certainly be a fine world indeed if, by merely opening wider the spigot of credit, the Federal Reserve could increase the flow of goods and services sufficiently to meet all human wants at any time. If the Federal Reserve possessed such magic, I assure you it would use it. But of course there is no such magic, and all of us will be better off if we do not act as if there were.

What is this Federal Reserve policy that some people are so anxious to change?

It is a policy of endeavoring, at all times, to assure monetary and credit conditions that will foster high levels of business and employment, maintain the stability of the currency, and promote sustainable growth in the economy.

It is a policy of combating, with equal vigor, the excesses of inflation and deflation alike. It is a policy that recognizes that inflation compounds its own cruelties by bringing deflation with its further cruelties—the cyclical progression we have suffered many times in the past with consequences heavy in human hardship.

Operations in execution of that policy must, of course, be adapted to the particular circumstances of an economy which, like everything else in life, is always changing.

As a central bank, the Federal Reserve System inevitably functions as an institution which itself has its most immediate contact with other institutions. But institutions are composed of human beings and are, over time, shaped by human beings. As I've sought to suggest in these few pages, this realization alone suffices to caution us toward great humility—especially humility about our ability to cope with transition through the use of mere logic and no more. We must not allow ourselves to be beguiled by our growing facility in gathering and juggling information, to succumb to the belief that information is a substitute for understanding.

We should not, in sum, fail to put the highest premium on the very special qualities of men such as Karl Bopp—men who have the cultivated mind and use it.

IMPACTS OF THEORY ON POLICY:
THE EARLY YEARS
OF THE FEDERAL RESERVE

LESTER V. CHANDLER

> . . . the ideas of economists and political philosophers, both
> when they are right and when they are wrong, are more pow-
> erful than is commonly understood. Indeed the world is ruled
> by little else. Practical men, who believe themselves to be
> quite exempt from any intellectual influences, are usually the
> slave of some defunct economist.[1]
>
> —J. M. Keynes

> The Federal Reserve Act was clearly not designed to create
> a monetary agency with ample powers for controlling the stock
> of money in accordance with any rational objective, although
> some of the provisions of the Act are not wholly unsuited to
> such a purpose.[2]
>
> —Lloyd W. Mints

How DIFFERENT the original Federal Reserve Act would have been
if it had been based on some sort of quantity theory of money, and
how different might have been the speed, if not the direction, of
evolution of Federal Reserve policies! The Act would undoubtedly
have referred repeatedly to the supply of money and to regulation of
its quantity in line with the needs of the economy for money
balances. And a natural line of evolution would have been to use
Federal Reserve powers ever more positively to stabilize price levels,
or perhaps to regulate some specific flow of expenditures, such as
MV. However, the Act was based not on a type of quantity theory
but on a commercial loan theory of banking, and its prime concern was not with money but with credit. A major purpose was to
adjust credit to "the needs of trade" as evidenced by demands for
commercial loans, not to adjust the supply of money to the economy's
demand for money balances; its infrequent references to quantities

---

[1] *The General Theory of Employment, Interest and Money,* (New York: Har-
court Brace and Company, 1936), p. 383.

[2] *A History of Banking Theory,* (Chicago: University of Chicago Press,
1945), p. 281.

were to the quantity of credit, not that of money; and it emphasized the "quality" of credit.

Though, as many of them claimed, other Congressional leaders influenced the new legislation, the original Federal Reserve Act bore the unmistakable imprint of Carter Glass and of his closest advisor on banking affairs, H. Parker Willis, the most unbending and best-known commercial loan theorist of the period. Nor did their adherence to the commercial loan theory or their influence end with the passage of the Act. For example, Senator Glass declared in 1931 that the Federal Reserve Act would never have permitted the Reserve Banks to lend on Government security collateral if its proponents had not believed that the Federal debt would continue to decline.[3] During the next year he agreed only reluctantly and under strong pressure to permit Government securities to serve as collateral for Federal Reserve notes, and he tolerated an amendment broadening the Federal Reserve's lending power only on condition that the ineligible paper not be used as collateral for Federal Reserve notes. Even at that late date Willis was still inveighing against "artificial" easing through Federal Reserve purchases of Government securities and was advocating passive adjustment of credit to the "needs of trade."

Many provisions of the Federal Reserve Act betray its origin in commercial loan ideas. The two enumerated purposes of the new System, other than to provide a more effective supervision of banking, were to furnish an elastic currency and to afford means of rediscounting commercial paper. Even the provision of an elastic currency was basically a credit rather than a monetary reform; its basic purpose was to prevent currency flows into and out of the banking system from having adverse effects on credit conditions. Only types of paper conforming to the commercial loan theory were eligible for discount at the Federal Reserve—"notes, drafts, and bills of exchange arising out of actual commercial transactions; that is, notes, drafts, and bills of exchange issued or drawn for agricultural, industrial, or commercial purposes, or the proceeds of which have been used, or are to be used, for such purposes. . . ." Only such paper and Federal securities were eligible as collateral for Federal Reserve advances. Specifically excluded were "notes, drafts, or bills covering merely investments or issued or drawn for the purpose of carrying or trading in stocks, bonds, or other investment securities, except bonds and notes of the Government of the United States." As

---

[3] *Hearings on S. Res.* 71, 71st Congress, 3rd Session (Jan. 20, 1931), p. 53.

examples *par excellence* of commercial loans, acceptances were given favored treatment; member banks were permitted to create them on the basis of "real transactions," and they were made eligible for purchase by the Reserve Banks. This, it was believed, would both adapt credit to the legitimate needs of trade and divert loan funds away from the stock market. To provide an appropriate elasticity of Federal Reserve notes to the needs of trade, they should be collateraled only by gold and eligible paper.

Thus the Federal Reserve Act clearly favored types of paper conforming to the commercial loan theory, intended that the Federal Reserve should issue and withdraw funds primarily by dealing in such paper, and implied rather vaguely that the System could control the use of funds created by it by regulating the types of assets acquired. However, the Act provided but little guidance concerning the amounts of funds to be provided or withdrawn, or the general principles which should guide discounting. Such guidance as was implied suggested a policy of more or less passive accommodation of "the needs of trade." For example, it stressed "elasticity" of Federal Reserve notes and provided that discount rates should "be fixed with a view of accommodating commerce and business." The following statement by Governor Norris, of the Federal Reserve Bank of Philadelphia, in September 1930, was not an unreasonable interpretation of the intent of the Act.

> *We have always believed that the proper function of the System was well expressed in the Tenth Annual Report of the Federal Reserve Board—"The Federal Reserve supplies the needed additions to credit in times of business expansion and takes up the slack in times of business recession." We have therefore necessarily found ourselves out of harmony with the policy recently followed of supplying unneeded additions to credit in a time of business recession, which is the exact antithesis of the rule above stated.*[4]

In view of the basic theory of the Act, it is ironic that the first large-scale provision of funds—that during the World War I period, 1917-1920—did not conform to the commercial loan theory at all. The Reserve Banks supplied funds not on the basis of commercial paper but on the basis of Government securities, and their prime purpose was not to "accommodate commerce and business" but to

---

[4] Except where indicated otherwise, quotations are from records and memoranda in Federal Reserve archives.

accommodate the borrowing needs of the Treasury. However, at the end of this episode commercial loan ideas again came to the fore and for the next decade and a half vied with new ideas for supremacy.

Commercial loan ideas, with their emphasis on the "quality" of credit, were one reason, though not the only one, for the deflationary policies of 1920-1921. Both Federal Reserve and commercial bank credit based on Government securities, which did not reflect "the needs of trade," should be eliminated in order to restore "normal" conditions. Many Federal Reserve officials accepted the definition of "normal" offered by Governor Seay, of the Federal Reserve Bank of Richmond, in October, 1920.

> . . . It would probably be fair to say that a normal credit condition exists when bank loans are made very largely, and loans from Reserve banks entirely, for the purpose of producing, purchasing, carrying, or marketing goods in one or more steps in the process of production, manufacture, and distribution.

The rise of open market operations in Government securities as a major policy instrument after 1922, sponsored primarily by Governor Benjamin Strong and his colleagues at the Federal Reserve Bank of New York, challenged the basic tenets of the commercial loans policy prescriptions in at least two ways. For one thing, such operations supplied Federal Reserve funds not on the basis of paper arising out of "real transactions" but on the basis of Government debt. Also, they supplied funds not in response to "the needs of trade" as reflected in applications for discounts but on the initiative of the Federal Reserve itself. They were "forcible insertions" or "forcible withdrawals," which were likely to lead to "artificial credit conditions," especially if purchases were made when "the needs of trade" were declining or if sales occurred when "the needs of trade" were rising. The fact that large Federal Reserve operations in Government securities did occur during the remainder of the 1920's might be viewed as an unqualified victory of the new concept of positive control on the initiative of the Federal Reserve over the older concept of accommodation of "the needs of trade." However, commercial loan ideas were by no means dead, and they continued to influence thinking, attitudes, and policies.

Neither open market operations in Government securities nor the positive use of Federal Reserve powers to promote stability of prices and business conditions enjoyed full support within the System. How numerous and strong were the dissents did not become fully apparent before the 1930's, though objections were voiced earlier. For example, Governor Roy A. Young, Governor of the Federal Reserve Board, stated in 1928 that the primary concern of the System should be to maintain "a healthy banking situation" and that "it would be unfortunate if the Federal Reserve System were to be charged with still further responsibilities which are not directly related to banking, such as responsibility for the stability of the general price level or for moderation of ups and downs in business conditions."[5] In the early 1930's, as Governor of the Federal Reserve Bank of Boston, he consistently opposed purchases of Government securities and favored allowing credit to adjust to the declining "needs of trade." Adolph C. Miller, another member of the Board, was generally unfavorable to open market operations until the depression had been under way for more than a year. He stated in early 1931:

> *I believe that our troubles will be enormously minimized—in fact I think we will pretty nearly get rid of most of them—if the Federal Reserve banks are operated as institutions of rediscount.*[6]

The commercial loan theory, or at least ideas consistent with that theory, continued to appear in various other ways during the remainder of the 1920's.

(1) In evaluations of the behavior of bank credit. Many writers referred to the "excessive" expansion or inflation of bank credit during the 1920's, usually inferring that a sound basis for recovery could be established only when the "excess" was eliminated. Empirically, it would be difficult, it not impossible, to establish that there was, in the 1920's, an "excessive" rate of growth in the quantity of either total bank loans and investments or of the money supply, whether narrowly or broadly defined. Those who found "excessive" growth appear to have based their judgments on "quality" rather than quantity. Commercial loans grew only slowly during this period; a far larger part of the increase of bank credit was in the form of loans on security collateral, real-estate loans, and bonds. To commercial loan theorists, this was clearly an "excessive" expansion;

---

[5] *Journal of the American Bankers Association,* October 1928, Vol. XXI, p. 281.

[6] *Hearings on S. Res.* 71 (January 23, 1931), p. 150.

it was an expansion in excess of "the needs of trade" as evidenced by demands for commercial loans. Also, some credit, including some bank credit, was used for speculation in securities and real estate. This, in itself, was convincing evidence of overexpansion for those who believed that only credit in excess of the legitimate needs of trade would flow into speculative uses.

(2) In contentions that the form of assets acquired by the banking system controlled the use to which the resulting money would be put—e.g., that money issued for commercial loans would remain in commercial uses and that issued on the basis of collateral loans or bonds would remain in the securities markets. Some believed this true of both the Reserve Banks and the commercial banks. Strong and others had shown the errors of such ideas in the early 1920's, yet they lingered on. For example, Adolph Miller testified as late as 1931:

> . . . when the Federal Reserve banks operate as investment banks, by buying investments, they force the member banks of the country also to operate as investment banks by buying investments or loaning against investments or by making loans of the kind here described as loans on real estate.[7]

Apparently such effects would not follow when the Federal Reserve supplied funds by discounting commercial paper or by purchasing acceptances or gold.

(3) In the Federal Reserve's concern, in 1928 and 1929, with the alleged "absorption of credit in the stock market." It is still not wholly clear why the Federal Reserve became so deeply concerned about the use of credit in stock speculation that it virtually abandoned its other objectives and adopted a policy of severe and prolonged restriction, with deleterious effects on the domestic and international economy. However, the idea stressed most at the time was that loans on security collateral led to "absorption of credit in the stock market" and to a decrease in the supply and increase of the cost of funds for legitimate business. They concentrated on the form of the loan and ignored subsequent uses of the money. It was, of course, clear that a lender, whether a bank or nonbank, on security collateral could not lend the same money to another borrower. But the money was not "absorbed" by the borrower; he passed it on to the seller of securities, who was free to use it as he

---

[7] *Hearings on S. Res.* 71 (January 1931), p. 139.

wished to finance his own consumption or productive activities, to lend to someone else, and so on. We do not know the net effects of the rise of bank loans on security collateral on the total supply of funds, both equity and debt, to "legitimate" business or on the cost of capital to business. But two things are clear. First, the fact that loans were collateraled by securities did not necessarily mean less money or higher interest rates for business. And second, the highly restrictive policies adopted to remedy the situation contributed far more to higher interest rates for "legitimate" business than did any "absorption of credit in the stock market."

The first years of the great depression brought a sharp conflict between those who believed that the Federal Reserve should use its powers actively and on its own initiative in an expansionary way and those who favored a more passive policy of "accommodation" or of allowing credit to adjust to "the needs of trade." Commercial loan theorists were highly prominent in the second group, though some others shared their policy views. This group was especially antagonistic to Federal Reserve purchases of Government securities, but it also opposed "excessively easy" policies of purchasing acceptances and lowering discount and bill-buying rates.

The failures of Federal Reserve policies, which allowed the money supply to decline by a quarter during the first three years of the depression, are well known. The rate of liquidation was especially rapid in the months following the international financial crisis which hit the United States in September 1931. However, the money supply had already fallen more than 10 per cent before the crisis impinged upon the United States and while the freedom of Federal Reserve action was not in any way limited by considerations relating to its gold reserve or free gold position or to the nation's balance of payments.

Why were Federal Reserve policies so inadequate and inappropriate in the early years of the great depression? One fundamental reason was the unsatisfactory, confused, and conflicting state of business-cycle and monetary theory, both within and outside the Federal Reserve System, and among professional economists as well as laymen. There was simply no valid, comprehensive, and generally accepted theory that could command a consensus and provide solid theoretical support for an appropriate and ambitious expansionary monetary program. The Keynesian Revolution was still years in the future. There was one type of monetary theory that suggested a positive policy of monetary expansion—the quantity theory. It is no coincidence that the principal proponents of large purchases of Government securities by the Federal Reserve were such well-known quantity theorists as Irving Fisher, John R. Conmons, Wilford I. King, James Harvey Rogers, and Harry Gunnison Brown. However, both their theory and their policy prescriptions were rejected by large numbers of other professional economists, including some of the most prestigious names of the time. Among them were H. Parker Willis of Columbia and most other commercial loan theorists; Benjamin M. Anderson, Jr., influential economist of the Chase National Bank; O. M. W. Sprague of Harvard, Economic Advisor to the Bank of England and frequent consultant to the Federal Reserve and the Treasury; most members of the Yale Economics Department except Fisher and Rogers; Edwin W. Kemmerer of Princeton, famed "money doctor" and author of the most widely read book on the Federal Reserve; and George W. Dowrie of Stanford.

Though members of this group were united in their opposition to positive and ambitious measures for monetary expansion, they offered a wide variety of reasons for their opposition.[8]

(1) Such a policy would be harmful and would prolong the depression by inhibiting the "natural process of liquidation." The depression was caused, it was claimed, by maladjustments created in the preceding period of prosperity, and a sound basis for recovery could be created only by liquidating these maladjustments. The preceding "inflation" and "excessive expansion of credit" had to be purged from the system. Expansionary monetary and credit policies would only prolong both the necessary process of liquidation and the depression.

(2) The appropriate policy was to allow the volume of credit to adjust to the needs of trade at "normal" interest rates, and it was healthful for the volume of credit to fall in response to a decline in the needs of trade reflecting a decline of business activity or price levels. Central bank attempts to manipulate interest rates "artificially" to induce recovery would generate troubles and lead later to excessively high interest rates.

(3) The Federal Reserve, as custodian of liquidity for the entire financial system, should conserve its own liquidity, and this could be assured only by limiting its earning assets to short-term, self-liquidating paper conforming to the commercial loan theory. Even

---

[8] The state of economic theory at this time is discussed more fully in a forthcoming study of American monetary policies, 1928-1941.

short-term Government securities were not self-liquidating, and longer-term Government securities were still less liquid. Even as late as 1935 a group of 69 economists sent a memorandum to Congress urging that:

> . . . The supply of non-commercial paper eligible for discount should be further restricted, not enlarged. . . . It is the function of a central banking system to maintain at all times a liquid portfolio, since the system holds the ultimate reserves of the nation's banks.
>
> All measures designed to correct weaknesses in the Federal Reserve System should seek . . . to increase, not reduce, its commercial nature. They should assure, not impair, its liquidity.[9]

(4) Even if an expansionary monetary policy did no harm, it had little chance of inducing recovery. For example, Kemmerer believed that the large Federal Reserve purchases in 1932 lowered "confidence," made business unwilling to invest and banks unwilling to lend, and lowered the velocity of money.[10]

Under the conditions of early 1931, Sprague stated, ". . . I am disposed to think that monetary agencies are almost helpless of themselves to stay the downward course of the price level, to say nothing of being able to induce an upward movement."[11]

Such wide differences in theory and in policy prescriptions were by no means confined to professional economists; they were also evident in Government, in the financial community, among businessmen, and in the community at large. In this confusion of theory and policy advice, Federal Reserve officials must have wondered: which advice should we take? Should we take positive measures to expand money and credit? Should we encourage "natural liquidation"? Should we simply respond passively to demands for credit at "normal" interest rates reflecting "the needs of trade"? Should our primary concern be to conserve the liquidity of the Reserve Banks themselves? Or should we relax because what we do or don't do isn't very important anyway?

---

[9] *Hearings before the House Banking and Currency Committee on H. R. 5357,* 74th Congress, 1st Session (March 1935), pp. 760-761.

[10] *American Economic Review Supplement,* March 1933, p. 134. See also same publication, March 1934, p. 99.

[11] *Minutes of Evidence Taken Before the Committee on Finance and Industry,* Vol. II, February 19, 1931, p. 312.

Theories and policy attitudes within the Federal Reserve System during the early 1930's were almost as diverse as those outside. A few officials were strong and consistent advocates of active expansionary policies, including both large purchases of Government securities and sharp reductions of discount and bill-buying rates. But these were few indeed. Of the members of the Federal Reserve Board, only one consistently took this position—Governor Meyer after his appointment in September 1930. Harrison of New York and Black of Atlanta were the only Reserve Bank Governors to advocate and support consistently active expansionary policies. Even these officials tended to think in terms of credit conditions rather than the money supply, and they sometimes, but not always, judged credit conditions by the behavior of interest rates. Thus they sometimes made the mistake of assuming that a decline of interest rates signified in some sense an "easier monetary policy" even if the fall of rates resulted largely from declines in demands for credit. Such a mistake would have been less likely if their guide had been the quantity of money or of total bank credit.

The ideas and policy positions of the other members of the Federal Reserve Board and of the other Governors of the Reserve Banks differed considerably. Some did on occasion support active expansionary policies. However, a large majority of them displayed a strong affinity for commercial loan ideas, including the desirability of "natural liquidation," passive adaptation of credit to the needs of trade, and avoidance of "artificial" easing measures. Their general approach was indicated in a recommendation made in January 1930 by Governor Norris of the Philadelphia Reserve Bank for the majority of the members of the Open Market Investment Committee.

> . . . the recommendation is made that we see no necessity for operations in Government securities at this time either to halt or to expedite the present trend of credit. The majority of the Committee is not in favor of any radical reduction in the bill rate or radical buying of bills which would create an artificial ease or necessitate reduction in the discount rate. If that reduction comes about naturally from further liquidation or reduced demand, all well and good, but we do not feel that there should be any active effort to bring that about. . . . We distinctly feel that no operation in bills should be undertaken for the purpose of either forcing or facilitating a reduction of discount rates by any bank.

These and other similar attitudes were expressed repeatedly by Reserve Bank Governors. For example, Governor McDougal of Chicago consistently opposed purchases of Government securities, complained that credit conditions had become so easy as to be "sloppy," and sometimes advocated sales of securities or reductions of bill holdings in order to firm money market conditions. Chairman Austin of the Philadelphia Reserve Bank objected to purchases of securities and bills in March 1930, noting that:

> . . . it lays us open to the apparent undesirable charge that the action is not justified by the demand for credit but for some other purpose, it may be for boosting business, making a market for securities, or for some other equally criticizable cause that will certainly come back to plague us.

In refusing to participate in purchases of Government securities in June 1930, Governor Calkins of San Francisco explained:

> With credit cheap and redundant we do not believe that business recovery will be accelerated by making credit cheaper and more redundant.
>
> We find no reason to believe that excessively cheap money will promote or create a bond market, seeing evidence in the recent past to the contrary, and, further, do not consider the promotion or creation of a bond market one of the functions of the Federal Reserve System.

In early 1930, officials of the Boston Bank preferred "to see things go along as they were for a time" because "there is more cleansing to be done." As late as August 1931 Governor Young voted against further purchases of Government securities, commenting that he

> . . . would rather see the portfolios of the Federal Reserve System composed of bills and discounts, and regretted to see two important functions nullified by operations in government securities.

Governor Talley of the Dallas Reserve Bank complained in March 1930:

> Everyone wants to keep business jazzed up all the time, and have it run along at boom figures. It seems to me the sounder course to pursue, after having done this for some time, is to catch up and let the public pay some of its debts.

He added later, "Satisfaction of a demand for further capital supplies would tend to increase overproduction."

Governors Seay of Richmond and Fancher of Cleveland sometimes supported positive expansionary actions, but on several occasions they objected that interest rates had been pushed too low.
Deputy Governor Atteberry of St. Louis expressed the view in mid-
1930 that "fictitiously easy money" might have adverse effects.

> *The discussion here develops the idea that excessive efforts
> in the interest of fictitious easy money may have just the op-
> posite effect from that intended. It has been suggested that
> such efforts have the psychological effect of increasing the
> feeling of uncertainty and thus discouraging buying other than
> necessity demands.*

Officials of both the Minneapolis and Kansas City Reserve Banks
usually opposed positive expansionary actions.

As noted earlier, Governor Meyer was the only member of the
Board who strongly and consistently supported positive expansionary
policies. The others were generally no more than reluctant supporters
of security purchases before September 1930; some became more
favorably inclined after that time. They were usually more favorable
to reductions of discount and bill-buying rates, though they often
favored less rapid and smaller reductions than those proposed by
New York.

The examples cited above suggest the wide variety of implicit
theories and policy attitudes which permeated the System during the
early 1930's, influenced policy decisions, and made it impossible for
the System to formulate and carry out strong and active expansionary
policies.

In concentrating on the influence of theory on monetary and credit
policies, I do not imply that policies can be explained wholly in
terms of theory, either of current theory or that of "some defunct
economist." A full explanation would require an investigation of the
entire intellectual, social, political, and economic environment. For
one thing it would have to explain why, when alternative theories
are available, one theory is chosen over another. Why, for example,
did so many adhere to the commercial loan theory, with its implications of relatively passive accommodation to private demands for
commercial credit, rather than to the quantity theory, which suggests
more positive control? Yet the commercial loan theory did have profound effects on the Federal Reserve. It influenced the very structure
of the System; no quantity theorist setting up an agency to control

the nation's money supply would have created 12 central banks, each originally expected to be largely autonomous. It influenced the powers granted to the System, and especially its emphasis on commercial credit. It influenced the thinking of professional economists and others outside, and thus the environment in which the System operated. And it had a profound effect on large numbers of Federal Reserve officials.

Nor can we be certain that this theory, with its remarkable ability to survive repeated refutations, is finally dead.

SOME CHANGES IN IDEAS ON
CENTRAL BANKING

ELMER WOOD

It was forty years ago that I first heard about Karl Bopp. North Carolina State College needed a teacher for a term while I was on leave and Harry Gunnison Brown recommended Karl as the most brilliant of the young men he knew. He had been doing graduate work at Missouri and (among other things) had had courses in the monetary field with Harvey Rogers. After finishing the term of teaching at N. C. State, Karl went to Wisconsin for further graduate work in economics and then came back to Missouri to work on his Ph.D. It was then that I first met him (as I had just joined the Department). From that time I considered him a friend and soon one of my closest friends. For ten years we were colleagues on the Missouri Faculty and during that time I had the advantage of free discussion with him. The things about him that appealed to me most were his complete objectivity and honesty and his fundamental kindness. In a discussion he made one feel that there was no gap to cross. I owe a great deal to Karl, both from my association with him over the years and for the ideas in his published work. His writings on central banking, particularly in the field of the criteria of policy, have become classics, as has his work on Reichsbank Operations, 1876-1914.

IN THIS PAPER I propose to comment on some of the changes in approach to central banking analysis that seem to me to have occurred during the past half century. Many of the ideas were not new in the sense that no one had ever thought of them before; it is rather that the order of importance of things changes until finally one realizes that the whole approach is different from that of former days.

Variations in Public Opinion About the
Capabilities of Monetary Policy

The public's views about what can be accomplished with monetary policy in maintaining prosperity and stabilizing the price level have varied considerably over the past half century. In the very early period of the System a limited stabilizing effect was expected— beyond the avoidance of panics; we had to follow the gold standard. During the twenties confidence picked up. The very large gold reserve seemed to give more freedom in developing policy, and central banks in the leading countries seemed willing to coordinate their policies. A few readers may remember the Stable Money luncheons at the national meetings of the A.E.A. Brown, Fisher, Kemmerer, and Young were often there. Strong told Congressional Committees that he was hopeful about the prospects for maintaining business stability but stated that there were causes of instability that monetary policy might not be able to deal with. Everything considered, however, including his record of accomplishment, one should count him among the optimists. It was a period of intense study of the business cycle—Persons's work at Harvard and Mitchell's at Columbia were widely known. On the whole, people were hopeful about what monetary policy could do in moderating the cycle—though in that era there was wide interest in fiscal policy also.

During the thirties there were many who advocated a very aggressive monetary expansion, and there was finally new legislation for this purpose. No short statement can summarize public opinion in that strange period. It was the beginning of a much greater reliance on fiscal policy for influencing the level of economic activity. As the depression wore on there was a widespread belief in the secular stagnation theory. Hansen referred to monetary policy as the "handmaiden" to fiscal policy. The ideas of Keynes's *General Theory* were taking hold.

It was not until the Korean war that confidence in the effectiveness of monetary policy was restored. The Federal Reserve, Congress, and the public feared serious inflation with a frozen rate structure. Monetary policy now shares the honors with fiscal policy, partly because the public understands monetary policy better and partly because the mammoth spending by national and local governments has driven people to search for means of reducing the rate of inflation, or to halt it.

Not long ago the use of monetary and fiscal policy to control the level of spending—with high employment and very little inflation—enjoyed more prestige than ever before. At the moment there is more doubt; there is a question as to whether public spending will be sufficiently restrained.

In an economy where the whole physiology is changing rapidly and where all sorts of decisions about spending and pricing are getting more into the hands of the Government and power groups—and where the political structure itself is changing—monetary controls have to be geared into the economic-political complex as seems best to an informed judgment.

Money in Existence and Money Potential in a Practical Sense

During the past half century there has been a shift in the way people view the monetary expansion potential; not perhaps in the way they formally state the matter, but in the way they reason and operate. The money concept we inherited from the past dealt with a quantity of money in being, precious metals. When paper currency of limited elasticity and deposits were included in the analysis, the amount of money in the hands of the public plus deposits seemed to give the best calibration of the independent monetary variable that the members of the public could not control but must adjust to.

The Federal Reserve System was given the rather vague assignment to accommodate commerce, industry, and agriculture, and through experience had to work out for itself a set of procedures and objectives. Its assignment certainly did seem to include the prevention of undue tightness of money, seasonally and generally, within the limits of redeeming in gold and meeting various legal requirements. In dealing with their day-to-day problems the officials developed a reliable procedure for governing conditions in the money market, against the background of other rates and business developments. Possibly some of those who guided operations did not at first understand the monetary implications of what they did. Some of their critics claimed that, in standing ready to lend at a price (with certain limitations) to banks needing reserves, they created money for reasons extraneous to the needs of the economy for money balances on social grounds.

But experience taught System operators what havoc they would create if they denied advances. They had the most convincing proof that they could not set their note circulation and deposit liabilities at some predetermined level. In addition to finding what instruments to use and how they might be worked together most advantageously, they gradually developed the criteria for deciding how to use them— measures of immediate results and indicators of business developments in the making. Finally they had to decide on the broad objectives they should aim at. Some of these seemed in partial conflict and the officials had to decide what weight to give them. The complex of the decisions they were likely to make and the way they would operate were what constituted the American monetary potential. It was not a quantity of anything. What they did had an impact on the economy, and the creation of money was the *modus operandi,* but they could not use the quantity of money as their immediate guide to action. This was because the economy did not respond mechanically, but cumulatively, and the quantity of deposits and currency depended upon the targets of the public for balances as well as the level of spending and the liquidity of the banks making the loans.

In 1840 S. J. Lloyd said, "The rate at which the Bank (of England) may lend money is a fallacious criterion by which to test its measures; the amount of its issues compared with the bullion is the only true criterion . . . ."[1] Events proved him to be mistaken.

In recent years some people have revived the idea that the central bank should take as its main criterion of action the volume of currency and bank deposits. If it attempted to do so, it would cause strange variations in the money market and confusing signals of its intentions. Another group of economists would go further and require a predetermined rate of increase in total deposits and currency. To at least some members of this group, it would be a serious mistake to deviate from their rule in order to maintain an orderly money market and avert a financial crisis.

When people work with something they gradually learn what they can do with it and what they cannot; sometimes this is quite different from what they previously thought. The implication is not that one should reject scientific analysis in favor of engineering, but that the analytical structure should be built on facts of special knowledge.

Congress can of course prescribe such standards as it chooses, e.g., introduce a price stabilization feature into the Employment Act, overriding other objectives. In that event the monetary potential would be specified within limits, but it seems doubtful whether a particular procedure would be tied to it.

The Shift Somewhat from Static Analysis

Economists have always realized that the rate of spending in the economy has a momentum that is only gradually changed by monetary conditions, as well as by other impacts. But during the past two generations there has been a tendency to work this approach further into the framework of the analysis and to shift somewhat from the idea of an equilibrium of static forces. This is true, for instance, in the explanation of the impact of monetary conditions on prices.

This shift in approach is exemplified also in many of the explanations that were developed within the System. Officials in discussing open market operations (during the 1920's) pointed out that the purchase of securities by the Reserve Banks might have little immediate effect on the total reserves of the member banks, but would

---

[1] *Letter to J. B. Smith, Tracts,* p. 169.

usually lead to a reduction of advances to members. (Many students, including Karl, used to read such passages in Burgess.) The reduction of advances, however, would tend to ease credit conditions and might contribute toward improved business conditions. It was then that deposits and required reserves would tend to increase. What seemed to be implied, though probably not stated explicitly, was that the inertia in the rate of spending worked back through deposits and required reserves. People do not change their spending plans quickly just because credit is easier.

Also, the explanation of the factors influencing the currency in circulation showed that the economy had a momentum that would be modified only gradually by changes in credit conditions. It was only as retail trade and payrolls and the like increased that more currency would be required.

Making appropriate allowances, a somewhat similar explanation could have been given for the behavior of deposits. At times it seemed implicit in some of the discussions. Perhaps there was not always a full appreciation of the relation between the demand for bank loans and the demands of the public generally for deposit balances. These demands for cash could not take effect immediately through a decline of aggregate spending for obvious reasons. The line of least resistance was for some people to borrow more from the banks.

A further example of the shift from the static analysis: in reasoning about the impact of fiscal policy we do not consider that the level of spending depends on an equilibrium of tendencies at a moment but on the cumulative effect on an economy already in motion.

Changes in Ideas About Interest Rates

Graduate students used to be taught that Hume was right and that the Mercantilists were fundamentally wrong in assessing the influence of money on interest rates. Financial writers and people in the money market, though they held that rates were determined mostly by natural forces, considered that a change in the gold reserve was a natural force. Teachers of economics tried to reconcile the two points of view. The economy, in their view, had little tolerance for rates that were depressed by monetary means; though in their practical discussions they were less adamant about it than in their formal theory. Depressing rates by monetary means would, with a metallic standard, require later correction, with rates higher than they had been to begin with; with a paper standard, inflation prospects would in time surpass in importance the direct effect of the monetary expansion. Rates might rise to fantastic heights.

One thing we have learned from the experiments of the past two generations is that interest rates can be administered by monetary means to a much greater extent, and for much longer periods, than people used to believe. Economies in very large monetary areas are relatively impervious to incorrectly administered policies, or policies imposed by the requirements of the international standard; they can get along in a fair state of prosperity for decades with rates that are too high—at least they used to—and avoid any frightening inflation for long periods with rates that are too low. Fiscal policy could be a moderating factor, but more often public spending has been large when rates have been too low. The historical backdrop, of course, makes a great deal of difference as to what the tolerance of the economy will be. (Smaller monetary areas naturally have less freedom of action in administering rates.)

There has been quite a swing in ideas on the matter during the past four decades. The very low rates of the middle and late thirties were in considerable part the accident of circumstances, though they were welcomed by the Treasury. The continuation of those low rates in the face of obviously inflationary conditions during World War II and the postwar period seemed shocking to some people, but they were very much in the minority. Most people seemed to believe there were far better means for avoiding inflation than raising interest rates—taxation and various kinds of direct economic controls. Chronic depression, they believed, was the real postwar danger to fear.

During the early fifties predominant opinion turned back again. Although by 1952 most middle-aged people could scarcely remember when rate levels on Government securities had not been approximately administered, in a short time the usual opinion expressed was that rates were determined by the natural forces of the market, i.e., when not interfered with by the monetary authorities. The latter should follow the market. This switch in financial opinion was somewhat surprising, but historically the consequences have on the whole been favorable. It helped the Federal Reserve to regain control of monetary policy and resist the gradual erosion of the dollar.

Debt Structure in Connection with Monetary Control

Interest in the volume and structure of debt is not new. Nineteenth century writers gave a great deal of attention to the matter, especially in connection with financial crises. During the 1920's brokers loans, especially those made by nonbank lenders, attracted wide attention and Congressional inquiry. Since the crisis of the early thirties there has been a more intensive study of debt as a whole and its relation to monetary control. The deterioration in the quality of debt led to the destruction of thousands of banks and their deposits, and much of the effort in reconstructing the economy following the crisis was devoted to restoring the debt structure and the solvency of financial institutions. Government agencies made loans or guarantees to corporations and individuals on a vast scale and under a wide variety of conditions. Many contemporaries regarded these accomplishments as the most important part of the monetary reconstruction. Since World War II the private and local government debt has become so vast and such an integral part of the economy that an analysis of all phases of it has become important to central banking direction.

The influence of debt on the economy has attracted attention from several angles. For instance, there was a time in the forties when some Federal Reserve officials thought that for a few years it would be dangerous to the economy to tighten credit to the point of causing appreciable capital losses to banks and other large holders of bonds.

At times there has been concern over the impact of new debt on purchases in particular areas of the economy, as well as on aggregate demand. The Federal Reserve has been given control over several different classes of debt at one time or another in addition to its permanent jurisdiction over margins for securities loans. While these regulations (delegated by law or Presidential order) were aimed especially to prevent excessive expenditure in particular areas, they were intended also as a reinforcement for general controls. The Federal Reserve has never been power hungry for these selective controls and for the most part prefers general monetary controls.

Then there is the liquidity angle, the effect on the holder of debt. Everyone is familiar with the use of debt instruments partly in place of cash on corporation balance statements. Also, the great supply of debt in general promotes the growth of financial institutions, which can issue liquid claims against it to the public. People have come to realize that it is not merely the supply potential of money that influences spending; the nonbank members of the economy can provide liquidity for one another in varying degrees. It is true that the debtor may have his liquidity reduced, partially offsetting the liquidity of the creditor, but the net effect is often great.

One needs a broader term than liquidity to describe the expansive potential of debt. In a large economy that is stable and resists rapid acceleration, an increase of debt can find placement easily; for the public collectively there is no immediate alternative but cash. Individually there is an escape into real assets, but a comparatively small rise of prices or business expansion usually deters one from going very far. The general growth of debt is nevertheless expansive. A tightening of credit can be used as a counteractive, but that has to be decided on the basis of all the guides to credit policy. The causes of expansion are not earmarked.

During the 1950's there was a widely held view that nonbanking financial institutions, since they were not required to maintain a reserve at the Reserve Banks, seriously interfered with the control of credit conditions by the Federal Reserve. Insofar as it referred to rate levels in the money market and other rates moving in sympathy, this was a mistaken view. There was still a minimum of a special kind of money required by the economy that only the Federal Reserve could provide, and the terms and conditions that it set for providing this amount would be reflected in the loan market as a whole. But though the nonbanking institutions were no threat to the System's grip on competitive loan rates, their activities did favor the growth of debt generally and in particular areas.

The properties of debt, as well as its volume, affect its expansive potential. At the present time (July 1969) one can be sure that the authorities are very much interested in how the quality of debt can stand up under the continued pressure of tight money. Everyone sees the possibilities of the cumulative effects of a change in attitude about the future safety of debt. A spasm of distrust might cause a flight toward cash and debt assets of unquestioned security. Yet there lurks a fear of inflation, the possibility of a panicky rush toward real assets. It is a rare thing for these two kinds of problems to be presented so close together. It is here that one sees the need for an intimate knowledge of what is going on in the financial world—even what is about to happen; and it is here that central bank technique has made great strides.

Changes in Ideas About the International Standard

The theoretical beliefs about the gold standard when the Federal

Reserve System was established were those which had been developed in England. Though the facts about London's position as the world financial center were certainly understood, it was not fully appreciated what influence England had on the world economy. Other countries used sterling balances and short-term investments as an important part of their reserves;[2] but the whole arrangement in turn depended on England's financial skill and upon her economic and political strength. Professor Clay (in recent years) emphasized that England always provided a source of international reserves by serving as a buyer of last resort. The formal theory of the gold standard, however, was that each country had to conform to the aggregate behavior; a country that got out of line would lose gold.

After World War I the special position of the United States was thought to be due to the currency disturbances abroad and to the strength of the American economy. The large gold reserve here gave this country a great deal of leeway in developing its policies, but this was not thought to be a permanent situation. United States policies were aimed at bringing about a return to gold by other countries and bringing about a "better" distribution of gold. There was a serious effort to promote cooperation among leading central banks, but there was not full appreciation of the dollar's new position as an international currency and how much influence it exerted on monetary action abroad. The Federal Reserve in raising the discount rate in November 1931 was following the rules of the game as they were then understood.

The Great Depression brought a complete revision of ideas about the gold standard in the world generally. We are all familiar with the wide variety of devices that were used to promote trade and revive employment in the thirties. Many of them seemed to be associated with nationalist ideology and state regulation of the internal economy. During the forties the problem shifted from unemployment to one of inflation and shortages of goods, but exchange controls, rate variations, and a wide variety of trade restrictions continued. The International Monetary Fund was intended to bring some order in the exchange network, gradually to get rid of exchange controls, and to provide temporary relief in balancing international payments, but it was not intended to restore the old mechanism of the gold standard.

---

[2] In *Indian Currency and Finance* (1913), Keynes pointed out that the gold standard was actually a kind of gold exchange standard.

To many observers in 1950 the nineteenth century theory of the gold standard seemed no longer applicable to modern arrangements. The standard had scarcely been restored in the twenties before it crashed, and it had not been in operation in a meaningful sense during the thirties and forties. Congress maintained its outward forms in the United States, but few people believed that the monetary systems of the world would be operated according to the state of their reserves. It would scarcely have been in keeping with the Employment Act and it would not have been in keeping with the then current ideas in other countries for maintaining full employment and for broadening the scope of the state control of economies.

With the remarkable recovery of European and many other economies in the fifties and sixties, their reserves of gold and dollar exchange improved strikingly. Scarcely had this position been attained before some of them raised questions about the soundness of the dollar. Considering the record of the dollar in maintaining purchasing power, relative to that of other countries, this seemed a very odd criticism.

Here in the United States financial public opinion seemed to shift quickly back to the old orthodoxy about the gold standard. In the light of later events, however, it seems doubtful that opinion within the System could be described in that way. Since the events of the past few years are so well known, there is no need to attempt a summary. The unfortunate part was that the press led the public to believe that the drain of gold for hoarding purposes was inseparable from the problem of the balance of international payments— that the payments deficit was the basic cause of the drain. All of the leading financial countries were concerned with the drain of gold. It would have harmed all of them for the United States to contract credit to the point of causing a world crisis in an attempt to stop the flow of gold into hoarding channels. The United States displayed no weakness in losing gold to hoarding channels; the reserve here was the main source available.

Once again the monetary authorities of the United States adapted methods to circumstances, maintaining the essentials and the desirable features of what has come down to us from the past. The dollar continued as an international reserve currency and the network of exchange rates was preserved. The leakage of gold into hoarding channels from the monetary reserves of the leading countries was practically stopped, while at the same time gold can still perform its traditional function as a means of payment among official institutions at a fixed rate. Under these circumstances the value of gold in the speculative market is of no great importance.[3]

There is still a problem of large foreign holdings of dollars. There are good grounds for believing that international reserves are not too large, provided confidence in the dollar continues. (The main reason given by the former Secretary of the Treasury for wanting approval of the SDR's was that there was need for greater international liquidity.) Confidence will depend on substantially reducing U. S. Government expenditure at home and abroad and stopping internal inflation.

One of the fruitful ideas of the present is that foreign holders of dollars should assume some of the responsibility for keeping supplies at appropriate levels. There are many kinds of restrictions on the use of dollars that they could ease. (Exchange controls, for instance, are by no means a thing of the past.) In ordinary times, however, there is good reason to believe that other countries, in their own interest, will invest and purchase here (directly or indirectly) with dollars beyond reasonable reserve levels.

*   *   *   *   *   *   *

A final word about Karl: If the country should ever face a great emergency, I hope he will be among those who decide what to do about it.

---

[3] It is hard to see what advantage there was to either the United States or Great Britain in restoring the London gold market in the fifties, aside from the profits to the dealers.

POLICY NORMS AND CENTRAL BANKING

ALLAN SPROUL

FROM THE EARLIEST DAYS of central banking in its primitive forms to the present era in which central banks, as the national monetary authorities, are charged with promoting the general economic interests of the nations they serve, domestically and internationally, there has been a continuous pursuit of a will-o'-the-wisp—a policy norm which would guide the operations of such banks with a minimum intrusion of fallible human judgment. The theory has been that a central bank, or any monetary control, must have a supreme norm of reference; that it cannot use more than one norm of reference.[1]

The modern beginnings of this passionate pursuit of an elusive object may be traced to misconceptions which have grown up concerning the operation of the international gold standard during the period 1880 to 1914. Prior to that period, the forerunners of present-day central banks were designed primarily to finance governments or acquired a tinge of public responsibility because of the magnitude of their private banking operations. In the years following 1880, however, most of the principal trading nations of the world had linked their currencies to gold—either they were on a "full" gold standard or a "limping" gold standard or a "gold exchange" standard or some combination of these standards—and the central banks of the financially developed countries had taken primary responsibility for maintaining the international convertibility of their national currencies, directly or indirectly, into gold at a legal parity.

Responsibility for a system of fixed exchange rates necessarily focused attention on international movements of goods and services, capital and credit, and on the rise and fall of the country's international reserves (gold or other legal reserves) which could be used as a buffer to confine fluctuations in the exchange rate within a narrow band around parity. The central bank's response to a fall in the exchange rate and a loss of reserves was usually an increase in its discount rate designed to reverse the movement and, with less uniformity, the response to a rise in the exchange rate and a gain of reserves was a reduction of the discount rate. But the timing and extent of such changes were matters of judgment and their effect on the domestic

---

[1] Unpublished paper of Robert B. Warren, Institute of Advanced Study, Princeton, New Jersey.

economy, while secondary to the primary objective, did not always go unattended, particularly in times of loss of public confidence and financial crisis. The whole working of the system depended upon a complex of institutions and techniques and economic conditions, domestic and international, favored by a period of relatively moderate shifts of trade and capital movements around multilateral balance, and fostered by the absence of great wars. To describe the system as an automatic gold standard, hardly touched by human hands, is to misrepresent it.

As the studies of Arthur T. Bloomfield have indicated, "Not only did central banking authorities, so far as can be inferred from their actions, not consistently follow any simple or single rule or criterion of policy, or focus exclusively on considerations of convertibility, but they were constantly called upon to exercise, and did exercise, their judgment in such matters as whether or not to act, the kind and extent of action to take, and the instrument or instruments of policy to use. . . . Discretionary judgment and action were an integral part of central banking before 1914, even if monetary management was not oriented toward maintenance of domestic economic growth and employment and stabilization of prices in the broader modern sense."[2]

The discussion in the United States concerning the creation of a central bank, or a central banking system, during the years before the passage of the Federal Reserve Act in 1913 took place in a period when belief in the automatic character of the international gold standard was little tarnished by later heresies; and gold redeemability at home and internationally was a widely accepted article of faith in this country. Attention was centered on changes in the national monetary system which would correct weaknesses in the domestic banking structure, but which would not interfere with domestic adjustment to "automatic" international monetary arrangements under the gold standard.

The principal purposes of the Federal Reserve Act in a monetary sense, and aside from matters of bank supervision and the pyramiding of bank reserve funds in New York, were as stated in the preamble to the Act: ". . . to furnish an elastic currency and to afford a means of rediscounting commercial paper." The panic of 1907 had focused attention on these problems. Subsequent studies had pinpointed the difficulty as being inherent in a currency largely in the form of gold certificates and national bank notes and in bank reserve requirements

---

[2] *Monetary Policy Under the International Gold Standard, 1880-1914*, published by the Federal Reserve Bank of New York.

which placed a limit on bank loans and investments more or less regardless of the appropriate and changing needs of the economy.

Although there was little specific reference in the final Federal Reserve Act to the promotion of general economic stability and stability of prices, there was a thread of theory running through the consideration of various drafts of the bill which saw in the legislation a means of automatically controlling the volume of currency and bank loans and investments in a way which it was thought would go far to accomplish these purposes. This theory found expression in the so-called "eligibility" provisions of the Act. The paper which the Federal Reserve Banks could discount or purchase ordinarily had to be, in the terminology of the time, "self-liquidating commercial paper"—that is, it had to be based on short-term agricultural, industrial, or commercial transactions which gave assurance of payment at maturity. This was the kind of paper which the Federal Reserve Banks could pledge as collateral (in addition to gold) for Federal Reserve notes, which were to become the elastic part of the currency, and this was the kind of paper which member banks could present to the Federal Reserve Banks for rediscount in order to acquire additional reserve funds with which to support additions to their existing loans and investments. Since the volume of such paper would rise and fall with the transaction needs of the economy, whether in the form of currency or bank deposits subject to check, excessive increases or decreases of currency circulation and excessive expansion or contraction of bank loans and investment would not occur. Or so it was believed.

This experiment in a species of automatic control of central banking operations did not long survive its inclusion in the Federal Reserve Act. It was first eroded because it proved to be impractical in the day-to-day operations of the Reserve Banks, and then was voided by amendment to the Act (in 1916) which permitted Reserve Banks to make advances to member banks on their promissory notes secured by deposit or pledge of United States Government securities.

This was done partly in preparation for financial needs which might arise if the United States entered the war then raging in Europe, but the permanence of the change was the result of an acquired awareness that the concept of eligibility was unrealistic. As stated by Goldenweiser: "Member banks borrow from the Federal Reserve Banks almost exclusively for the purpose of building up their reserve deposits (with the Reserve Banks) to the necessary (required) level. The banks lend money to such customers (and make such investments) as they choose and meet the currency requirements of their depositors.

If, as a net result arising out of all their operations, they find themselves short of reserves, they borrow from the Reserve Banks. . . . There is thus no relationship between the character of the discounted paper and the use to which the funds are put." Furthermore, ". . . the theory disregards the fact that banks can expand at a multiple rate on the basis of Federal Reserve credit; consequently paper representing the movement of goods to market, when discounted with the Federal Reserve Banks, can become the basis of several times its value in loans of an entirely different character."[3] Self-liquidating commercial paper as an automatic means of controlling the expansion and contraction of bank credit or adjusting the money supply to the productive requirements of the economy was a theoretical and mechanical failure. It provided neither a quantitative nor a qualitative norm of central bank policy.

Along this chronological road, the idea that central bank policy should find its normal guide in stability of prices was never far from the surface of discussion. It had been around for a long time, but it received increased attention in the United States following World War I, when there was a sharp increase and then a sharp fall in prices, and when Professor Irving Fisher of Yale became a champion and articulate advocate of a dollar of "invariable purchasing power."

He held that the only unstable unit of measurement in civilized countries was the unit of money, that this was a survival of barbarism, and that it was manifest that an economic system which is largely based on agreements made at one date to pay money at another date would have to find a way to adjust its contracts to changes in the purchasing power of money. (The problem is still with us.) This, he argued, had become possible because a means had been devised for measuring the aberrations of an unstable monetary unit, to wit a representative index number of prices. And his specific proposal was that the monetary authorities should use such an index number of prices as a guide for adjustments (perhaps every two months) in the weight of the gold content of the dollar so as to keep its purchasing power invariable. If prices tended to rise or fall the movement would be corrected by "loading" or "unloading" the gold in the dollar.

This idea of a "goods dollar" or a "market basket dollar" or a "compensated dollar," in the form suggested, sounded academic and impractical in a country (or a world) which had become accustomed to the idea (if not the practice) that, if external price levels were unstable, it could not keep both its domestic price level and the exchange rate

---

[3] *American Monetary Policy* (1951), p. 126.

of its currency stable and that (under whatever form of the gold standard it adhered to) it must put stability of the external exchange ahead of stability of the internal price level.

The idea was opposed on other grounds than those growing out of habit and custom, however. It was argued that (a) no price index, no matter how comprehensive, could include all of the things for which money is spent; (b) that the relation between the volume of credit and the level of prices is not precise and determinable but is indirect and inconstant; (c) that things which do not enter into the price-money relationship, such as an increase or decrease in the efficiency of production and distribution, and changes in quality of product would affect an index of prices; and (d) that the movements of a price index which might be used to trigger monetary counteraction would usually be late, since they would refer to past rises or falls in prices, whereas it would be future price moves which should be counteracted.

Despite its break with gold-standard thinking and the defects of the proposal itself, it had a simple and direct appeal which led to its consideration by the Congress at hearings of the Committee on Banking and Currency of the House of Representatives. The proposal was put forward and was the subject of hearings of the Committee in 1926, that all of the powers of the Federal Reserve System should be used to promote stability of the price level.

A principal witness opposing such a statutory instruction to the Federal Reserve System was Governor Benjamin Strong of the Federal Reserve Bank of New York. Governor Strong was aware of and used the various arguments which had been advanced in opposition to legislation that would order the Federal Reserve to use all of its powers to stabilize price levels, but the main thrust of his testimony was that there could be no mathematical formula for the administration of Federal Reserve policy nor for the regulation of prices. He accepted the view that credit is a major influence on prices and that the promotion of price stability should be a major policy objective of the Federal Reserve, but his views had a broader scope, comprising ideas later finding expression in the Employment Act of 1946. They were that the Government, through its various agencies, has a responsibility for maintaining maximum employment and production and promoting economic growth, and that the objective of credit policy should be to insure that there is sufficient money and credit available to conduct the business of the nation and to finance not only seasonal increases in demand but also the annual normal growth of the economy. He was willing to have the powers of the Federal Reserve System used to promote stability of the price level, but he also recognized that choices and compromises had to be made between various objectives at various times and that, in the end, human judgment has to govern the decisions which are made.

Stability of prices as a norm of central bank policy as a supreme norm of reference did not survive. (Although the Employment Act of 1946 does include promotion of maximum purchasing power in its policy declaration.) Other candidates for that honor have arisen or persisted, however. The doctrine of "bills only" (common name) or "bills preferably" (botanical name) may be placed in this category, not because when viewed as a technique of Federal Reserve open market operations it deserves this prominence, but because its proponents came to place so much stress on the avoidance of price and yield effects of open market operations that they finally asserted (and made it a part of the operating directives of the System Open Market Account) that the sole purpose of open market operations is the provision and absorption of reserves (excepting the correction of disorderly markets in Government securities). This was an attempt to elevate what first had been advanced as a matter of technique to the eminence of a mechanical rule of Federal Reserve policy—a "supreme norm of reference" for the principal element of flexible and effective central bank policy in the United States.

The controversy which this doctrine aroused for several years until it was abandoned in 1961 resulted in a considerable literature and involved emotions which seemed to widen and distort the differences of those who favored and those who opposed the policy. In a broad survey such as this, no extended discussion of all of the arguments which were brought forward on both sides can be attempted. Only a summary presentation of its life history from birth to death is possible. The formal birth certificate was recorded in May 1951 when the Federal Open Market Committee voted to authorize its Chairman (William McC. Martin) to appoint a committee to make a study of the Government securities market. But the idea had been conceived earlier by members of the staff of the Board of Governors (and of the Open Market Committee) who not only were interested in the operation of the Government securities market as a channel through which to reach and regulate the reserve position of the member banks, but who also were dissatisfied with the performance of the management of the System Open Market Account at the Federal Reserve Bank of New York and with the power distribution involved in the linkage between policymaking by the Federal Open Market Committee at Washington and the execution of policy by the New York Bank. The study committee, which became known as the Ad Hoc Subcommittee, was set up and began its work in May 1952, and its findings and recommendations became a subject of discussion at a meeting of the Federal Open Market Committee in March 1953, after a delay which was reported to have stemmed from the fact that it had become apparent that "the issues involved in the Committee's terms of reference are of a most fundamental and far-reaching character. They involve not only the most complicated problems of technique and organization, but profound problems of a more theoretical or philosophical nature."

And yet, at the March 1953 meeting of the Federal Open Market Committee there was unanimous approval of the two most important statements of policy with respect to the operations of the System Open Market Account which had been suggested by the Ad Hoc Subcommittee. (Underlining supplied).

> (1) *Under present conditions, operations for the System account should be confined to the short end of the market (not including correction of disorderly markets);*
>
> (2) *It is not now the policy of the Committee to support any pattern of prices and yields in the Government securities market, and intervention in the Government securities market is solely to effectuate the objectives of monetary and credit policy (including correction of disorderly markets).*

The second of these ordinances, which really should have been first, put a seal of disapproval on any future pegging of prices of Government securities such as had been practiced during World War II, and in the postwar period of readjustment in the Government securities market while the consequences of financing the war were being unwound. The first ordinance represented a consensus that, *in most circumstances,* the Open Market Committee would be able to attain its policy objectives by operating in the market for Treasury bills and other short-term Government securities.

The apple of discord became apparent later when there was a creeping movement to give constitutional permanence to the doctrine which had become known as "bills only," and to engrave it permanently in the public mind, and particularly in the minds of Government securities dealers, by a dribble of statements of individuals concerning the "ground rules" for all future open market operations, even though the question of publicizing ground rules had been deferred by the Open Market Committee for further study.

At the September 1953 meeting of the Open Market Committee[4] the phrase "under present conditions" was dropped from the directive that operations for System Account be confined to the short end of the market, and replaced by the clause "until such time as (it) may be superseded or modified by further action of the Federal Open Market Committee." And, at the December meeting of the Committee in 1953, the general statement with respect to System intervention in the Government securities market was changed to read "transactions for System account in the open market shall be entered into *solely for the purpose of providing or absorbing reserves,* except in the correction of disorderly markets."[5]

The major differences of opinion, at least within the Federal Open Market Committee, had now become (1) whether it was misleading and undesirable to promulgate a capsule version of the whole theory of central banking, and the whole purpose of open market operations, which mentioned only the providing and absorbing of reserves and omitted the essential linkage between such actions and the cost and availability of credit; (2) whether it was unnecessary and undesirable to endow the doctrine of "bills only" with an air of permanence as a norm of System open market operations, no matter what changes in economic conditions and in the market structure of interest rates might occur; (3) whether it was desirable to attempt to provide the Government securities dealers with a continuing set of "ground rules" for System open market operations, which would seek to protect the market from the hazards of there being a central banking system whose policy decisions, and whose every action to make its policy decisions effective, must influence the cost and availability of credit throughout the economy and, therefore, the movements of interest rates and prices

---

[4] There was a June meeting of the Open Market Committee at which there were five presidents of Federal Reserve Banks and four members of the Board of Governors, and at which the March directive relating to confining operations for System Account to the short-term sector of the market was rescinded, with the understanding that the Executive Committee of the Federal Open Market Committee (which was later abolished) would be free to determine how operations should be carried on in the light of the current general credit policy of the full Open Market Committee. The five presidents voted for the motion to rescind and the four Board members voted against it (following the meeting, the Executive Committee, consisting of three Board members and two presidents, decided to confine *current* operations to Treasury bills). By the time of the September meeting of the Open Market Committee, three of the presidents had changed their minds concerning preserving such limited freedom of action and the March pronouncement, as amended, was restored by a vote of nine to two.

[5] This change had a special application to so-called "swap" transactions in connection with Treasury financing, but it also was an attempt to nail down permanently a general philosophy of open market operations.

through the whole range of maturities in the Government securities market.

In the running debate which followed, a great deal of discussion was devoted to elucidating the obvious necessity of having a properly functioning Government securities market in which to conduct System open market operations; to trying to prove that confining such operations to the short end of the maturity scale would improve, or had improved, the "breadth, depth, and resiliency" of the market; and to asserting that substitutability was more important than arbitrage in carrying impulses throughout the whole range of maturities. But the major questions involving the promulgation of a norm of central banking and the publication of permanent "ground rules" for the conduct of open market operations tended to be neglected, while the Federal Open Market Committee annually voted to perpetuate the views of its satisfied majority. It is ironical, perhaps, that the so-called "bills only" policy, which was hailed by one of its chief architects in October 1960 as "the greatest advance in central banking technique in the last decade," was overtaken by events and abandoned in February 1961. The Federal Open Market Committee then announced that the System Open Market Account was purchasing Government notes and bonds of varying maturities "in the light of conditions that have developed in the domestic economy and in the U.S. balance of payments." The question of "bills only" may arise again, of course; its abandonment can be endowed with no more real permanence than its adoption, but it is unlikely that it will ever be revived as the basis for the sweeping assertion that transactions for System Account in the open market shall be entered into solely for the purpose of providing or absorbing reserves.

It is reassuring on this score that the latest Joint Treasury-Federal Reserve Study of the U.S. Government Securities Market (April 1969) recommends that "System purchases of intermediate- and long-term U.S. Government coupon issues should be continued—even apart from use in correction or forestalling disorderly market conditions—as a useful supplement to bill purchases in providing reserves to the banking system and, when compelling reasons exist, for affecting to the extent consistent with reserve objectives interest rate pressures in specific short- or long-term maturity sectors of the debt market."

The mechanical purpose formula for Federal Reserve open market operations which grew out of the doctrine of "bills only" is a not too distant relative of what is, at the moment, the most virulent form of norm addiction, the "money supply" addiction. Both would rely wholly on market forces to produce desired effects flowing from Federal Reserve action affecting a single monetary aggregate. The present virulence of the money supply proposal for getting rid of the fallible judgment of central bankers, and substituting a mechanical formula for their gropings, may be ascribed to the existence of a "school" for the propagation of the faith and to a combination of circumstances relating to the respective merits of fiscal and monetary policy in helping to order our economic affairs which has stirred up academic dispute and endowed the views of the "school" with a modicum of public attention and political acceptance.

Once an energetic and forensically formidable economist assembles a massive collection of empirical historical evidence to provide apparent support for his opinions, and indoctrinates enough disciples who then go forth and preach the gospel, a "school" becomes established. If there happens to be another "school" of followers of another leader whose views have found wide professional and political acceptance in the past, and which now may be attacked with some hope of success, the stage is set for a rash of academic and journalistic coverage of the battle. The whole subject then comes to the attention of a growing group of men of affairs in politics and in business, and the risk arises that a shaky hypothesis may become something more than a source of academic argument and journalistic enterprise.

We are not concerned here, however, as to whether Keynes or Friedman is the economic messiah of our time, but with the claim of the monetarists that the money supply should be the sole or, at least, the supreme norm of reference of monetary policy. We are concerned with the proposal that the Federal Reserve should content itself with attempting to increase the money supply at a fixed annual rate (4 or 5 per cent a year is suggested) calculated on the average to be consistent with stable prices, thus providing a stable monetary framework in which other economic goals may be realized and avoiding the hazards of trying to use monetary policy as a flexible and sensitive instrument for influencing our economic affairs.

In the more restrained versions of this theory, it is admitted that monetary growth is not a precise and infallible source of future economic stability but that, on the average, (which conceals much variability in both the time delay and the magnitude of the response) there is a close relationship between the rate of change in the quantity of money and the rate of change in national income (at current prices) some six months or more later.

This is an appealing doctrine which "rolls up into one simple explanatory variable all of the many complex forces which determine aggregate demand." No wonder political interest has been aroused and a public following has emerged. But the economic peers of the monetarists are skeptical. They have raised many questions concerning the money supply theory which the monetarists have yet to answer convincingly. Drawing on the work of those who have addressed themselves to the problem and are competent to discuss it as professional economists, I shall list some of these questions.

First and foremost is the question of whether the asserted causal connection between cycles of growth of the money stock and cyclical movements of the economy runs from money to business activity or from business activity to money. It is akin to the question phrased by a British writer: "Did man begin to lose his general covering of hair when he began wearing clothes, or did he begin wearing clothes when he noticed he was going into a permanent moult?"

Second, what monetary aggregate is to be used as the guide of monetary policy; is it the money stock narrowly defined as currency in circulation and demand deposits at banks, or is it currency and demand deposits plus time deposits at banks, or is it the "monetary base," or is it the money supply which is "currently most meaningful in indicating monetary influence in economic activity"? Recent revisions of the most commonly used money supply series, and the patent sketchiness of such series stretching back into the historical and statistical past ("over a century") add point to this basic question.

Third, are the econometric models which the monetarists use to demonstrate how the transmission process proceeds from money to business activity adequate for the purpose?

Fourth, are not both price and quantity of money important; do you not have to take into account shifts in demand and in interest rates?

Fifth, do the observed variations in monetary time lags and monetary velocity cast doubts on the suggested simple causal relationship between the money supply and general economic activity; do they not suggest that there are unpredictable variables other than the money supply which influence the level of economic activity and which must be taken into account in devising monetary policy?

Sixth, the suggested monetary framework for the economy is put forward most precisely in terms of a closed economy, although it is admitted that it should involve a free foreign exchange market (floating exchange rates) in the open economy of which this country actually is a part. Is this a practical directive for monetary policy?

Even if some of these murky areas are cleared and the monetarists become less rigid in their formulations, experience suggests that the money supply norm of central bank policy eventually will take its place on the library shelves along with the policy norms of the past. With improvement of our knowledge and understanding of the present state of the economy and its likely future course, the money supply norm may leave a trace; the use of annual rates of change in the money supply as a navigational aid for central bank action (channel markers indicating maximum and minimum rates of growth to be sought) cannot be ruled out, but the discretionary band would have to be wide enough to accommodate the flexible requirements dictated by experience.

Practicing central bankers (and the governments to which they are responsible) cannot afford to be confined by formulae which attempt to cope, in precise measure, with the actions and anticipations of millions of human beings exercising a high degree of economic freedom of choice. Monetary policy can continue to make its contribution to the goals of vigorous sustainable economic growth, maximum attainable production and employment, and reasonable stability of prices, if its practitioners continue to sharpen their analyses of complex economic developments and continue to base their actions upon a balanced view of total situations. They cannot be relieved of this difficult task by doctrinaire policy norms.

REAPPRAISING THE FEDERAL RESERVE
DISCOUNT MECHANISM

ROBERT C. HOLLAND*

PRESENT-DAY AMERICA is replete with examples which emphasize the necessity for institutions to undergo periodic reevaluation and reform if they are to serve the needs of an evolving society. As one of the nation's key institutions, the Federal Reserve System has been subject to a wide variety of such revisionary efforts, internal and external; and, even if these may not always have been so timely, so objective, so organized, or so comprehensive as some may have wished, nonetheless they have been essential contributors to the evolution of a central banking mechanism that has come a long way from the institution envisioned by the drafters of the Federal Reserve Act.

The mode of organization of the Federal Reserve System contains enough different power centers and accommodates enough diverse points of view to generate a continual flow of internal reappraisals of one aspect or another of relevant theory and practice. Some have been modest, some have been major—depending on the criticalness of the issue and the time and resources available for its investigation.

One of the most ambitious of recent System exercises of this type has been a reappraisal of the philosophy and operations of the Federal Reserve lending function, popularly termed the "discount window." Karl Bopp was intimately involved in this reappraisal, as indeed he was in most of the significant internal studies of Federal Reserve operations over the past three decades—one concrete indication of the value his colleagues have placed on his judgment and his scholarship.[1] I was also a participant in the discount window reappraisal,[2] and I should like to draw on that experience to outline in following pages the general approach to the study, environmental considerations dictating the design of the discount mechanism, and the manner in which the proposed revision of the discount window is expected to

---

* Unless otherwise indicated, the views expressed in this essay are the responsibility of the author and do not necessarily represent official Federal Reserve positions. Special acknowledgment is due Miss Priscilla Ormsby of the Board's staff for her assistance in the preparation of this paper.

[1] Mr. Bopp served as a member of the top-level Steering Committee that was responsible for the overall direction and resolution of the discount study.

[2] As chairman of the staff Secretariat that was responsible for implementing the discount study under the guidance of the Steering Committee.

overcome deficiencies in the present operation and deal with prospective challenges in years ahead.

Scope of the Study

Because discounting problems giving rise to the study were not so much immediate as progressive, the investigative effort could be extensive and time-consuming, with a deliberate orientation toward fore-handed preparation to deal with future developments. In the interests of a complete consideration of all possible alternatives, the study, at least initially, assumed away all current legal restraints. The intent was to study what the ideal role and design of the discount mechanism would be in the financial system, and secondly to determine what legal changes would be needed to achieve this design and/or what compromises would be necessary in that ideal design to make it legally and politically feasible. On the other hand, the specific recommendations of the study, intended as they were for fairly prompt implementation, were designed to be completely within current law.

As had been done for several preceding major studies of discounting and open market operations, a wide range of talent was brought to bear on the subject. Top-level direction was supplied by a steering committee consisting of three members of the Board of Governors and four presidents of the Federal Reserve Banks, under the chairmanship of Governor Mitchell. Under this steering committee a secretariat composed of research, discount, legal, examination, and operating personnel from within the System was responsible for developing proposals for steering committee review and implementing the study outline as determined by the parent committee.

Over 20 individual research projects were commissioned to provide historical perspective and quantitative and theoretical background for considering policy alternatives.[3] Most of these projects were undertaken by members of the research staffs of the Board of Governors and the Reserve Banks. Academic economists were asked to prepare several formal papers, and also to contribute advice and suggestions more informally through an exploratory seminar and written communications. Central bankers abroad were consulted concerning their lending experience, and added insight into domestic

---

[3] Most of the research papers prepared in this connection have subsequently been published by the Board of Governors; see the September, 1969 *Federal Reserve Bulletin*, p. A100 for a list of currently available papers.

commercial banker attitudes was obtained from a survey conducted by the American Bankers Association.

Drawing upon the results of these investigations, and suggestions received from a variety of other sources, the staff secretariat formulated specific proposals for the redesign of the discount window. These proposals with amendments and refinements growing out of further discussion within the steering committee and by other System personnel, were presented for System and public consideration in a July 15, 1968, report of the steering committee.[4] Since that time comments have been received from a wide segment of the financial community, and a Congressional Committee hearing has been conducted on the proposals. Following further study to take into account these outside reactions as well as experience in the intervening period, the report, with limited suggested modifications, is now awaiting consideration and action by the Board when the general monetary climate is regarded as appropriate.

Need for Discount Mechanism

A comprehensive study of the appropriate role of the discount mechanism must begin conceptually with the basic question of whether in fact there exists such a role. As is well known, a few respected academic scholars have argued that the discount window no longer serves a useful function and can and should be eliminated. Federal Reserve officials have consistently opposed this view, but not even this long-established position was taken for granted in the recent study.

In reaffirming the need for a discount mechanism currently and predicting that this need would grow rather than diminish in the foreseeable future, the study identified and examined pertinent characteristics and underlying trends in the financial system. Probably the most important of these is the continued fragmentation of the United States banking system. In contrast to many other countries with only a relatively few commercial banks, this nation has almost 6,000 banks that are members of the Federal Reserve System, the vast majority of which are small and relatively isolated from day-to-day dealings with the central money market. The result is a serious lack of homogeneity in financial pressures and flows.

All banks are at times subject to day-to-day, temporary, seasonal,

---

[4] "Reappraisal of the Federal Reserve Discount Mechanism: Report of a System Committee," Board of Governors of the Federal Reserve System, July 15, 1968.

cyclical, and emergency shifts in the supply or demand for funds which may be either unanticipated or larger than anticipated. Since in many cases an outflow for one bank represents an inflow for another, the net of these shifts for the banking system as a whole seldom appears very large. However, the gross size and distribution of swings in fund flows can produce abrupt pressures on individual banks for which they can prepare only at the cost of excessive liquidity and a significant limitation on the credit resources they make available to their communities. Moreover, the liquidity instruments used are dependent on financial markets and mechanisms which often do not function with sufficient speed and elasticity to guarantee that a bank can always effect its desired adjustments through these means. And not all member banks have adequate access to such markets.

The size of these fluctuations impinging on individual banks has grown over time, while the banking system's ability to deal with them has tended to lag behind and in fact may actually have declined in many individual circumstances. In most years since World War II, private debt has expanded rapidly relative to public debt and to income and locally generated savings. Bank portfolios have reflected these developments, with holdings of easily salable unpledged Government securities dwindling relatively and the asset side of bank balance sheets becoming dominated by much less salable business, consumer, and mortgage loans and municipal obligations. With demands for these loans rising steadily and almost all of the once-typical sources of funds—investment sales and deposit growth—proving inadequate, many banks have been caught in a funds squeeze

The most striking and innovative bank response to this squeeze has been the increasing issuance of liquid liabilities. This development can be seen in the rapid growth of the Federal funds and Eurodollar markets, in the intense competition for negotiable certificates of deposit (when such competition is not inhibited by the effect of Regulation Q ceilings), and most recently in the use of repurchase agreements, sales of loan participations, and sales of commercial paper through parent holding companies.

These developments have unquestionably been accelerated by the effects of monetary stringency but nonetheless are responsive in part to underlying trends. In contrast to the sale of Government securities, however, bank issuance of liquid liabilities places a clear and direct premium on attributes which many banks lack—namely, geographic proximity to the central money market, adequate informational flows, national reputation, and the ability to trade in large blocks of funds.

As a result, such "disadvantaged" banks have been unable to participate effectively in the growing reliance on new methods of funds transfer and, in order to be even minimally prepared to meet the shifts in funds flows mentioned earlier, they have been forced to continue holding fairly substantial portions of their assets in liquid or near-liquid form despite the constantly growing credit needs of the communities they serve. This necessity has put smaller banks in particular at a competitive disadvantage with other financial institutions which may serve the same communities, or in the absence of such institutions has sometimes left the communities' needs unfilled.

Under these conditions, some limited direct bank access to Federal Reserve credit can contribute to more homogeneous credit availability by cushioning what otherwise might be seriously destabilizing movements arising in the short run from the structural inequities and market imperfections now existing.

A corollary attribute of the discount window—and one of key importance to the implementation of Federal Reserve monetary policy—is its functioning as a "safety valve" for open market operations. Since reserves are provided through the window at the initiative of member banks, there is an opportunity for individual banks to cushion, partially and temporarily, operations by the Open Market Account that impinge with excessive stringency on particular banks. It is not accurate to argue, as some do, that the discount mechanism dilutes the effectiveness of open market operations. In practice, the discount mechanism enables the Federal Reserve to conduct its open market operations more freely in response to overall market conditions, without being inhibited in these decisions by any unevenness in the impact of its operations within the banking system and the possibility that individual banks will be hurt excessively.

Another important although seldom called-upon function of the discount mechanism is in carrying out the System's role as lender of last resort to the economy. In a complex and heavily layered financial system subject to strong surges of demands, there is impelling need for an ultimate source of pinpointed liquidity available in instances when damaging disruptions threaten. The Federal Reserve is the only institution capable of assuring such liquidity. The carrying out of this responsibility may in rare instances require loans to institutions other than member banks; however, it should be expected that such loans would be carefully circumscribed, with an interest rate above the discount rate, and would be extended only when their absence would almost certainly cause significant damage to the economy's financial structure. Nonetheless, the means of extending this type of loan and thereby placing the funds directly in the institutions or sector involved, rather than relying on normally effective market mechanisms for reserve distribution, need to be ready for contingent use.

The discount window can also serve as an incentive to membership in the Federal Reserve System. So long as the present voluntary membership arrangement is retained, the Federal Reserve needs to extend advantages to its members sufficient to offset the burden of meeting reserve requirements. Access to discount credit can represent one such advantage. There are clearly limiting considerations which constrain this role. To serve this purpose, the terms and conditions for member bank access to the window must be significantly more favorable than those available to would-be nonmember borrowers under the lender-of-last-resort function outlined in the preceding paragraph; yet the general public interest argues against such liberal terms as to give a major subsidy to the member banking system. But the stakes involved in adequately offsetting the costs of membership, and therefore in providing meaningful borrowing assistance to member banks, are considerable; the protracted decline in Federal Reserve membership, if not stemmed, could eventually threaten the ability of the System to effectively implement monetary policy.

Another function that the discount mechanism can serve—one that is clearly secondary but still useful—is the provision of an opportunity for direct communication between Reserve Banks and member banks. While the impersonality of reserve injection through open market operations has obvious advantages, the more direct communication involved in discount operations can also prove useful on occasion. This does not mean that the discount window should serve as a primary vehicle for bank supervision; that task is appropriately reserved to the bank examination function. The potential rather lies in helping to increase member bank understanding of Federal Reserve views as to policy issues at the aggregate level, and bank liquidity and soundness considerations at the individual bank level. Opportunity is also provided at the window for a reverse flow of information, making the Reserve Banks more aware of and responsive to developments at the individual member bank level.

A last reason for keeping and improving the discount mechanism is simply uncertainty about the future. While the policymakers try to look ahead as far as possible, the banking system is constantly changing and no one can confidently describe what it will look like

20, 10, or even one year from now. In such an uncertain world there are clear advantages to "keeping options open." What may seem superfluous today—and the discount window clearly did not to those involved in the study—may nonetheless become vital tomorrow. For instance, to cite an extreme example, in a war emergency a decentralized discount mechanism might become the only practicable way of providing (and absorbing) reserves if normal open market operations were rendered impractical.

Changes Needed in the Discount Mechanism

Giving varying weight to all of the considerations outlined in the preceding section, the recent study concluded that the discount mechanism must be preserved as a means of reserve injection and, further, that it should be strengthened and brought into closer touch with the prevailing and prospective economic climate.

As presently designed, the discount mechanism accommodates only minimal use. The volume of borrowing from the Federal Reserve is at least in theory held down to narrow dimensions by banker reluctance to borrow, although this reluctance is in practice reinforced if not replaced by Reserve Bank application of subjective administrative discipline whenever bank use of Federal Reserve credit is deemed to have become "inappropriate." This design, clearly outdated in an era when banker reluctance to borrow from other sources appears in many cases largely eroded—or at best reduced to the minimum allowed by soundness considerations— is already generating a good deal of misunderstanding and hostility, permitting nonuniform accommodation of banks in similar circumstances, and further eroding member bank interest in borrowing from the Federal Reserve, even at strikingly attractive interest rates. Moreover, one can only expect that projected trends in banking will leave the window, as it presently exists, even more out of date. A redesign is therefore imperative if the discount mechanism is to remain viable and to encourage the more active use which would be involved in making a significant contribution to an effectively functioning monetary system.

The precise details of the changes proposed in Federal Reserve lending facilities by the steering committee report are summarized in a table at the end of this article. In general terms, that proposal can be thought of as introducing two major and interrelated changes in emphasis from current discount operations. The first of these is the articulation of several complementary arrangements for borrowing at the window, designed to provide credit for short-term adjustment needs, seasonal needs, and emergency needs, respectively.

Short-term adjustment credit would be further divided into two parts. First, there is the "basic borrowing privilege"— which would provide credit on a virtually automatic basis, within preset relative limits on amount and frequency, to all member banks meeting minimum specified conditions. On top of this would be provided what is termed "other adjustment credit." The latter would be available, under administrative control much akin to what is now applicable, to meet needs larger in amount or longer in duration than could be accommodated under the basic borrowing privilege. Seasonal credit would be provided, under the title of a "seasonal borrowing privilege," to accommodate recurring intra-yearly demands for funds over and above a minimum relative amount, for such amounts and duration of months as the applying member bank is able to demonstrate a need.

The proposed redesign provides that the Federal Reserve would continue to supply liberal help to its member banks in general or isolated emergency situations. In addition, it recognizes a Federal Reserve responsibility to be lender of last resort to other sectors of the economy—and it provides that the System will stand ready, under extreme conditions, to provide circumscribed credit assistance to a broader spectrum of financial institutions than member banks.

The second major change included in the proposal is a move toward more objectively defined terms and conditions for discounting. This would be accomplished first by introducing specific quantity and frequency limitations on a part of borrowing from the Federal Reserve—the basic borrowing privilege and the seasonal borrowing privilege, as has already been mentioned. Secondly, more reliance would be placed on the discount rate as an influence on member bank borrowing. This would require a closer alignment of the discount rate to the general level of market rates, almost certainly calling for more frequent changes in the discount rate than have been typical up to now.

Hopefully, this sought-for greater objectivity in the provision of discount credit would achieve several results. Member banks would be able to achieve a much clearer understanding of the limitations on their borrowing from the Federal Reserve. This should relieve confusion and irritation, and should permit banks to evolve better plans for meeting the ebb and flow of demands upon them. Furthermore, keeping the discount rate more closely aligned to relevant national market rates should produce more rational and hence more predictable recourse to the various borrowing arrangements proposed without socially undesirable subsidy. It should also allow room for the development and improvement of market mechanisms for the transfers of funds, whenever and wherever private institutions can produce innovative efficiencies.

One of the most visible effects of adoption of these proposals would probably be a generally higher level of borrowing being done by changing groups of member banks. But such a higher level of borrowing would not necessarily mean a corresponding increase in total reserves, because the increased borrowing would be expected to be offset to the extent necessary by correspondingly smaller net System purchases of securities in the open market, thereby maintaining an overall level of reserve availability appropriate to existing conditions.

The proposed redesign also contains a potential for the introduction of a fairly stable element into the larger borrowing total which can serve as a base of reserve injection upon which open market operations can build. Up to now the discount window has acted somewhat in the role of a sponge, soaking up or releasing reserves on a net basis chiefly in response to the underlying cyclical forces in the economy and/or policy-induced pressures. To be specific, in an inflationary situation, when credit demands are high and the System is squeezing the reserve positions of the banking system through its open market operations, one result is that a limited but cyclically high volume of cushioning reserves oozes out through the discount window. On the other hand, when the economy slows down and the System loosens its grip on bank reserves by increasing its open market purchases, a part of these reserve injections are used to repay indebtedness at the window. Thus the analogy is completed, with the discount window soaking up a part of the reserves put in.

There can be a second kind of discounting, however, less responsive to the tides of contracyclical policy, which serves to provide more in the nature of a stable building block of reserves from the point of view of the banking system as a whole. This kind goes on today to the extent that needs largely seasonal but also shorter-term are being met which reflect regular operational needs of the economy which continue regardless of the fluctuations in overall economic activity and policy. It is of course impossible to draw a clear dividing line between the aggregate component of discounting which is sponge-like cyclically and that which is more of a stable building block. While the credit needs satisfied by the latter kind of discounting may not vary a great deal from one year to the next, the relative attractiveness of different means of filling them inevitably does.

Nevertheless, there can be a useful place in the Federal Reserve kit of monetary tools for such a category of discounting, consisting of a continuously changing collection of limited-term loans but representing in the aggregate a relatively stable block of reserve injection into the economy. And the proposed redesign of the window moves in a direction which should encourage the evolution of such a block, especially through the innovation of the seasonal borrowing privilege. While the size of the block might be modest initially, it could be expanded if and as it proves a useful development by relaxing the terms for a qualifying seasonal loan and perhaps by making it a more general source of intermediate-term credit. In time it could come to represent a fairly significant proportion of the ongoing reserve base of the banking system as a whole.

An Evolutionary Philosophy

This last comment illustrates a philosophy which pervades the recommendations of the recent discount study. The proposed redesign was at no stage viewed as the ultimate, destined to remain appropriate indefinitely in a constantly changing financial system. Rather it was regarded as an evolutionary step, constrained both by uncertainty as to the future and by currently applicable law, in a continuing effort to bring the discount mechanism more closely into line with developing needs and conditions. In line with this goal, an attempt was made to create a proposal which, in addition to breathing new vitality almost immediately into what in recent years has become a relatively minor tool of reserve injection, would establish worthwhile new directions for discounting philosophy and contain the seeds for further growth and adaptation as that proves desirable and practicable.

Certainly this study did not exhaust all the possibilities for useful innovations at the discount window. Many others will undoubtedly be put forward from time to time in response to the emerging needs of the banking system. Continual reappraisal and reevaluation will be necessary to assure that the design of the discount mechanism remains appropriate to its implicit objective—helping the banking system to extend credit on a homogeneous basis in forms that serve the public interest and in dimensions that comport with overall stabilization policy. Such reappraisal ought to be conducted with enough sense of developing trends so that it anticipates needs and does not wait until they are immediate and already causing problems. Furthermore, it ought to deal with these needs by measures that complement market allocation and that can wax and wane as a compensating adjustment to the success, or lack of success, of the private credit market itself in evolving mechanisms to meet developing credit demands.

The spirit of inquiry appropriate to this kind of appraisal has rarely been better expressed than by Karl Bopp, himself, in his essay entitled, "Confessions of a Central Banker":

> *The world in which we live never quite measures up to the world of which we dream. This does not mean either that we should cease to live or that we should give up our dreams, but, rather, that we should strive constantly both to enrich our vision and improve our performance.*[5]

---

[5] Pinkney C. Walker, *et al, Essays in Monetary Policy in Honor of Elmer Wood* (Columbia, Missouri: University of Missouri Press, 1967), p. 17.

SUMMARY OF PROPOSAL FOR REDESIGN OF DISCOUNT MECHANISM*

Item	Basic borrowing privilege (1)	Other adjustment credit (2)	Seasonal borrowing privilege (3)	Emergency credit to member banks (4)	Emergency credit to others (5)
Definition	Member bank access to credit upon request, within precisely stated limits on amounts and on specified conditions.	Supplemental discount accommodation, subject to administrative procedures, to help a member bank meet temporary needs that prove either larger or longer in duration than could be covered by its basic borrowing privilege.	Member bank access to credit on a longer-term and, to the extent possible, prearranged basis to meet demonstrable seasonal pressures exceeding minimum duration and relative amount.	Credit extended to member banks in unusual or exigent circumstances.	Credit extended to institutions other than member banks in emergency circumstances in fulfilling role as lender of last resort to the economy.
Rate	Discount rate	Discount rate	Discount rate	Discount rate.	Significantly higher rate than discount rate.
Quantity limitations	—(20-40) per cent of first $1 million capital stock & surplus plus—(10-20) per cent of next $9 million, plus—(10) per cent of remainder.	None specified.	Seasonal needs in excess of—(5-10) per cent of average deposits subject to reserve requirements in preceding calendar year.	None specified.	None specified.
Frequency or duration limitations	—(6-13) of any—(13-26) consecutive reserve computation periods.	None specified.	Need and arrangement must be for more than 4 weeks. Maximum 9 consecutive months.	None specified.	None specified.
Administrative procedures	None other than general discouragement of net selling of Federal funds by borrowing banks.	Appraisal and, where necessary, action broadly similar to procedures developed under existing discount arrangements.	Prearrangement involves discussion between discount officer and bank management concerning amount, duration, and seasonality of need. Administrative review maintained during borrowing to prevent abuse or misuse.	Continuous and thoroughgoing surveillance. Require that bank develop and pursue workable program for alleviating difficulties.	Continuous and thoroughgoing surveillance (may have to be through conduit). Require that institution develop and pursue workable program for alleviating difficulties.
Other restrictions	Must not have been found to be in unsatisfactory condition.	None specified.	None specified.	None specified.	Required to use all other practicable sources of credit first.
Method of provisions	Direct.	Direct.	Direct.	Direct.	(1) through central agency; (2) direct; (3) conduit through member bank.

* "Reappraisal of the Federal Reserve Discount Mechanism," *Federal Reserve Bulletin*, July 1968, p. 551.

THE 1966 CREDIT CRUNCH

ALFRED HAYES*

IN AMERICAN FINANCIAL HISTORY 1966 will probably long be remembered as the year of the "credit crunch," when the nation's vast and complex credit system appeared to teeter on the brink of collapse. Admittedly the term "credit crunch" inadequately captures the deep uncertainties, the genuine fears, and the real hardships experienced by borrowers and lenders during that time. Yet I think most of us feel that it expresses, as well as any one or two words can, what was happening in the summer of that year. Although the crunch involved in the first instance a sharp drop in deposit flows to thrift institutions that resulted in a real wrenching of the mortgage market, I would define it largely in terms of psychology in the financial markets. Generated in an atmosphere of virtually unmanageable credit demands from the Federal Government and its agencies, and severe and increasing Federal Reserve restraint, there was a widespread and growing apprehension as the summer wore on that various kinds of credit might become unavailable at any price, perhaps leading to a general financial panic with drastic consequences for financial and even nonfinancial institutions.

In view of New York's unique position in the country's financial structure, we in the Federal Reserve Bank of New York were especially well-situated to keep a close watch on these developments. I am trying in this article to set forth a few observations on this whole phenomenon as we observed it from our vantage point.

Although the entire 1966 financial experience is now popularly described as "the" crunch, in fact there were two such episodes separated by several months and even more widely in terms of their origins, psychological impact, and consequences. The first, the mortgage-market crunch, occurred from about April through June; the second, the short-lived securities and money-market crunch, came in the latter days of August and the early days of September. The first of these two financial disturbances impinged primarily on the nonbank thrift institutions—the savings and loan associations and mutual sav-

* I wish to acknowledge my debt to many colleagues at the Federal Reserve Bank of New York who offered valuable comments and suggestions during the preparation of this article. Special thanks are due to A. M. Puckett, S. V. O. Clarke, and Linda Karagosian of the Bank's Research and Statistics Function.

ings banks—and involved massive outflows of interest-sensitive deposits from these institutions. The most obvious result of this loss of competitive position by the thrift institutions was an abrupt drying-up of funds to the residential mortgage market and a drop of great severity in home building. So extensive were the deposit and share losses that a good many institutions during that time became keenly apprehensive about their ability to meet further deposit drains, and some probably considered themselves in imminent threat of insolvency.

The securities market crunch began to evolve during the summer of 1966, as Federal demands on the credit markets soared at a time when the Federal Reserve System sought to apply steadily increasing restraint to the overheated economy. The major lending institutions and many borrowers became increasingly apprehensive about the ability of our complex financial system to continue to meet the demands being placed on it in an environment of monetary restraint greater than had been experienced in the memory of many market participants. These fears fed upon themselves. They provided an incentive for potential borrowers to accelerate their demands on the market and threatened a scramble for liquidity that would make money unavailable at any price. This atmosphere of crisis, which gradually built up through August and at its peak lasted for only a few brief days, reflected to some degree a misplaced feeling on the part of the market that the Federal Reserve System would not or could not stem the tide of financial pressures, which were believed to be largely out of control.

Prelude to the Credit Crunch

Before discussing the actual events of 1966, it may be worthwhile to discuss briefly the developments leading up to that period which appear to have contributed in a major way to the crunch. In retrospect, it is apparent that the financial markets and institutions at the beginning of 1966 in many respects were more vulnerable to tight money and high interest rates than they had been in a number of years. In some specific areas of the market this fact was well-recognized before 1966 began, but other areas of weakness in the financial structure came to light only as the events of 1966 unfolded.

The potential vulnerability of the thrift institutions and residential mortgage market was being widely discussed prior to 1966. It had become almost a matter of fashion, as the first half of the decade wore on, to "point with alarm" at the deteriorating quality of mortgage credit in general and of residential mortgage credit in particular. Many observers were especially apprehensive about the soundness of the huge mortgage portfolios of the thrift institutions. Defaults and delinquencies in the mortgage portfolios of thrift institutions were running at postwar highs, and there were scattered instances throughout the country of failures of savings and loan associations due to slow and defaulted loans. The concern was heightened by the steady shrinkage during the 1960's of these institutions' holdings of liquid assets and, in the case of savings and loan associations, by their growing reliance on money borrowed from the Federal Home Loan Banks.

These developments at the thrift institutions were only symptomatic, however, of broader financial and economic trends during the first half of the 1960's. The period from 1961 through mid-1965—before the Vietnam war began to intensify—was one of strong economic growth, but for most of the period the economy remained well below its full output potential. Business spending for plant and equipment, while increasing, could for the most part be financed with only modest resort to the credit markets. In this environment, the supply of funds to the credit markets was more than ample to meet demands. This situation was reinforced by a relatively easy monetary policy, as the Federal Reserve System sought to encourage the economy's growth and to reduce the high rate of unemployment.

Reflecting the ease in the financial situation, interest rates in the securities markets, which were already considerably below their 1959 peaks as economic growth resumed in early 1961, generally edged lower until reaching stable levels around 1962 and 1963. However, largely because of great demand for mortgage funds, the rates paid by the thrift institutions did not fall during this period—in fact they increased gradually. Indeed, by late 1962, savings associations on average were paying interest (dividend) rates on their liquid share accounts fully as high as those available on new corporate bonds and considerably higher than those available on long-term United States Government securities. In some regions of the country, such as California, savings associations were offering far higher rates on their liquid obligations than could be obtained on almost any other relatively low-risk investment and thus were attracting a large volume of interest-sensitive funds from faraway points.

The result of this development in the structure of interest rates available to individuals and other small- to medium-sized investors was a flood of money into the thrift institutions—a flood that later was to prove to contain a substantial proportion of highly interest-sensitive money ready and able to move out in response to the emergence of better alternatives elsewhere.

The thrift institutions and the mortgage market, however, were not the only areas of the financial structure to experience an increase during the early 1960's in their vulnerability to a tightening of credit conditions. Many commercial banks also became more vulnerable, and the sharp expansion of commercial bank lending and investment activity throughout the early 1960's extended that vulnerability into the municipal and other securities markets.

A major banking development of the early 1960's was the emergence of the large certificate of time deposit (CD) as a means of attracting loanable funds. The growth of this means of bank finance in the early 1960's was remarkable, and it had widespread effects on the breadth and depth of commercial bank participation in the credit markets. One apparent consequence of the growth of CD's was a much greater bank role in financing state and local governments. The sharp growth of interest-bearing CD's placed bank profits under some pressure, and the tax-exempt status of municipal obligations offered one means of offsetting that pressure. Banks also began to reach for higher-yielding, less liquid loans. Term lending to business rose sharply, and banks also penetrated more deeply into mortgages and consumer finance. Additionally, many banks sharply reduced their holdings of liquid United States Government securities during the early 1960's, placing those funds in better-yielding loans to help cover their mounting deposit costs.

It would be possible to argue that the decreasing liquidity, a reaching out for less liquid, higher-yielding investments, and a deterioration in loan quality were characteristic of almost all classes of financial institutions during the first half of the decade. The period generally was one of sharply increased competition among financial intermediaries, paralleled by a growing reliance of all borrowers on funds obtainable from financial institutions. As a result, the facilities of the securities markets for distributing issues to noninstitutional investors were weakened, and those markets tended to lose some of their resiliency.

The 1966 Mortgage-Market Crunch

Around mid-1965 the stage for 1966 was set when the decision was made to increase sharply this country's involvement in the Vietnam war without at the same time providing for higher taxes to finance the heavy cost involved. The Federal income tax reductions of 1964 and 1965 had provided a strong stimulus to the private sectors of the economy, and by mid-1965 the remaining idle resources available for growth were being absorbed by a sharply rising civilian demand for goods and services. The imposition of large-scale military purchases on an economy already operating close to its peak output capability brought a dramatic end to the long period of growth with stability that had lasted since early 1961.

The economic effects of the country's widening involvement in the Vietnam war began to emerge even before 1965 came to a close. Unemployment declined steadily in the closing months of that year, and price pressures became increasingly apparent. Against this background, the Federal Reserve System in early December raised the discount rate from 4 per cent to 4½ per cent and increased the maximum interest rate permitted on time deposits to 5½ per cent. These actions coincided with, and helped to spur, a growing public awareness of the impact of soaring military demands for manpower and material on the country's economy and financial markets.

The financial markets had already sensed the impending strains on the country's financial and economic resources well before 1966 began. Interest rates moved steadily higher throughout the last half of 1965. However, following the discount-rate increase in December, interest rates soared as market awareness of the swiftly changing financial climate became full blown. By the late winter of 1965-1966, the level of interest rates had in three short months risen a half percentage point or more from the level prevailing in November 1965.

To many of us, these developments pointed ever more clearly to the need for restrictive fiscal action to support the policy of monetary restraint if the effort was to be effective. Unfortunately, however, the Congress and the Administration were slow to react to the swift increase in the Federal deficit and the inflationary pressures that were being generated. A major factor in the steep rise of interest rates early in 1966 was the growing concern about the ability of the markets to absorb the sharp increase in Federal borrowing that lay ahead.

In the early months of 1966 it was quite evident that responsible banking and other financial executives were growing increasingly restive and concerned about the outlook. Many banks had begun to tighten loan policies even before the turn of the year and later were able to point to substantial turndowns of loan requests from new customers or for patently speculative purposes. Nevertheless, loan requests from good customers were still usually being met without question. The banks were understandably eager to satisfy the borrowing needs of customers who had maintained excellent deposit balances over the years, and the potential drain on funds from greater use of existing credit lines and formal commitments loomed as a major worry. A number of leading bankers with whom I talked at this time were much concerned over a growing tendency of corporate treasurers to convert existing credit lines into formal legal commitments in order to feel a little "safer" about getting funds when they might be needed. Other customers were already indulging in "scare" or "anticipatory" borrowing. Some big banks had been approached by major insurance companies for credit facilities in case the drain from heavy policy loans should become too large. Commercial bankers were also aware of the fears of savings bankers and, in some instances, were beginning to arrange large special credits for the savings institutions in case deposit losses were to burgeon.

As the bankers surveyed their sources of loanable funds over the coming months, the prospects were anything but encouraging. Certificates of deposit, while holding up rather well early in 1966, were generally expected to run off at an accelerating pace—though there were some bankers who still felt optimistic on this score. Remaining securities holdings of the banks consisted in large part of longer-term tax-exempt securities showing large potential capital losses, so that the banks hoped they would not have to sell many of these securities and at the same time were beginning to worry about a very thin market in case sales could not be avoided.

Not surprisingly, the banks were reaching for ways to back their efforts to ration credit more effectively. One obvious help might be an increase in the prime rate, but the bankers were acutely conscious that Washington might not take kindly to such a move. While generally approving of the Federal Reserve's tough stance on monetary policy, several bankers felt that further tightening by means of the usual policy instruments (principally open market operations) was no longer feasible as it would doubtless invite a financial crisis. In a number of conversations it was suggested to me that some form of informal credit selectivity program should be initiated by the System. Views varied as to details. There was some thought of a revived set of "guidelines" of the kind used in the Korean war. It was even hinted in one talk that the banks might welcome a more formal limitation of the volume of bank lending, if this was the price of avoiding a banking crisis.

Such was the atmosphere in which we had to formulate monetary policy. Let us turn now to the actual unfolding of events.

For the securities markets, the soaring of interest rates in early

1966 caused little disruption in the flow of funds and, indeed, the functioning of the markets for the most part seemed little affected by the sharp adjustment in rates. Commercial banks, by raising their offering rates on large CD's and aggressively bidding for consumer savings through smaller denomination certificates of time deposits, were able to remain competitive in the financial markets. However, the same was not true of the thrift institutions and the mortgage market. The leap in market rates of interest brought them substantially above the rates the savings banks and savings associations were able to offer. The result was a predictable one. Highly interest-sensitive money that had found its way into the thrift institutions earlier in the 1960's, when their deposit rates were among the highest available, now moved out rapidly. In April of 1966, following quarterly interest crediting, deposit outflows surged, fully offsetting the inflow of new money on a seasonally adjusted basis. This was a dramatic shift away from the 8 per cent to 10 per cent annual rate of growth enjoyed by these institutions in earlier years.

The April deposit losses were a traumatic shock for the thrift institutions. With their liquidity low and many of their mortgage loans subject to slow repayment or outright default, they became acutely concerned. To help calm these fears and to relieve the stresses on the mortgage market caused by a virtual drying-up of loans from the thrift institutions, the Federal Reserve Banks, with the approval of the Board of Governors, quickly arranged to make emergency discount-window facilities available to those institutions if needed to prevent temporary insolvency.

In the event, the fears of a collapse of the thrift industry proved greatly exaggerated, and not a single institution found it necessary to use discount-window funds. The deposits that had moved out of the thrift institutions in April proved to have contained a good part of the interest-sensitive money accumulated in earlier years of exceptionally attractive deposit rates. Thus, in July, following midyear dividend and interest crediting, deposit losses—while as large as April's—were less than had been generally expected, and calm began to return to the industry. Also, Congress had become increasingly concerned with the situation facing the thrift industry and, although legislation permitting the Federal agencies to set competitively uniform ceiling rates on thrift deposits and smaller denomination bank time deposits was not enacted until September, the thrift institutions were encouraged as the legislation gathered support in Congress through the summer. Nevertheless, the mortgage markets remained exceptionally tight, and the home-building industry entered into one of the steepest declines on record.

The Securities-Market Crunch

After the critical midyear interest and dividend crediting period for the savings banks and savings associations had been traversed with far less savings loss than had been feared, concern with their financial solvency generally abated. However, pressures in the remaining areas of the financial markets continued to mount as the Federal Reserve System pursued its policy of restraint amid ever-rising credit demands from business and the Federal Government.

Open market operations in the opening months of the year had been conducted with the aim of easing the adjustment to higher interest-rate levels that followed the December discount-rate hike and the liberalization of Regulation Q ceilings on bank time-deposit rates. But in May, open market operations began to place increasing pressures on bank reserve positions, and those pressures were gradually intensified through the summer. In July, the Federal Reserve Board increased reserve requirements against time deposits in excess of $5 million at each member bank. The steadily mounting strains on member bank reserve positions coincided with increasing limitations on the banks' ability to attract funds through issuance of consumer and large CD's. The System in July had acted to reduce the rate banks could offer on small multiple-maturity time deposits—those that competed most directly with nonbank savings accounts. At the same time, banks were finding it increasingly difficult to attract and retain funds obtained through large CD's as competing market rates began to surpass the Regulation Q ceiling on new CD offering rates.

The squeeze on banks that began to develop in the summer of 1966 was quickly transmitted to the securities markets. Just as banks had stepped up their acquisitions of state and local obligations earlier in the 1960's in response to a rapid growth of CD's, they began to withdraw from this market as their competitive position in the time-deposit markets started to decline. Total bank holdings of municipal securities increased little in June and then began to decline in July as banks sold these tax-exempt obligations in volume to make room for intense loan demand from business borrowers. The municipals sector was thus the first to feel the impact of a gathering storm in the securities markets. Indeed, while the tone of the money and corporate bond markets remained fairly steady, the climate in the municipal market began to reflect pessimism in June, and by early July the market was disorderly and confused. The situation continued to worsen when, around midmonth, the market felt the full effects of the swing of commercial banks from principal buyers of state and local issues to net sellers. The selling by banks was described by one commentator as "continuously undermining the market by a heavy volume of securities that has nowhere to go even at distress prices."

In July, business loans at banks grew very sharply, in part because of large special tax payments to the Treasury required in connection with the placing of payments on a more current basis with accrued liabilities. This tax acceleration had the effect of shifting, from the Treasury to corporate businesses, a part of the borrowing that had to be done to supply the Federal Government with funds. At the same time, the Federal Government throughout 1966 diverted much of its borrowing away from direct Treasury issues, resorting instead to increased agency borrowing and sales of participation certificates. The result of all this was to place considerably more pressure on the capital markets than would otherwise have been the case and, in the case of the tax speedups, to focus that pressure more directly on the banking system by increasing corporate demand for funds.

The System became increasingly concerned with the rapid growth of bank loans to business. For some in the System, this concern primarily reflected the role business loans were playing in the excessive rate of growth of bank credit. Others stressed the fact that these loans, while partly tax-related, were also helping to finance a huge, inflationary increase in capital spending. Still others were concerned that a disproportionate share of bank credit was going to businesses, creating especially severe hardships for other borrowers such as state and local governments and homebuilders.

The System's desires for more bank rationing of credit to business borrowers and reduced sales of securities, especially tax-exempt obligations, were expressed candidly during the summer of 1966. The banks, however, were reluctant to take the strong measures needed to curtail their lending to businesses, which they felt might jeopardize valuable customer relationships built up over time. They also pointed out that they were faced with very heavy commitments, entered into earlier. One important result of this loan situation was a growing reluctance of many banks to resort to discount-window borrowings as a means of relieving unusual strains on their reserve positions. They feared that seeking discount-window accommodation might bring their portfolio decisions, and particularly their business lending policies, under close scrutiny by the Federal Reserve. Many banks thought such fears were confirmed when, in announcing the July increase in reserve requirements against time deposits, the Board of Governors said that, while the discount facilities would be available to assist banks in making an orderly adjustment, "such adjustments will be expected to emphasize increased restraint in lending policies and maintenance of an appropriate degree of liquidity on the part of the borrowing banks."

In the face of prospective heavy bank losses of large CD's, restrictive open market operations, and mounting demands for credit throughout the financial markets, the gloom that infected the tax-exempt markets in July began to spread to other sectors in August. Early in August, the word "crisis" began to be used with reference to the liquidity squeeze potentially faced by banks if maturing CD's could not be rolled over. The first half of the month was, however, a period of relative calm before the storm. A routine Treasury financing proceeded without difficulty, and a nationwide airlines strike tended to ease banks' reserve positions temporarily by creating unusually large amounts of check float.

During August, I talked with officials of most of the principal New York banks and found a growing feeling of grave concern. Investment bankers and brokers also telephoned me on several occasions to warn that we might be on the brink of a financial crisis. Banks had already sharply curtailed their lending to brokers and dealers, and there were fears that this kind of lending might dry up altogether. Along with the gloomy atmosphere in the tax-exempt market, pessimistic views were heard as to a probable surge of mutual fund redemptions that would put the stock market under heavy pressure. I was told that Washington was not sufficiently aware of the danger of a financial panic and was urged to issue some form of assurance that the Federal Reserve would be ready to meet seasonal needs as usual and would move promptly if necessary to prevent any financial crisis. One banker thought that a crisis might come later in the autumn, while others felt that it might be much more imminent.

On August 17 the Board of Governors announced a second increase in reserve requirements against member bank time deposits to take effect around September 15 when the banks were expecting to be under the greatest pressure from CD runoffs and midmonth tax borrowing. This was taken—correctly—as an indication that the System had decided to press its battle against inflation to the fullest. Thus, the Federal Open Market Committee's August 23 directive to the Trading Desk was the most restrictive of the year. The directive told the Desk to supply "the minimum amount of reserves consistent with the maintenance of orderly money market conditions and the moderation of unusual liquidity pressures; provided, however, that if bank credit expands more rapidly than expected, operations shall be conducted with a view to seeking still greater reliance on borrowed reserves."

Market psychology deteriorated seriously further as August neared a close. Market interest rates scaled up sharply following the ¼ percentage-point increase on August 16 in the bank prime rate and broker loan rate, and were given a further boost by the announcement of the increase in time-deposit reserve requirements. The period was characterized by a flood of other depressing news and rumors. The flow and calendar of expected corporate bond offerings were increasing; there were rumors that a huge sale of agency participation certificates was being planned for September, and news about the prospects for fiscal action continued to be gloomy. At the same time, it was becoming increasingly apparent to bankers that the Federal Reserve System was not prepared to ease the pressures on their flows of loanable funds by raising the Regulation Q ceiling on large CD issuing rates.

The bond market reached frightening lows on Friday, August 26. One observer described the market psychology as "the coldest, bleakest I have ever experienced on Wall Street." Later, on August 30, another described "old timers" on Wall Street as "scared." At the Federal Open Market Committee meeting on September 13, I summarized the conditions in the market as follows:

> The financial markets were marked by convulsive movements and an atmosphere of great uncertainty. At the nadir of the bond market about two weeks ago there is no doubt that the financial community was experiencing growing and genuine fear of a financial panic. This fear seemed to stem mainly from the conviction that credit demands would remain very strong (with corporate and government needs for funds unabated), that fiscal policy was making no contribution toward a dampening of the economy, that the agency financing program was actively stimulating higher interest rates, and that the Federal Reserve System was determined to push its restrictive policy ruthlessly.

Government securities dealers were particularly hard hit during the latter days of August by the sharp decline in the prices of their securities holdings and by a shrinkage of their usual bank sources of finance. The market was rocked on August 25 by the auctioning of new one-year Treasury bills at a discount rate of 5.84 per cent, nearly a full percentage point above the rate set in the previous month's auction and, at the time, the costliest short-term borrowing by the United States Government since the early days of the country. Following this auction, the market focused nervously on the next Monday's auction of three-month and six-month bills.

However, on the day of the auction, August 29, the Trading Desk took the unusual step of asking for bill offerings from dealers as early as 10:30 in the morning. The action was the first in a series of rapid-fire events that were to turn the tide of market psychology. It helped to assure the markets that, contrary to the opinions being expressed in some quarters, the System was keenly aware of the deterioration of market psychology and had both the means and the intention of preventing a market crisis.

The second piece of good news to hit the market came on August 30 when the then Under Secretary of the Treasury, Joseph W. Barr, told the House Rules Committee: "We can't rely on monetary policy much more. . . . If we have to do more, we will have to do it by taxing or [reducing] spending. There is no other way." This statement, which indicated a growing recognition on the part of the Administration of the excessive burden being placed on monetary policy and the financial markets by a lack of fiscal restraint, resulted in a substantial improvement in market psychology. Thus, *The New York Times* reporter described the bond market on that day as "encouraging."

A third step toward easing market tensions came on September 1, when the Federal Reserve System published a letter to all member banks requesting their cooperation in moderating the growth of business loan demand and reaffirming the availability of discount-window credit assistance. While the intent of this letter was subject to some misunderstanding and erroneous interpretation that may have increased some banks' reluctance to use the discount window, the letter was interpreted more favorably outside the banking system. In particular, by stating that the System sought orderly bank credit expansion in the context of a moderation in the rate of expansion of loans, the letter helped to ease fears of further large bank sales of securities in the Treasury and tax-exempt markets. Moreover, the letter also helped to counter rumors of further "drastic" System action that had emerged toward the end of July, when it had become known publicly that the System was contemplating a statement regarding the administration of the discount window.

The improved tone that began to develop in the money and capital markets on the final two days of August carried over into September.

To be sure, there were occasional setbacks, but it was apparent that the worst was over. The announcement on September 9 of President Johnson's program of fiscal action provided the final turning point. That program included (1) a cessation of agency borrowing and sales of participation certificates, (2) the temporary suspension of the investment tax credit and accelerated depreciation on business capital spending, and (3) a $3 billion reduction in nonessential Federal spending.

For the most part, interest rates by the end of September had almost fully reversed the steep increases of August. This reversal was encouraged by growing evidence pointing to a slowdown in business later in the year, although such views were by no means unanimous. The major exception was Treasury bill yields, but the further climb in these rates past mid-September reflected in part anticipations of greater supplies as more Federal borrowing took the form of bill issues. And, shortly after mid-September, these rates also began to drop sharply.

Thus, the credit crunch was over, and monetary policy was soon destined to ease in response to the important changes in the economy that presaged the modest economic pause of early 1967.

Let me add one closing observation: It may appear ironic to be dramatizing the 1966 crunch at a time when money is probably tighter, and interest rates certainly much higher, than they were three years ago. Yet, at the time of writing (late September, 1969) we have not seen any such crunch as 1966 brought forth. This is due in part to the fact that the business and financial community was better prepared this time, as a direct result of the 1966 experience. I would not want to rule out the possibility that a crunch may yet occur before the current anti-inflationary campaign succeeds. But we must all hope that this will not happen, and a full understanding of the events of 1966 may help us avoid a repetition of history.

NEW STANDARDS FOR CREDIT AND MONETARY POLICY*

GEORGE W. MITCHELL

INNOVATIONS IN COMMERCIAL BANKING in recent years have been numerous and significant. Many of the changes were overdue or inevitable in light of the nation's economic development. Several have implications for monetary and credit policy because the banking system is the primary transmission link for the Federal Reserve's monetary and credit actions.

At least three such facets of postwar banking developments emerging in the 1960's appear to foretell significant trends in the 1970's. These are: (1) changes in commercial banking structure and function; (2) the introduction of new and varied intermediation instruments of both a deposit and non-deposit character; (3) the progress toward computerizing monetary transactions.

My comments on new standards for credit and monetary policy are organized around these unfolding developments in commercial banking because they will determine to a considerable degree the efficiency and effectiveness of alternative monetary techniques and devices.

Banking Structure and Function

It was becoming more and more apparent in the 1950's and early 1960's that banking's growth was being constrained by geographical confinement of major conventional types of banking activity. Stunting the growth potential has been accomplished by limiting the economies of scale realizable in a modern corporate organization. For banking these economies and efficiencies are significant in such diverse areas as data processing, capital adequacy, resource allocation, management succession, portfolio management and planning.

Banking organizations today ordinarily compete in the markets for checking, saving, and loan services only in areas around their banking office locations. There are exceptions, of course. Banks are continuously active in the impersonal money and capital markets. They also provide services to remote corporate and individual customers whose balances are large enough to justify a competitive effort. But, by and

---

* This essay was originally given as a talk before a Conference on Money and the Corporation sponsored by *Business Week* on December 8, 1969.

large, most banks grow either by extending their service areas or as the communities around their existing locations grow. And a community might, in these terms, be a neighborhood, a city, a county, or a group of counties. If economic growth in a community is slow relative to that in the nation, its banks are also faced with relatively sluggish growth prospects. As the higher rates of population and industrial growth in the past 20 years have been in the South and West, banks in those regions have had the greater growth potentials. The established financial institutions in the East and Midwest, on the other hand, have had to develop new activities, markets, and sources of funds in order to show significant rates of growth.

Aggressive banking organizations of sufficient size to exploit economies of scale have extended their operations and competitive positions in many ways. Results of their efforts are manifest in the accelerated growth of registered holding companies and in the recent spurt in the organization of one-bank holding companies. Their efforts have borne fruit in relaxed branching restrictions and quickened merger activity in a few states; in the development of new lending and borrowing services; and in the expansion, mainly through subsidiaries and affiliates, into related and financial services such as equipment leasing, mortgage servicing, data processing, insurance, factoring, international finance, and mutual funds.

Some of the thrust of these developments can be seen in the comparative statistics over the past decade. There has been a decline in unit banking, a drastic shift in the balance in the dual banking system, and an erosive change in the influence of correspondent banking connections. The main fact though is that banking's structural horizons are changing in ways that will be more apparent in the statistics of the 1970's.

For the banks that are participating, the extension in markets has been both geographical and in broadened services. In general, the competitive effects on both bank and nonbank competition have been salutory although there is much apprehension evident in the congressional deliberations on the one-bank holding company bill that larger banks will, by these means, become too dominant in too many markets.

Coming now to the implications for credit policy. As banking organizations become more diversified in form, function, and geographical extent they become more resourceful in coping with regulatory constraints and more protean in their resistive capacities. Shaping or confining the resource-gathering and credit-granting activities of banking conglomerates through interest-rate ceilings, reserve requirements, and other regulatory restraints might be likened to punching a bag of sand into an erect position. And many doubt it is possible, necessary, or even desirable to do so.

Most sectors of the United States financial structure are less hampered by regulations affecting credit conditions than banks, but the banking sector has been so pervasive in its influence on other financial institutions and market participants that it has had the capacity to pass on or "lay off" restraint. This action is not costless so far as the bank and its customers are concerned. But a bank can, for a market-determined price, sell assets, borrow money, or attract deposits and use these resources to meet its loan and investment commitments. This ability to transmit restraint to the market and other intermediaries has meant there has been no real difficulty in making public credit and monetary policies work even though many institutions and their customers are not directly touched by Federal Reserve policies.

Recent trends toward conglomerate corporate complexity indicate the possibility of stripping some activities and functions away from the banks proper and lodging them in subsidiaries, affiliates, joint ventures, or trusteed stock arrangements. These moves would, at least temporarily, frustrate regulatory constraints and might serve other corporate objectives, but they would, if thought to be running counter to the overall public interest, invite further regulatory complications. My expectation is that financial conglomeration will remain peripheral to a banking system which will retain credit market shares in the neighborhood of those realized in the late 1960's. In that case there seems to me to be little cause for concern that existing forms of credit and monetary control will be hampered by the functional and structural developments under way today.

On the other hand, banking as it has existed for most of the 1960's may be forced into a role of steadily diminishing importance if regulatory constraints on attracting funds are long continued. In that case, financial conglomerates, or spun-off elements of such conglomerates, are the most likely inheritors. They have the expertise to take over many banking activities. It is hard to see how they could not in some form or manner retain the use of techniques which would afford them continuing access to financial markets for the disposition of assets or the purchase of liquidity. The ensuing fractionization of financial intermediaries might not be without parellel in world experience, but it would seem highly unsuitable to the well-developed financial markets and for long-established financial institutions in the United States.

Time Deposits and Liability Management

A drastic decline in the major component of money—demand deposits—has occurred in the 1950's and 60's. Such deposits have long been regarded as the life blood of commercial banking; they have also been the source of predictable stability in loanable resources. In mid-1947 the net contribution of such deposits to commercial banking's resources was equivalent to 37 per cent of the then-current GNP; in mid-1957 to 25 per cent; in mid-1969 to 17 per cent.

Banking had a response to the 50 per cent decline relative to GNP in check-book or noninterest-bearing bank money. It was the development and promotion of a variety of interest-bearing deposits and other liability instruments. The long-established passbook accounts were glamorized and their rates made more competitive. Negotiable and nonnegotiable certificates of deposit were tailored in size, maturity, rate, and name. In a variety of forms they have been suited to the needs and convenience of the banks' regular customers as well as customers of other intermediaries. These certificates have also appealed to large numbers of money-market participants.

In the aggregate these measures worked to extend banking's share of credit markets from roughly 20 per cent in the late 1950's to around 40 per cent in the late 1960's. Within banking, the relative roles of demand and time deposits in providing loanable resources have shifted from a 2.4 to 1.0 relationship in 1947 to an 0.8 to 1.0 relationship in 1969.

Experience with monetary restraint in 1966 showed banks how regulatory ceilings on rates of interest for deposits might become a threat to their capacity to retain contact with the sources for funds they had developed in the early 1960's. In consequence, new channels of communication with markets were developed in the form of non-deposit liabilities which were subject neither to interest-rate ceilings nor reserve requirements. Among the devices used, Euro-dollar borrowings, repurchase agreements, and commercial paper sales by holding company affiliates and banking subsidiaries have been the most important or promising.

As banks extended in scope and magnitude their access to money and credit markets in 1969, apprehension that such techniques would undermine the force of monetary restraint grew despite the magnitude of the decline in their deposit flows.

On July 24, 1969 the Board of Governors restricted the use of repurchase agreements by commercial banks. This was done by making the bank liabilities on such agreements deposit liabilities, provided the agreements had been entered into with nonbanks and on assets other than Treasury securities and agency issues. The purpose of the regulation was to prevent banks from borrowing on their portfolios of loans, mortgages, and municipal securities and thus obtaining funds for other lending and investment or to meet liquidity needs. The constraint of Regulation Q ceilings applied to such transactions as it would to time deposits generally.

This action had the effect not only of limiting the banking system's access to money and credit markets but also of downgrading mortgages and municipal securities as liquidity assets relative to Treasury and agency issues.

On August 13, 1969 marginal reserve requirements were imposed on Euro-dollar borrowings and the sale of outstanding loans to foreign branches. And subsequently a regulation imposing interest-rate ceilings on commercial paper sold by banking affiliates was proposed by the Board.

Without doubt regulatory policies have been aimed at insulating the banking system from money and credit markets. This has been done with rate ceilings, regulations curbing banks' ability to substitute other liabilities for deposits, and restrictions on contingent sales of assets. In total, these measures have limited the banking system's ability to lend to its customers, a fact that is abundantly clear from the magnitude of the decline in market shares of funds going to banks in both 1966 and 1969. The same rate ceilings have hampered the savings and loans and the mutual savings banks in serving their customers, too, although their plight in 1969 has been ameliorated by the operations of FNMA and the lending policies of the FHLB Board.

The policy of reinforcing monetary restraint by constraining banking's access to money and credit markets may be more controversial than its practical significance at this writing (December, 1969) warrants. But for the long run it clearly raises important issues relating to financial structure and the role of credit policy.

As seen by their proponents today, regulatory constraints have forced a sharp contraction in the rate of bank and other intermediary lending and investment. The rationale for this approach is that Q ceilings, by limiting bank access to funds, have led to greater restraint on business loans than would otherwise have occurred—a desirable distributional effect on credit availability in view of the role of business investment in generating excess demand and inflation. Furthermore, since intermediaries are more efficient in their credit allocative function than direct lenders and markets, the reduction of intermediation is seen as the quickest and surest way to slow and restrict the availability of credit and thus to bring about the modification of spending and investment decisions. All of those borrowers who are exclusively dependent on intermediaries encounter credit restraint even though they may be preferred customers.

The main argument against sealing off the intermediaries from markets is that the effectiveness of overall restraint is not significantly diluted as a result of its being shifted by a bank—whether it is shifted to the market or to another intermediary, however different the incidence. As banks disperse monetary restraint, and they cannot disperse all of it, they force borrowers other than their customers to pay higher prices for credit and to face uncertain availability. Their action in selling assets, raising interest rates paid for funds, entering into repurchase agreements of assets and the like does not result in much diminution of overall restraint. Even if intermediaries were given unlimited access to money and credit markets they would themselves be increasingly restrained by the market environment they would be creating. The argument continues that the channeling and confinement of restraint to intermediaries and their customers results in the unnecessary dislocation of credit patterns, in inequities in the distribution of credit and inefficiencies in the operation of the financial system.

The differential effect of forcing intermediaries to contract their lending operations has the most certain and serious effect on smaller customers who do not have significant access to capital and credit markets. Shutting off or restricting the flow of bank credit to large corporate borrowers only means they become more dependent on markets. And since such borrowers are better able than most others to obtain funds in the market using such nondepository credit instruments as commercial paper, it can be argued that corporate borrowers were more favorably situated with respect to credit availability as a result of bank disintermediation.

While I am persuaded that intermediaries should have had more ready access to markets, the contrary position is not without merit from a pragmatic short-run standpoint. However, I believe the real problem is not one of making monetary and credit restraint effective at some given time but the longer-run effect of such tactics on the process of intermediation and the institutions providing this service.

A significant change in the financial environment during the 1960's has been the greatly expanded role for intermediation. Liquidity services have been shifted on a large scale to intermediaries or specialized intermediary devices. There has been a resulting relative decline in demand deposits and nonintermediary holdings of nonintermediary debts. If long-run policies are adopted to cut off their access to markets, intermediaries will be greatly handicapped in fulfilling their liquidity function. In this view, they are more in need, from a public policy standpoint, of being assisted in dispersing restraint than being constrained from doing so.

Looking beyond the current period and its requirement of monetary restraint, therefore, I believe the view that banks should be barred from access to financial markets by regulations of one type or another presents neither a stable solution to the problem nor one that is in our long-run interest. It is unstable in the sense that the banking system can develop quite an array of alternative techniques for maintaining contact with sources of funds and users. While it may be true that commercial banking "cannot fight city hall" very effectively in the short run, given time it can develop flexible instruments and durable relationships to break down most of the barriers regulators can think up. And if it cannot and the belief prevails that banking must in the public interest be isolated from financial markets, many of commercial banking's present-day functions will be scattered to other intermediaries and financial agencies.

But, it seems to me, this, in addition to being undesirable, is entirely unnecessary to the objective of monetary restraint. If, in fact, it should be determined that monetary restraint ought to be aimed at selected types of institutions or specific uses of credit, it would be better to impose differential reserve requirements on all such institutions and assets. While I believe we need not shrink from being concernd with the social objectives served by the economy's use of credit, I question whether this period of monetary restraint is one in which to launch such a policy explicitly or by indirection.

We would improve the effectiveness of the linkages by which monetary restraint is transmitted if we could develop techniques for bringing commitments to lend under pressure more promptly. No reasonable application of monetary restraint is intended to bring about "fails" on prior commitments. The process is aimed rather at prospective spending and investing decisions. The tardy response to monetary restraint in 1969 can be traced to the weakness of its initial impact on commitment policy of lending institutions.

Computerizing and Scheduling Monetary Transactions

I noted earlier the decline over the past twenty years, in relative terms, of the demand deposit component of the money stock. A similar decline has occurred in currency. Coin usage, on the other hand, has stepped up about 25 per cent in the same period, primarily as a result of requirements for meter hoards.

Money serves two basic functions: as a transaction tool and a source of liquidity. Technological changes in the past decade have greatly extended money's efficiency as a transactor and greatly reduced its relative attractiveness as a liquidity source.

The relative decline in currency can be linked to the expansion in consumer checking accounts, charge accounts, and credit cards. Non-cash sales make up over two-thirds of the transactions of many of our largest retailers. Convenience credit is widely available via vendors' credit facilities and, more recently, through bank, oil company, and travel and entertainment cards. It has been estimated that by late 1970 at least 50 million bank credit cards will have been issued. There are 75 million charge accounts in use today.

The most striking decline in holdings of demand deposits has occurred in business accounts. These are no higher today than they were in the early 1950's. Actually corporate demand balances today probably reflect more than anything else compensating balance requirements for check processing, loan, and other banking services. Theoretically, a skilled money-managing, computer-equipped treasurer, unhampered by compensating balance requirements, could manage his firm's checking account so that toward each day's end he would know if he had a balance large enough to cover the transaction costs for an overnight investment. And if he had, his resultant late-day investment action might, under certain circumstances, indirectly turn out in effect to be lending that residual in his account to his own bank. Electronic facilities for check processing will make possible much closer management of cash positions, particularly if scheduled credit transfers become commonplace.

The best information we have on the ownership of the demand deposit component of the money supply indicates that households own about $70-75 billion, nonfinancial businesses $45 billion, financial businesses $15 billion, and State and local government $13 billion. About $4 billion is in foreign accounts. It is safe to say that all professionally-managed accounts are at or near minima established by banking rules or practices.

Households these days are managing their money position more closely, too—many use a fee-no-minimum balance-type account. They have become increasingly sensitive to interest costs and interest yields. Their response to the promotional efforts on the advantages of time and savings accounts has been to progressively reduce demand balances to the minimum levels consistent with the timing of income receipts. Such attitudes are evident in the average holdings in household checking accounts. According to mid-1968 data, the latest we have, there were 79+ million demand deposit accounts. Most of these were owned by households. Sixty-four million accounts had balances of less than $1,000 and the average holding was only $240!

Computer facilities becoming available will enable households to schedule regular periodic payments through pre-authorization arrangements even more precisely in relation to the timing of their salary and wage credits. This will bring within their reach still more of the money economies that corporate treasurers presently enjoy.

The reduced relative attractiveness of money—currency or demand deposits—as a source of liquidity arises chiefly from the competition of near monies—mainly savings and time deposits in commercial and mutual savings banks and savings and loan associations, but, of course, including short-dated Government debt and money market paper. Since these interest-bearing deposits or paper have instant liquidity or conveniently scheduled maturities they can serve as both liquidity reserves and earning assets.

The relevance of these facts on deposit trends and prospects is to the controversy over the use of money supply as a guide for monetary policymakers or as an indicator of their actions. In recent years rates of change in various financial aggregates have been increasingly recognized for their analytical value in both of these roles.

For example, the Federal Open Market Committee has, since 1966 and regularly beginning in 1968, used an aggregate called the "bank credit proxy" to quantify intervention limits on monetary or credit expansion or contraction arising out of a directive couched in terms of money market conditions and interest rates.

The primary instructions to the Manager are for "no change," "firmer," or "easier" posture supplemented by specified ranges in marginal reserve measures and short-term interest rates. This pattern is internally consistent, so far as can be foretold, with a projected range for the "credit proxy." But if the proxy begins to move outside of its range this fact begins to modify the Manager's reserve supplying actions.

Our experience using aggregative measures as supplementary operating guides has not been spectacularly successful but it has been good enough to encourage further development and use. Since the only measurable monetary action the Committee can take is to alter the amount of reserves supplied to the banking system, it is necessary to estimate how quickly a change in reserve injection will affect changes in various aggregative measures. The relationships are far from stable and the results have been necessarily approximate and subject to significant errors.

Another example is from the Joint Economic Committee of the Congress. This Committee in recent years has urged greater attention to a particular monetary aggregate—M_1, the narrowly defined money supply. In its 1969 report it said:

> Over the long run, the increase in the money supply should be roughly at the same rate as the growth of U.S. productive capacity. As indicated by this committee in its report, the expansion of the money supply should be somewhat above the long-run real growth rate during periods of high unemployment and excess capacity. On the other hand, monetary expansion should be below real growth in periods of inflation. We recommended a rate of increase ranging from 2 percent to 6 percent. The principle of harmony between the rate of growth of the money supply and the rate of growth of the economy has been recommended by the committee for many years. . . .
>
> As long as inflation continues at a high rate, the pace of expansion in the money supply should remain near the lower end of the range suggested; that is, near 2 percent per annum.

By the Committee's standards the Federal Reserve's recent performance may or may not be in the ball park. For 1969 as a whole (up to December) money supply rose at a 2.7 per cent rate but the growth in the first half was 4.3 per cent and in the past five months was 0.8 per cent.

There is no doubt, in my opinion, that financial aggregates will steadily become more useful in guiding policymakers and the judgments of those who are searching for clues to policy changes. But I believe we are a long way from being able to specify a particular aggregate as a "North Star" for monetary navigation. Nor would I expect that in our researches we will be able to find for our constantly changing environment a single aggregate—monetary or credit—of predictable durability and reliability.

On the other hand, if the analytical insights that can be gained from the study of the Flow of Funds were available on a more current basis our reliance on changes in credit aggregates and aggregates generally would be significantly extended.

The most popular of all the aggregates—M_1—seems, given present technological and institutional trends, to have the shortest life expectancy. Its significance for policy is being chipped away, on the one hand, by steadily increasing variety and attractiveness of near monies and, on the other, by the long-continued and prospective further rise in velocity being made possible by computer and communications technology. Turnover (velocity) in demand deposits has been increasing steadily: it more than doubled in the 1960's and has increased 7 per cent through October of 1969.

The technological obsolescing of M_1 does not mean that money supply is dead or only alive in St. Louis. If it were to be rid of its transaction component and become primarily a liquidity measure its meaning and interpretation would be in the tradition of M_2 and M_3, and, in my judgment, this would add significantly to its stature as an important financial aggregate.

BANK COMPETITION AND
MONETARY POLICY

GUY E. NOYES

IN 1920 PROF. CHESTER ARTHUR PHILLIPS published a book entitled *Bank Credit: A Study of the Principles and Factors Underlying Advances Made by Banks to Borrowers*.[1] Directly or indirectly every student of money and banking since has been reared on Phillips. While Phillips's book itself has been little used as a text since the 1930's, it has literally been rewritten a thousand times in texts on money and banking that have been the basis for courses in our colleges and universities—and his analysis has survived the years very nearly intact.

In many ways this has been a good thing. Certainly the Phillips analysis represented a great advance over that of his predecessors— it is more accurate to think of the loan as the father of the deposit than *vice versa* and it is well to understand that a 10 per cent reserve requirement (O, happy day!) permits the commercial banks taken all together to parlay their loans and deposits tenfold on the basis of an infusion of new reserves, but a single bank, the "Mad River National Bank of Springfield, Ohio," can expand its loans by only $122,000 on the basis of $100,000 borrowed from the Federal Reserve Bank of Cleveland, assuming the 10 per cent reserve requirement and an automatic 20 per cent reciprocal balance (O, still happier day!). These are good things to know and it is well that millions of eager young minds have learned them.

But along with these venerable truths the students who grew up on Phillips, directly or indirectly, have also acquired a wholly unrealistic notion of the almighty market power of the commercial banker over his customers. It may or may not have been true in the 1920's, but it certainly isn't true today. Prof. Phillips's banker had no problem in expanding or contracting the loans of his bank—he simply said "yes" or "no" in a positive, if courtly, manner. His style is well-illustrated in a little discussion of "derivative" balances. "You are straining your credit" says the banker to the credit-seeking customer, "and, with tight money staring us in the face, I shall have to ask you to keep a more

---

[1] The Macmillan Company, New York, 1920. Page references are to a 1931 reprint.

liberal balance in relation to loans than previously, as a requisite to additional accommodation."[2]

This snug little monopolist who ran Prof. Phillips's Mad River National in Springfield, Ohio, has been taken as a microcosm for the banking industry by several generations of students who have grown up to be Congressmen, Federal Reserve Board members, Federal Reserve Bank presidents, Comptrollers of the Currency, and Chairmen of the FDIC—to say nothing of the thousands who are professors of money and banking; some of whom are intermittent members of the President's Council of Economic Advisers. And, of course, like Keynes and Friedman, Phillips has suffered at the hands of his followers. Phillips never said it, but there is hardly an economist now alive, who, confronted by the uncomprehending faces of the eight o'clock section of Economics A or the friendly, but confused, countenances of the local Rotary, has not blurted out, in the course of an effort to explain deposit creation, "Think of the banking system as one large bank." In fact, there is hardly an economist now alive who hasn't blurted it out so often that he has slipped into the habit of thinking that way himself.[3]

Of course, we all know that the commercial banking system in the United States isn't one large bank and can't be expected to behave like one. But I am not sure we are as acutely aware as we should be of just how misleading this "simplifying" assumption has been and continues to be.

Except in a few rural areas—and they are fast becoming fewer and farther between—competition among banks is intense, in fact, fierce. This is, when one considers it, hardly surprising. From the earliest days of our national existence competition among banks has been protected and nourished by public policy. As every high school history student knows, the dragon of nationwide banking, in the form of the Second Bank of the United States, was so effectively slain by Andrew Jackson in 1836 that it has been hard to even make much political capital out of the issue since. The threat of a "money monopoly" has been rolled out from time to time as a subject of campaign oratory, as it was by the Populists in the late 19th century, but the old dragon has properly

---

[2] *Op. cit.,* p. 51.

[3] To those who know that I had the good fortune to take my first course in economics under Karl Bopp in the summer of 1931, let me say that I am not accusing him of using this pedantic crutch. On the contrary, I seem to recall a very vigorous and earnest young man filling a blackboard that covered one whole side of the room with individual bank T accounts before he finally unveiled the magic 10 to 1.

been regarded by the public with about as much awe as the balloon version of a comic strip character in a Thanksgiving Day Parade.

The pervading and overpowering philosophy was well-expressed by the Banking and Currency Committee of the House of Representatives in its report on "The Bank Holding Company Act of 1955" when it said, "The United States early in its history . . . adopted a democratic ideal of banking. Other countries, for the most part, have preferred to rely on a few large banks controlled by a banking elite. There has developed in this country, on the other hand, a conception of the independent unit bank as an institution having its ownership and origin in the local community and deriving its business chiefly from the community's industrial and commercial activities and from the farming population within its vicinity or trade area." If this bucolic ideal is not precisely the reality of today, it is certainly closer to it than the "monied oligarchy" Jackson "exterminated" in the words of Bostonian David Heughon—who may have been slightly prejudiced, as were many New York financiers of the period, because the Second Bank was headquartered in Philadelphia.

In fact, of course, competition reaches its pinnacle in the efforts of larger banks to attract and hold a share of the business of large national and multinational corporations. Because of the legally enforced fragmentation of the commercial banking system, no single bank is large enough to accommodate alone the financial needs of any of our larger corporations. Most large companies have four or five continuing banking connections, and some have hundreds ranging over banks of all sizes. In terms of market power this puts the corporate treasurer in an extremely favorable position. He can always play the banks with which he has established relationships off against one another, or, alternatively, play all or any of them off against 100 more or less identical banks that would be delighted to provide him with more or less identical accommodation. Moreover, quite aside from the practical problems that the intensely competitive banks would have in trying to deal jointly with a large customer, they are legally prohibited, except with explicit permission of the customer, from even discussing with one another the terms and conditions on which they will lend to him. At least in the initial stages of negotiation banks must rely wholly on the integrity of the borrower for any information as to the terms and conditions on which other banks are prepared to accommodate him.

In these circumstances bankers who deal with large corporations are, if not exactly in, very close to the position one New York banker described when he said "Sure, we would turn down a loan to a good corporate client who had maintained good balances with us over the years, but not until after we had sold our building and all the furniture."

What are the implications of this for monetary policy? It depends, of course, on what monetary policy is trying or should be trying to do. If one feels that the task of monetary policy is to establish some desired rate of increase in the narrowly defined money supply, the consequences are comparatively minor. The problems of measuring the rate of increase in money that has been or is actually taking place or in determining what rate of increase is optimal are magnified only very modestly by the intensity of competition for "business" business. In this case, as in others, the pressure to accommodate business borrowers may produce allocative effects that will cause the monetary authority to falter in its determination to adhere to a given money supply objective when credit demands are generally strong, but in the view of the true monetarist this is only evidence of human fraility—not the product of the competitive process. This problem of the contribution of hyper-competition to the selective impact of general policy will be touched on again in connection with other alternative objectives of policy where it appears to play a more important role.

If one leans to the broader money supply, or the closely related bank credit proxy, as the appropriate objective of policy, the problem is more complicated, especially if one includes in the defined objective all or part of the claims arising from the money market fund raising activities of banks. These problems become overwhelming if one injects the further complication of a sub-market Regulation Q ceiling, but that is another story. Sub-market Q ceilings are a sufficient evil unto themselves and have amply demonstrated their capacity to produce such massive distortions as to make rates of change in any of the conventional broad measures of bank credit and money practically meaningless. In these circumstances the modest contribution to the confusion that stems from the relative market power of banks and their customers seems insignificant.

If we abstract from the Q ceiling distortions (which is difficult to do in the current setting in which their impact is so pervasive), it does appear that the inability of banks to ration credit to large business borrowers, especially in the early stages of a move toward credit restraint, operates to lessen the precision and increase the time lag with which the monetary authorities are able to control the rate of growth of total bank credit, the bank credit proxy or the broadly defined money supply. In the long run the availability of reserves must operate as a limiting factor, but for a considerable period footings on both sides of bank balance sheets can expand at a rather high rate even in the face of an extremely parsimonious policy of new reserve creation by the central bank. The reasons for this do not have to be explained to the typical reader of this sort of paper who is doubtless thoroughly familiar with the factors affecting member bank reserves and their relation to the volume of money and bank credit. Suffice it to say that in the circumstances set forth and in the short run, banks are prepared to go far beyond the optimal, equilibrium or profit-maximizing point in the intensity with which they utilize total reserve balances and the extent to which they pull reserves normally occupied in other ways into the "member bank balance" component of the uses of the monetary base.

How much this delays the ability of the central bank to achieve control over monetary aggregates, such as the broadly defined money supply, depends importantly, of course, on how ruthless it is prepared to be in the pursuit of its objective. Even the most strong-willed, broad-definition monetarist would doubtless find himself compelled to employ some gradualism in stemming an excessive rate of growth in bank credit or broadly defined money, and there can be little doubt that the willingness of banks to compete for funds, among themselves and with others, to satisfy the borrowing demands of their customers enhances this problem. But even so, the problem is one of timing and the determination of the authorities and one would conclude that, if control over the broader banking system aggregates is the appropriate objective of policy, then competitive conditions in the banking industry aggravate only modestly the difficulty of achieving that objective.[4]

Substantially the same conclusion emerges if one accepts interest rates or some other broad measure of credit conditions as an objective.

---

[4] There has been very little empirical work in this field. While I would not pretend to have researched the literature thoroughly, I am encouraged to believe that I have not overlooked any highly significant contributions by the fact that a recent article on the subject did not refer to anything that had escaped my attention. This article, "The Banking Structure and the Transmission of Monetary Policy," by Sam Peltzman in *The Journal of Finance*, Volume XXIV, No. 3, June 1969, pp. 387-411, addresses itself primarily to the question of how the market structure affects the speed with which deposit growth is influenced by changes in reserves or reserve requirements. The results cannot be directly related to the judgmental observations in this paper, since the categories used by Peltzman do not necessarily reflect the differences in market power as between banks and their customers. In a general way, however, the fact that the differences in bank structure which Peltzman explores make only modest differences in the speed with which policy changes are transmitted would seem to support the proposition that if the rate of deposit change is the objective of policy, the intensity of competition among banks plays a comparatively unimportant role in the efficiency with which policy operates.

In fact, it can be argued that a desired level of market rates can be achieved more rapidly than might otherwise be the case because of the intensity with which banks are prepared to compete in funds markets. But the problem of selective impact, or burden sharing, is more visible, if not more acute, and, therefore, more likely to interfere with policy formulation. If the authorities are focusing on general credit conditions as the objective, it is hard for them not to be aware of conditions in the separate markets and succumb to the temptation to moderate their general objectives in order to relieve what seem to be unduly harsh conditions in specific markets—and again, the intense competition among banks to accommodate business borrowers tends to amplify the problem. The wide swings in bank participation in the market for state and local obligations is an obvious case in point.

But while the highly competitive structure we have chosen to maintain and encourage in the United States banking system may complicate the problems of conducting a general monetary policy directed to any of the above objectives—and increase the temptation to superimpose selective controls to "even out" the burden—it cannot be said to frustrate such policy or even make it significantly less effective.

However, there is one objective that appears to be literally beyond the reach of general monetary policy under present competitive conditions. This objective is the more or less precise regulation of the rate of increase in business loans at commercial banks. If this is taken to be an appropriate immediate objective of monetary policy, i.e., if effective control of the rate of bank business-loan expansion is assumed to be the essential financial link through which monetary policy makes its contribution to overall economic stability, then monetary policy simply cannot do what it is supposed to do with the tools it has to work with, given the present distribution of market power as between banks and their business customers. If one goes further—as, once started down this path he might logically proceed—and adopts the objective of regulating the *total* flow of credit to business borrowers from all sources, then the attainment of the objective in present circumstances and with the present policy tools is even more remote from reality.

Thus, if one sincerely believes that it is essential to stable economic growth that the monetary authorities be able to influence directly and promptly the availability of credit to business borrowers, he must conclude either that a basic change in banking structure is needed which will re-allocate market power in such a way as to permit banks to pass on to business borrowers more effectively restraint imposed on them by the monetary authorities or that the monetary authorities should have the explicit power to regulate selectively the volume of business borrowing, probably from nonbank as well as bank sources. Meanwhile it makes no sense to belabor either the central bank or the private banking system for not doing something neither of them has within its power.

While the change that would be needed is put above in terms of two alternatives, it could just as well have been expressed in terms of two ways of doing the same thing—reducing the market power of the corporate borrower. If we move toward any form of selective regulation of bank lending, it would be, in effect, an abridgment of the benefits borrowers enjoy as a result of the banking competition we have pursued so vigorously through legislation and regulation. The fact that it would be done under the banner of public policy does not change its character. It is for this reason that jurists have always concluded that efforts to regulate business credit, like the "voluntary" credit restraint program of the Korean War period, can work only under the protective umbrella of an exemption from the Sherman Act. In order for selective regulation of bank lending to work, some sort of collaboration among banks with regard to which loans are appropriate and which are not, would be unavoidable even if broad guidelines were provided by a Government agency. Business credit simply cannot be regulated by the type of "down-payment" and maturity regulations that have been used in the case of consumer installment credit and real-estate credit regulation.

Doubtless some students of the monetary mechanism will conclude that the national interest requires a de-intensification of the zeal with which banks compete with one another for business customers and accommodate their credit needs even at times when policy is limiting the growth of total money and bank credit. They also will reason that this can be most equitably done by superimposing some form of selective regulation on top of the existing general authority to regulate the growth of broad aggregates or influence general credit conditions. But we should all be very clear just what we would be doing if we follow that path—we would be impairing with one hand the competitiveness that we have so zealously protected with the other. One would want to be very sure that regulating business-loan volume is an essential objective of monetary policy. I, for one, am not.

COMMERCIAL BANKING AND THE
FEDERAL RESERVE:
A RECORD OF MISUNDERSTANDING

WILLIS W. ALEXANDER

CENTRAL BANKING in the United States has a rather unusual history. It was not until well into the twentieth century that it was possible for this nation to establish a central bank, much later indeed than other modern nations and then only after considerable controversy.

Perhaps the major problem and the reason for much of this delay was the strong and pervasive antagonism toward concentration of economic power, especially where financial institutions were involved. The unit banking system, which still characterizes much of American banking, testifies to this attitude. So far as central banking is concerned, the difficulties attached to its eventual establishment are best illustrated by the struggle over the Second Bank of the United States. This institution, which lost its Federal charter in 1836, gave evidence of eventually becoming a full-fledged central bank. But the violent political controversy which swirled around its operations, as well as around its president, Nicholas Biddle, derived much of its support from the egalitarianism of the frontier with its fear of monied monopolies.

Three-quarters of a century were to pass after the demise of the Second Bank of the United States before it was possible to establish a central bank in this nation. Even then, when the Federal Reserve System came into being in 1913 it was a regional system, reflecting still the distrust of "Wall Street" and the centralization of financial power.

Commercial banks have always had an ambivalent attitude toward the Federal Reserve. At the outset, and to some extent yet today, banks in major financial centers regard the local Federal Reserve Bank as a possible competitor. At the same time, bankers work quite closely with the Federal Reserve at all levels and of course rely heavily on its principal services.

The attitude of commercial bankers toward the Federal Reserve today is a rather curious mixture of affection, respect, and irritation. It is worth considering the reasons for each of these attitudes.

Affection is basically an emotional attitude and thus the most difficult to explain. Essentially, it may stem from the fact that the Federal Reserve System is, after all, comprised of 12 regional Banks with many of the characteristics of commercial banks. Accordingly, to some extent, bankers are more likely to view Federal Reserve officials as colleagues rather than as supervisors or central bankers.

Few would question that the regional structure of the Federal Reserve has contributed to this attitude. Individual Federal Reserve Banks have a long history of involvement in the welfare and problems of their respective areas. By making their research facilities available to help solve local problems or to plan for future economic growth the various Federal Reserve Banks provide major assistance to local economies.

Finally, we should not overlook the fact that in common adversity there is likely to be, if not affection, at least a feeling of camaraderie. The continual criticism leveled by the populists in the Congress at the banking system makes little or no distinction between the Federal Reserve and the banks themselves. First one and then the other is the principal target, but neither is ever entirely overlooked.

The respect which commercial bankers hold for the Federal Reserve is based on certain well-recognized facts. More than any other Governmental agency, Federal or state, the Federal Reserve is regarded as above politics. At a time when cynicism as to Government is rampant, rarely if ever does one hear even a whisper of undue influence or politically motivated decisions when the Federal Reserve is discussed.

The respect which bankers have for the Federal Reserve is based on more than the System's ability to free itself from the political thicket. The record of the System, whether it be in the management of monetary policy or the regulation of banks is one which commands respect, though not always agreement or admiration. There are, of course, the usual exceptions, but generally speaking an examination of the reasons for Federal Reserve actions reveals a painstaking and thorough analysis which can only be impressive.

The publications program of the Board and of the Banks is one with which every banker has some familiarity, whether or not he is a member of the System. Indeed it would be difficult to be involved in any financial activity without being aware of the volume and quality of information made available by the Federal Reserve System. Since this reflects a large and capable staff under competent direction, a banker does not have to be personally aware of the existence of this staff—although of course many are—to recognize the solid research underpinnings for much of what the Board and the Banks do. Add to this the frequent exposure of member banks to Federal Reserve bank examiners and supervisory personnel, which along with those of the other

Federal agencies are known to be of high quality, and another good reason for banker respect for the System is apparent.

But perhaps the most important explanation for the respect which bankers accord the Federal Reserve is attributable to the decisions which come forth, particularly from the Board. Whether it be a new set of regulations, a bank merger application, or a particular action having to do with monetary policy, there is rarely if ever any question that the decision reflects the Board's and the Banks' view of the best course in the public interest. This does not mean that these decisions or actions *are* unanimously accepted as being in the public interest, but simply that it *is* the public interest which the Board or the Banks are seeking when these decisions or actions are taken.

From the foregoing account of banker attitudes toward the Federal Reserve, it would seem most unlikely that one would be irritated with the System, aside from a few congenitally disgruntled individuals. But the fact is that bankers have always been critical of many of the actions taken by the Board or the Banks, and never has this attitude been more pronounced than in recent years. Indeed, the respect and affection to which I made reference earlier must be working overtime at the moment to keep the large majority of bankers from becoming bitter critics of the Federal Reserve.

One reason for this irritation is monetary policy. This is a complex subject, not easily understood. Nonetheless, bankers and the general public today are much more sophisticated on these matters than even a decade ago. The popular press now carries, as a matter of course, articles on economics, finance, and monetary policy which, 10 or 20 years ago, would have been required reading in college economics courses. Together with this increased awareness, must stand the observation that Federal Reserve monetary policy at certain times during the past few years has not been on target. The 1966 crunch and the excessive expansion in the money supply in 1968 have caused serious dislocations in the economy; the latter in particular has led to serious problems in 1969. And the financial press has not been very far behind the academicians in pointing this out.

It is doubtful, however, that monetary policy is the major source of irritation for bankers. For many bankers, what the Federal Reserve does in its open market operations is not so clearly identifiable and therefore nearly so important as what it does in the regulatory area. A decision involving a holding company acquisition, a bank merger, or the formation of a subsidiary corporation can be of particular importance to a bank, largely because the effect of such a decision can be measured rather precisely in terms of cost and potential profits. Here again, in its regulatory activities, the record of the Federal Reserve leaves something to be desired.

The major criticism is that the Federal Reserve is so ponderous in its decisionmaking process, and so wedded to what may be described as a "strict constructionist" philosophy of the banking laws, that it has lost sight of the fact that the banking industry, notwithstanding its extensive regulation, is, or at least would like to be, a dynamic and rapidly expanding industry. Bankers today feel that the Federal Reserve is a major roadblock in their drive to become more competitive and to react more promptly to the changing demands of a burgeoning economy.

Recently the Board has given some indication that this posture will change. The decisionmaking process is apparently being speeded up through passing more responsibility back to the regional Banks. Statements made by Federal Reserve officials, as well as certain recent actions, suggest a more enlightened view of present and future problems of the banking industry. Nevertheless, there are many who, based on past performance, are dubious.

From the banker viewpoint, the curious mixture of attitudes toward the Federal Reserve naturally results in misunderstandings. Too often, bankers simply cannot reconcile the Board's action or decision with its demonstrated abilities and its concern for the public interest. One would assume that there are equivalent misunderstandings on the part of officials of the Federal Reserve, who must wonder why it is that bankers frequently fail to comprehend what the Board or the Banks are trying to do. Is it possible that there can be any resolution of this matter?

Doubtless there can and will be better understanding and quicker resolution of difficulties as each side becomes more aware of the interests and concerns of the other. However, it is doubtful that the time will ever come when the Federal Reserve System and the banking industry will see eye-to-eye on all matters. The major reason for this is the fact that the Federal Reserve is, after all, a public agency whereas banks are private institutions operated with a different set of objectives in view.

Beyond this, however, there lies a question as to whether this history of misunderstanding between the System and the banks may not be indicative of a structural defect within the System itself. Specifically, is it possible for one agency to be both a central bank and a regulatory agency? If one were talking of another nation, particularly a European nation, the answer might be a quick "yes." However, there are some rather unusual factors to take into consideration when it comes to the United States.

First, there is clearly a need for the central bank to maintain a relatively independent posture within Government. The degree of independence has been frequently overstated but, in general, there should be some kind of arm's length dealing between the agency which must obtain funds for the Government—the Treasury—and the agency which is responsible for the quantity of money within the economy. Certainly the two cannot be so independent as to be unconcerned as to each other's problems but neither should they be merged.

Another rather unusual feature of the American banking system is its essentially competitive nature. This is not a system with only four or five major banks but, rather, one with more than 13,000 banks, a situation unique in the modern world. Of course, not all 13,000 banks are in direct competition with one another but, nevertheless, banking is still an industry for which entry, while difficult, is reasonably possible. It is likely that in a city of any size, and in most counties, there are more individual banks in this country than there are in an entire nation overseas.

Given the desirability of some degree of independence for the Federal Reserve, is it possible for that agency to be an effective regulatory agency when dealing with thousands of individual banks? Can it afford to operate in the manner traditional for United States bank regulatory agencies, that is, with a maximum emphasis on informal procedures and quick action? The answer would seem to be "no" if, at the same time, the Federal Reserve must guard its flanks from critics who would destroy its monetary independence. Put another way, one method of insulating one's self from the hurly-burly of politics and entanglement in dangerous political issues is to rely heavily on formalistic procedures, rule making, hearings, extensive and thorough research, and, in general, a kind of deliberateness that is characteristic of much of what the Board does. These are the very characteristics of which banking is most critical and, indeed, for which banking's case is particularly good. Yet to ask the Federal Reserve to change because it is a regulatory agency may, at the same time, be asking it to endanger its ability to remain independent within Government in carrying out its central banking responsibilities.

The foregoing would suggest that the record of misunderstanding between the Board and the banking industry might well be seriously diminished if consideration were given to eliminating much if not all of the regulatory functions now exercised by the Board. Indeed, a rather strong case can be made for doing this on purely mechanical grounds; there is, after all, little real need for the Federal Reserve to be engaged in examining some state banks while the FDIC insures virtually all banks and has adequate funds and resources to take over the Board's responsibilities in this regard. There may well have been need for bank regulation by the Board in 1913, but certainly not since 1933 with the establishment of FDIC.

There is, of course, a case which can be made against transferring Federal Reserve regulatory powers to another Federal agency. It is not within the scope of this paper to debate that particular issue. Rather, we simply point to the fact that any analysis of banker attitudes toward the System would suggest that there is an important reason for at least re-studying the present bank supervisory structure.

NEW TOOLS OF MONETARY
CONTROL ABROAD

GEORGE GARVY

GOALS, INSTRUMENTS, AND PROCESSES of monetary policy all have undergone considerable change since World War II. These changes reflect a variety of factors, some of wide impact, others characteristic of individual countries. Even where trends of broad applicability are involved, the timing of changes has differed. Innovations originating in one country underwent mutations and adaptations to meet the specific conditions, traditions, constraints, and challenges operating in another. In attempting a few generalizations within the limited scope of this short essay, I am acutely aware of the pitfalls of such an undertaking, in particular in an area where superficially similar arrangements operate in a considerably different environment.

It is not the array of available instruments but their actual use, singly or in combination, that is significant for an assessment of the conduct of monetary policy. But drawing the distinction between what a central bank can do and what it actually does would require a thorough review of actual country-by-country experience. My attempt to identify the nature of, and the reasons for, the broadening of the range of tools available to central banks since World War II is thus nothing more than a modest beginning. It is limited to the group of leading industrial countries, roughly coinciding with the "Group of Ten" (although some comments on developing countries are also ventured). Since innumerable variants are encountered even in this limited group, and in some cases numerous changes and refinements have been made in the application of individual instruments, only the main lines of development can be put into relief, and no attempt can be made to indicate in each case where and at what time individual techniques have been used or introduced.

Postwar Setting in the Advanced Countries

Central banks of the industrially advanced countries found themselves after World War II operating in a substantially different domestic and international environment from that of the thirties. In most cases, the institutional setting, the problems, and the policy goals had changed. However, the degree to which the central banks sought new powers and undertook to adapt old tools to new tasks varied a good deal, not necessarily in relation to the newness of problems and the magnitude of the challenge.

Since World War II, central banks have been faced with the problem of meeting new policy goals designed to promote broader and more specific national goals in economies that have been growing more complex and integrated among themselves and with the rest of the world. Acceptance by most of the developed countries of national goals similar to those embodied in our Employment Act required a reorientation of policies of the older central banks. Central banks began to direct their efforts increasingly towards contributing to conditions conducive to optimum economic growth, to maintaining adequate aggregate demand, and to achieving socio-economic objectives which, while differing from country to country, typically encompassed a greater equality in living standards and also a reduction of inequalities in welfare and opportunity between various parts of the country. Achieving a desired composition of output has been frequently regarded as a means for achieving these goals. Partly as a result of capital destruction or under-maintenance during World War II, the older central banks, such as the Bank of France, became increasingly concerned with domestic capital formation, frequently using traditional tools of monetary control to stimulate the flow of financial resources into favored sectors of the economy.

Another consequence of events precipitated by World War II was the nationalization of important segments of industry in several countries and the nationalization of central banks. The fact that significant segments of industry are government-owned, while other important units involve some degree of government participation or sponsorship (or official tutelage, as in Japan), has become an important consideration for the conduct of monetary policy in most countries. Municipal ownership of public utilities is widespread, and communications as well as the main railroad, air, and shipping lines are usually publicly owned, directly or indirectly. A considerable part of assets owned by commercial banks (including those publicly owned) consists of credits to publicly owned units, even though the form of accommodation extended may be indistinguishable from that available to private borrowers. In effect, they represent loans extended to, or guaranteed by, government institutions that implement official economic policies.

After World War II, the central banks of Western Europe, as well as of Japan, were nationalized. The newest of the leading central banks, the Bank of Canada, was created in 1934 as a government bank, while the oldest of the central banks, the Swedish Riksbank, was a State bank from the very beginning of its history. The change in the institutional setting altered the *modus operandi,* thinking, and style of central banks surprisingly little.[1] Even prior to nationalization, while they also operated for the profit of shareholders and carried on substantial private business, the banks of issue were banks of their respective governments, cooperating in various degrees in the implementation of economic policy objectives, as then established or understood. Government ownership of central banks and changes in central banking legislation, involving in some cases creation of administrative, advisory, or planning bodies for formulating and coordinating credit policy, have not necessarily by themselves resulted in radical changes in the position of the central bank *vis-à-vis* the government.

In most industrial countries, the central problem of the postwar period has been to limit and, as necessary, neutralize the effects of excess liquidity inherited from the war and, later, increasingly, from temporary or persistent balance-of-payments surpluses. In many instances, the range of tools of monetary control available to the central banks was not adequate to cope with excess liquidity. Confronted with the huge task of reconstruction while coping with the monetary overhang of war and occupation, the central banks of Europe improvised. Of necessity, whenever new expedients were tried in extraordinary circumstances, direct and administrative measures emerged, even where conservative attitudes counseling reliance on indirect and general measures had typically dominated.

As a new environment gradually emerged after the immediate effects of the war were overcome, there was a natural tendency to seek a return to "normalcy" by liquidating the restrictive measures imposed by the financial collapse of the Great Depression, war economics, and the exigencies of reconstruction. The dismantling of war and postwar controls seemed to pave the way for a return to traditional reliance on general monetary controls. In the international sphere, it was expected that the return to convertibility at the end of 1958 would lead to less rather than greater need for innovation in the management of international liquidity. Before long, however, controls introduced to cope with wartime problems of scarcity of goods and abundance of money proved handy in dealing with new objectives of directing credit into areas favored by macro-economic priorities. At the same time, the growing integration of economies following the acceptance of convertibility and the freer flow of capital across national borders created its own problem for monetary policy.

In spite of the broadening of domestic goals, external equilibrium

---

[1] As Karl R. Bopp had anticipated in his "Nationalization of the Bank of England and the Bank of France," *The Journal of Politics,* August 1946.

remained a principal focus of monetary policy. Even in the nostalgic memory of the simplicity of pre-World War I days, defense of the exchange value of the national currency was, of course, a primary concern of central bank policy. But since the return to convertibility, in a world with a considerably greater economic interdependence and a vastly enlarged financial structure, defending fixed exchange parities and protecting the proper functioning of the monetary system has become considerably more complex. While proper behavior became codified on an international scale by the Bretton Woods institution and various other group arrangements, such as the European Payments Union and the European Monetary Agreement, and the exchange provisions of the Treaty of Rome, individual central banks still had to devise and operate appropriate defense, neutralizing, and adjustment mechanisms as wartime exchange controls were dismantled.

Because the general framework of public policy gives little scope to price and employment flexibility, equilibrating capital flows have been assuming a greater role since World War II, in particular since the return to convertibility. Thus, the task of central banks widened from defending exchange parities through operations in exchange markets and the skillful management of international reserves to concern with the regulation of financial flows across international borders. Such regulations usually required close cooperation among the central bank, the Ministry of Finance, and other parts of the government. Indeed, while, typically, the central bank continued to supervise exchange controls and to manage exchange stabilization funds, the national government usually appeared on the scene whenever broad problems of international monetary cooperation were under discussion. Thus, the growing complexity of international financial interrelationships became one of the main reasons why concern with the financial environment emerged more and more as a part of overall governmental policy.

Discovery of fiscal policy as a potent tool of economic policy was the other main reason for closer coordination of monetary and other policies. The burden which monetary policy had to carry diminished as fiscal and income policies, as well as a variety of direct and indirect controls, were applied in individual countries, with varying success, to cope with the problems of excessive domestic demand and external disequilibrium. But advanced as well as developing countries continued to place considerable reliance on monetary policy as a means of influencing aggregate demand.

The following sections briefly review the main lines along which

monetary policy instruments have developed since World War II.
Space does not permit dealing with the coordinated use of these tools,
with the problem of aligning monetary and fiscal policies, or with the
increasingly felt need for coordinating both kinds of public policy
within the Common Market.

The Need for New Tools

With notable exceptions, changes in tools available to central banks
of the advanced countries arose largely from improvisation and adaptation of existing tools, rather than as the fruit of systematic efforts based
on comprehensive inquiries. Monetary control techniques which the
central banks had at their disposal as they confronted new problems
at the close of World War II were forged essentially at a time when
belief in the inherent tendency of the economic system to return to
equilibrium was strong, and faith in automatism was not deluded by
suspicion that the response might be capricious, or even perverse.[2]
The role which central banking should play in achieving the newly
accepted or gradually evolving goals of government economic policy,
and the changing policy environment and credit needs of the economy
required a searching re-examination of the financial structure, monetary policy, and of its tools and processes. In some countries, broad
official inquiries were undertaken which produced monumental reports
that vastly enriched our knowledge and offered new insights and interpretations, such as the Radcliffe Report in England and the Report of
the Royal Commission in Canada. In France, a series of reports by
special committees of experts probed into the need for changing the
financial structure as well as monetary policy tools, thus laying the
groundwork for important reforms. Official as well as private inquiries
were also conducted in some other countries, but in many cases the
initiative for obtaining new tools or developing new techniques was
left to the central banks themselves. Nowhere has monetary policy and
the changing financial structure been subject to the kind of continued
and searching examination it has received in the United States, largely
as a result of continuing Congressional interest, as well as numerous
private initiatives. And it was in the United States that most of the
new monetary techniques used by central banks around the world

---

[2] In his study of the pre-World War I policy of the Reichsbank ("Die Tätig-
keit der Reichsbank von 1876 bis 1914," *Weltwirtschaftliches Archiv,* 1954),
Karl R. Bopp was struck by the difficulties the German central bank had encountered in reconciling, in day-to-day operations, its frequently conflicting rate
objectives as well as by its failure to pay adequate attention to controlling the
reserve base of the banking system.

originated, transforming "banks of issue" in the advanced countries into one of the most important channels through which public policy affects the economy.[3]

Closer integration of monetary and overall economic policy requires shifting from commercial banks to the central bank the initiative for injecting and withdrawing reserves, and open market operations emimently suits this purpose. Effective use of open market operations has remained, however, limited to the United Kingdom and Canada, in spite of the more recent endeavors in Japan, West Germany, France, Sweden, Austria, and elsewhere to develop such operations. The narrowness of their money markets and the limited number of instruments traded in them hinder a more vigorous use of this tool. Indeed, in no other country is the debt of the central government so widely held by individuals, business firms, lower-level governmental units, and others as in the United States. Nowhere is this debt so actively traded, and its yields subject to day-by-day changes in demand or to reassessment by money market participants as the Treasury undertakes frequent new financing or refunding operations. There is, indeed, a great difference between the willingness of the central bank to buy or sell government securities at infrequently changed posted rates, as in West Germany, or to make periodic purchases of certain previously announced amounts of government securities, as in Japan—with the initiative for transactions left to the market—and a broad, impersonal market in which the central bank can operate as merely one of the major participants, buying and selling on the market to affect bank reserves rather than being the market.

Since relying on open market operations for controlling the liquidity of the banking system was not feasible in most countries because central bank portfolios were not suitable and the money market was too narrow, central banks had to seek other means for influencing the reserve base. One such new tool was the introduction of mandatory minimum reserve ratios[4] (Italy). More frequently, however, the oldest tool of monetary control—the discount mechanism—was adapted to achieve the desired policy objectives, frequently as a means of direct-

---

[3] How distant, indeed, appears the time when the National Monetary Commission commissioned a translation of a series of monographs on banking in various countries to help decide how the new central bank to be created in the United States could benefit from foreign experience!

[4] References to individual countries are to well-known or early examples of the techniques referred to. They are not meant to be complete. For more details, see George Garvy, *The Discount Mechanism in Leading Industrial Countries Since World War II*, Board of Governors of the Federal Reserve System, 1968.

ing the purposes for which bank credit was used and not only to control its total volume (France).

Where central bank control traditionally focused primarily on the level of interest rates rather than on the volume of bank credit, the approach of setting the discount rate and letting the banking system determine how much central bank credit it wanted to use at any given time was, by and large, replaced by a system which combined qualitative and quantitative limitations to achieve control over the total volume of bank credit and to influence its use. The shift of emphasis from avoidance of undesirable developments, such as excessive cyclical swings and loss of international reserves, to positive goals, formulated in terms of employment, growth, or social welfare, seemed to make exclusive reliance on indirect tools inadequate. The narrowing of the range of socially acceptable rates, possible conflicts between domestic and external objectives and, in some cases, pressure for fostering preferential or subsidy rates in certain sectors of the economy caused central banks to seek additional tools for achieving overall objectives of monetary policy. Thus, in many advanced (as well as developing) countries, considerable reliance has come to be placed on controlling expansion of bank credit directly, mostly by quantitative limitations on loans (Belgium, France, Switzerland). Quantitative controls operate largely through the imposition and manipulation of absolute bank credit ceilings, which continue to be supported by more traditional tools of credit control aimed at liquidity and rate objectives.

In most advanced countries, even where quantitative controls are used, central bank policy continues to be guided by rate objectives, as authorities attempt to achieve rate levels that will stimulate capital formation and avoid undesirable short-term international capital flows. In most recent years, rates of growth of the money supply and bank credit have been given more attention. This is true even in countries which have traditionally focused on rate objectives and in which the discount rate has served as an anchor for the entire structure of interest rates. Since the 1950's, for example, the Bank of England has expanded its means of controlling the banking sector. In addition to the traditional cash and liquidity ratios, a system of special deposits for the clearing banks was introduced in 1965 as a means of influencing bank liquidity, and a cash deposit scheme for other banks was established in 1968 (although it has not been used). Loan priorities and quantitative controls (initially introduced by means of letters issued by the Governor) to achieve nonrate bank credit rationing have also been used.

Widening of the Scope of Controls

In most advanced countries, institutional changes since World War II have affected the place of money in the spectrum of liquidity, and of commercial banks as the main source of credit. Commercial banks themselves have been operating in an atmosphere of greater freedom from traditional inhibitions and of fewer rigidities in legal restrictions. Fairly universally, the emergence of new financial institutions and processes, or the greater willingness of the older institutions to compete with banks for deposits as well as loans, presented new challenges to central banking. It has become evident in many industrial countries, although to different degrees, that it can no longer be assumed that the central bank can exercise adequate control over total credit by affecting reserves of commercial banks. As the financial environment and objectives of public policy changed after World War II, reliance on the rate mechanism and manipulation of access conditions to central bank credit in order to affect the liquidity of the banking system became increasingly more difficult, and at times inadequate.

The growth and proliferation of nonbank financial institutions and the emerging importance of money substitutes introduced significant changes into the environment for the conduct of monetary policy. The role of financial intermediaries, which first became the subject of a lively debate in the United States, has become a problem for most advanced countries in the application of monetary controls. Its acuteness varies, largely as a function of the degree to which institutions other than commercial banks can issue deposit-like liabilities which, in fact, are an adequate substitute for money, or can compete with commercial banks for various categories of credits traditionally associated with the sphere of banking activities in a given country. As a result, there was a need to adapt traditional techniques of monetary control to new objectives, to forge new tools, and to widen the area of concern from commercial banking to a wider and widening circle of financial institutions and instruments.

By and large, the range of institutions subject to monetary controls has grown, as financial intermediaries multiplied, and older institutions, such as savings banks, tended to broaden the scope of their operations. Central banks began to seek powers (or use existing powers) to regulate institutions issuing money substitutes. They did so largely because they became convinced that the size and direction of total credit flows was a financial variable most relevant for the achievement of national economic goals, rather than because they became convinced that there was no significant distinction between money and near-money. The solutions adopted vary, but more and more countries have found it necessary to extend the scope of at least the main monetary controls to savings banks and various types of specialized credit institutions catering to individual segments of the economy, such as agriculture. When the scope of power of the older central banks was redefined by new legislation, it was often expanded to include a range of financial institutions other than commercial banks.[5] When this was not done, central banks found themselves compelled to find ways of controlling credit flows that increasingly bypassed institutions subject directly to central bank policy actions and/or supervision.

Where considerable reliance continues to be placed on voluntary compliance, as in the United Kingdom, the Governor of the Bank of England found it necessary to address his requests to limit credit outstanding to a widening circle of credit institutions. Thus, when in 1955-1956 the Bank of England limited advances by clearing banks, it later sought to limit growth of commercial paper as well, and also to extend loan ceilings to banks other than clearing banks. In countries in which monetary mechanisms were supplemented by a variety of quantitative restrictions, it was also found necessary in many cases to extend such restrictions beyond the area of traditional commercial banking. And, indeed, one of the aspects of the cash deposit scheme recently developed, but as yet not implemented, is to extend control of the Bank of England to nonclearing banks.

Evolution of the Discount Mechanism

The choice of instruments used by an individual central bank is normally a function of the degree of precision that may be expected from using any of them, singly or in combination, to achieve the desired effect. Frequently, however, the role of any particular monetary tool depends on the availability of alternative control mechanisms. By and large, granting of new controls to the older central banks tended to lag behind changes in economic and financial structure, and in the objectives these banks were supposed to pursue. As a result, the oldest tool of central banking has been given in many countries new functions requiring adaptations far beyond the original mechanism,

---

[5] The Bundesbank, for instance, applies reserve requirements to savings banks; the French National Credit Council has jurisdiction over a wide range of financial institutions, including credit unions and discount houses. The Canadian Porter Commission recommended imposition of cash reserve requirements on all financial institutions issuing near-money claims.

which is closely linked to the oldest theory of central banking—the commercial-bills doctrine. In most advanced countries, the discount mechanism remains the centerpiece of domestic monetary controls. In most, it was, until very recently, almost the only significant tool available to the central bank. The precise form of its current use, of course, varies, ranging from the traditional coordination with open market operations in England to the preservation of archaic trappings, such as the local discount committees of leading merchants and wealthy citizens in Belgium.

From the very beginning, the discount mechanism had two aspects —rate and eligibility requirements. For a variety of reasons, the use of the rate as a price, and thus as a rationing device, has declined since World War II. The diminished role of the bank rate as a signal of the central bank's wishes stemmed, in part at least, from changes arising out of socio-political, as well as purely monetary, considerations.[6] Thus, in England, the discount rate remained unchanged from July 1932 through October 1952, with the exception of a short episode during which it was raised immediately before the outbreak of the war and then lowered in two steps to the original level a few weeks later. A more recent example involves Italy, where the rate was raised in 1969—the first change since it was lowered in 1958—while in Norway at this writing (July 1969) the discount rate remains at the level set almost fifteen years ago. In a broad sense, it is not improper to speak of a "politicization" of the discount rate.[7] Yet, rediscounting with the central bank (or obtaining advances from it) remains the only routine and generally used means for adjusting short-term— and in some countries also cyclical—fluctuations in reserve positions (Italy).

With the revival of monetary policy in the early fifties, most industrial countries, however, have again been using changes in the discount rate for domestic as well as for international reasons.[8] Indeed, moves in either direction by one of the leading countries are now usually

---

[6] Linking the discount rate automatically to a market rate—the Treasury bill rate—as was done in Canada between 1956 and 1962, was another attempt to escape constraints on moving the discount rate.

[7] Karl Bopp, who has devoted so much of his attention to studying policies of the leading central banks of Europe, had no difficulty in documenting that "Napoleon viewed the Bank rate as a political tool." "Bank of France Policy: Brief Survey of Instruments, 1800-1914," *The American Journal of Economics and Sociology,* Vol. II, No. 3.

[8] In the less-developed countries, in which a large segment of commercial banking frequently consists of government- or foreign-owned institutions, the effectiveness of the discount rate as a rationing device is limited and the rate typically serves primarily as a signal.

followed by similar defensive or coordinated moves by other countries. In some countries the discount rate remains an important element in the credit situation, even though it is changed infrequently, because deposit and/or lending rates are tied to it by custom (United Kingdom), practice (Belgium, Italy), or agreement (Austria, Japan). Recently there has been a tendency to relax the resulting rigidity, in part because it imposes additional constraints on the use of the rate.

Eligibility requirements governing access to the discount window are easily traced to the commercial-bills doctrine. To a surprising degree, central banks have retained traditional forms and practices by continuing to give preferential treatment to credit extended by means of discounting customer notes. In some cases, as in France, formal compliance with the rule that central bank credit should be extended on the basis of short-term paper only was achieved by interposing special primary discounting institutions; such institutions issue short-term instruments discountable at the central bank against medium- and even long-term claims which they keep in their portfolios; thus, in fact, acting as primary discounting institutions.

In spite of the survival of the trade bill as the single or preferred instrument of short-term accommodation at the discount window, central banks use their considerable discretionary powers to regulate access to discount facilities by varying eligibility requirements in accordance with policy objectives (Germany, Netherlands). This increases their ability to influence commercial bank behavior in the direction consistent with the objectives of monetary policy. Indeed, in some countries the discount mechanism has also been used as an enforcement mechanism—access to the window is dependent on compliance with overall objectives of monetary policy attuned to achieving specific national policy objectives. Even in countries where access to the window within ceilings is considered a right, differentiated variations in such ceilings have become a means of inducing or enforcing compliance.

In countries in which the discount window has been used for influencing credit flows by means of differentiated discount rates, compartmentalized discount procedures have been used to implement a variety of official programs. In countries which use this technique, it is believed that by controlling the cost (rather than the quantity) of credit, differentiated discount rates can be helpful in directing the use of credit and in influencing the direction of growth of the economy. Such use of the discount window to stimulate investment in certain sectors, to finance farm price-support programs or in other ways to substitute for budgetary financing, resulted, in fact, in the provision of central bank credit on a semi-permanent basis. The techniques used include giving preferred categories of credits automatic access to the discount window. Where discount quotas applicable to individual banks exist, preferred paper may be discountable outside such quotas or within special, additional quotas.[9] Perhaps the most outstanding example of this technique is the Bank of France's use of preferential status at the discount window and of a lower discount rate to stimulate residential construction and the re-equipment of industry. Preferential treatment of foreign-trade credits goes back to the period between the two world wars, but the extent to which central bank facilities have been made available for this purpose expanded considerably after World War II. Preferential access may be formalized by giving prior approval ("visa") to such paper (Belgium, France, Italy, Japan), in which case the paper is often discountable at a lower rate.

Progressive rates at the discount window are usually applied in combination with quantitative limitations rather than as an alternative to quantitative restrictions. Scaled rates are usually a function of the size and duration of borrowing, or they may be applied to borrowing in excess of basic quotas (France). Access to the discount window now usually involves a complex structure of discount rates, but in recent years there has been a clear tendency (France, Japan) away from excessively complicated multi-rate structures and from extreme penalty rates.

In some countries, advances obtainable on credit instruments not eligible at the window incur a higher cost, but continue to provide a safety valve for obtaining central bank credit for reserve or liquidity adjustment purposes and at the same time set an effective ceiling on money market rates (Belgium). Where the conceptual difference between discounts and advances is being maintained, there has been a clear tendency to confine the role of advances to the provision of a temporary safety valve—if necessary, by imposing rigid restrictive conditions on its use (Germany). In some cases, when the scope for open market operations still remains very limited, as in France, discount window operations at the initiative of the central bank, designed to relieve excessive market tightness, have been used as a substitute for such operations.

---

[9] Interestingly enough, Yugoslavia, the only socialist country which has separated the central banking from the commercial banking function and introduced rediscounting, also uses eligibility requirements and discounting outside the quota as a means of selective credit control.

The complexity of the discount mechanism has stemmed largely from endeavors to channel credit into uses to which economic or social priorities were assigned by government policy, rather than to achieve broad objectives of monetary policy. However, the use of the discount mechanism as a tool of selective credit control tends to render the implementation of overall monetary policy more difficult, especially when the discount window is used to stimulate particular activities. In recent years, therefore, there has been a tendency away from using the discount mechanism as a tool for achieving multiple and, at times, conflicting objectives. Conditions of access and administration have been simplified, especially where they had become exceedingly complex and involved a wide range of rates, including several penalty rates, and highly differentiated conditions for access, as in France and Japan.

At the same time, the availability of new control tools, in particular the introduction of minimum reserve requirements, has tended to reduce the need for relying heavily, or even excessively, on the discount mechanism and on the related "Lombard loans" (advances). In several advanced countries, the development of a true money market (and in some countries, of an impersonal market for reserve balances) also served to reduce the need for relying on borrowing from the central bank (Netherlands). Concentration of banking resources in a diminishing number of banks, and the concomitant growth of branch systems, which tended to reduce seasonal and cyclical fluctuations in deposits and loan demand, had a similar effect on the need for day-to-day recourse to central bank credit.

Reserve Requirements

While the discount rate affects the cost of credit, minimum reserve requirements affect its availability. Legal reserve requirements have emerged as a most important tool of monetary control, supplanting in many countries the primacy of the discount mechanism.

Liquidity ratios have traditionally played a role in central banking as an instrument of control or as a requirement deemed essential to assure adequate performance of the banking system.[10] In the latter case, they are enforced primarily from a bank-supervisory rather than

---

[10] Formal liquidity ratios, instead of, or in addition to reserve requirements, have been imposed in a few instances (Belgium, France), to be satisfied by the holding of assets otherwise eligible for discounting or as collateral for advances. (Proposals for imposing similar "security reserve requirements" were made in the United States after World War II.)

policy-oriented point of view (Switzerland). In some countries, as in France, liquidity ratios (where they had to be satisfied by holding specified percentages of government obligations) had been introduced after World War II to neutralize (sterilize) the effect of excessive liquidity inherited from wartime developments. In others, with England as the classic example, they have been viewed as a means for controlling total bank liabilities. But even in England, voluntary observance of traditional liquidity ratios, which after World War II were formalized by the Bank of England, was supplemented first (when the need for additional restraint arose) by special deposits for clearing banks and more recently by cash deposit requirements for other banks. In Canada, liquidity reserves have been introduced as a supplement to minimum reserve ratios.

Minimum reserve ratios (legal reserve requirements), and the authority to vary them within stipulated ranges, gave the central bank a new tool for controlling the base of deposit creation and thus of bank credit expansion. The requirement that reserves be maintained at the central bank in amounts related to commercial bank deposit liabilities makes the central bank share in the growing role of banks in the creation of money. Part of the monetization of debt associated with the creation of demand deposits can thus be used for the public benefit. Legal reserve requirements, first introduced in the United States, are an integral part of monetary powers conferred upon new central banks by laws passed since World War II; the older central banks have gradually acquired such powers and learned to use them effectively and to devise variants specifically suited to conditions in their countries. In some countries, the use of reserve requirements has been hesitant and intermittent and their level so low as to be of slight significance. In Japan, the burden of a low requirement was made even less onerous by payment of interest by the central bank. Other countries have moved toward making minimum reserve ratios more effective by requiring observance on a continuing (average) basis and not only on the last day of the month or some other report period.

Several countries have effectively used reserve requirements to prevent undesirable inflows of foreign funds by imposing such onerous requirements on foreign deposits as to make it unprofitable for banks to accept them (Germany). In fact, imposition of requirements in amounts of up to 100 per cent on marginal increments is tantamount to direct control of additional foreign liabilities that banks can incur. Lesser percentages applied to total or marginal amounts permit the central bank to vary the degree of profitability of such deposits for commercial banks.

Quantitative Controls

Since World War II, quantitative controls have been used frequently to reinforce or replace reliance on discount policy as a means of regulating the banking system's lending base. Central banks in several advanced as well as developing countries have resorted to such non-price rationing, often because social and political constraints or international considerations interfered with the full and effective use of more general controls. In some countries, the scope of selective controls, introduced to achieve limited objectives, has simply been extended. Where adequate legislation to impose formal controls is not available, quantitative restrictions have occasionally been introduced and enforced by means of moral suasion—"window guidance" in Japan and the "gentlemen's agreements" between the commercial banks and the National Bank of Switzerland being conspicuous examples. In some cases, quantitative restrictions are quite congenial to the broad philosophy of governments which apply controls to other economic activities as well. But it would be wrong to identify the use of quantitative credit or other monetary controls as a concomitant of an economic policy committed to planning or "dirigisme," as the case of Germany clearly demonstrates.

Not all monetary controls involving quantification are quantitative controls. This term is best reserved for techniques that involve the establishment either of quotas for individual (or groups of) banks for specific categories (or the total amount) of credit obtainable at the central bank (France, Germany, Italy, Japan), or of absolute limits on the growth of various types of loans or of the total amount of credit extended by individual banks to their customers (Belgium, France, Japan, Netherlands, Switzerland). Several central banks have concluded that using discount quotas as a means of regulating the total volume of bank credit and as a fulcrum against which rate policy becomes effective is inadequate. In some countries, therefore, discount quotas have been supplemented or replaced by ceilings on total loan volume, or other quantitative controls applying to total (or selected) bank assets, most commonly taking the form of maximum limits for permissible expansion during specified periods. In some cases, loan ceilings have been extended to a variety of other financial institutions as well.

Many of the quantitative controls have been built around the discount window, in particular where discounting remains the primary means of access to central bank credit. Others have been grafted onto liquidity ratios, by freezing a certain volume of bank assets eligible at the discount window. Discount quotas for individual banks may be made quite complex by using changes in such lines not only to permit secular growth, but also to discipline banks that do not adhere to rules laid down by the monetary authorities. Separate, but more flexible, quantity limitations on advances frequently supplement quantitative rules at the discount window. In addition, a certain degree of flexibility is usually provided by permitting banks to exceed discount quotas at their option at the cost of a severe penalty rate, or under specified special conditions only, and then usually for limited periods. The cost of such "overline" borrowing at the discount window has at times been pushed to such extreme levels as to make it prohibitive and, therefore, inoperative.

Quantitative restrictions applied to the volume of discounts, to total bank loans or credit, or to bank liabilities may be linked to overall national economic targets or merely represent the judgment of the central bank as to the extent to which further credit expansion is compatible with internal and external equilibrium. In several countries, they are used almost exclusively to combat the development of inflationary pressures (Belgium, Switzerland). In some cases, control over domestic credit is reinforced by separate controls over the foreign positions of commercial banks (Netherlands).

Obviously, the administration of credit lines at the central bank, and of quantitative rules in general, requires frequent review by the monetary authorities of various problems, such as the equity of the system and its potentially stifling rigidity. Linking discount quotas or credit ceilings to some "objective" variable, such as bank capital or some measure of past performance, may reduce, but can never completely remove, the area of administrative discretion. The use of complex formulas, no less than of informal guidelines, for setting quantitative limits usually involves central banks in close supervision of the actual performance of the banking system and, indeed, of the entire range of financial institutions subject to central bank control. Pursuance of multiple goals by countries using quantitative credit tools results at times in complex schemes under which the overall effectiveness of ceilings is undermined by various exceptions.

Defending the International Value of the National Currency

After World War II, the central bank's traditional concern for the external value of the national currency became institutionalized within the framework of an international organization. With the creation of the IMF, stability of exchange rates became a matter of codified international behavior. Inevitably, strains developed in a system which failed to acknowledge that maintenance of stability requires prompt adoption of appropriate adjustment policies. Since the return to convertibility, individual countries have experienced disequilibria of varying degrees of seriousness. Demand pressures have at times led to balance-of-payments strains (periodically in Japan) and occasionally to confidence-shaking deficits of major proportions (as in the United Kingdom, Canada, Italy, and, more recently, France).

In contrast to the years prior to World War I, when central banks relied primarily on rate policy to defend the external value of national currencies and to cope with international capital flows, the post-World War II period has witnessed the development of a host of special policies and devices. Reduced price, wage, and employment flexibility make it necessary to rely more heavily on capital flows as a means of equilibrating the balance of payments. Central banks have had to find new techniques to deal with capital flows and in some cases, with embarrassingly large balance-of-payments surpluses. New techniques had also to be developed, and some old techniques adapted to minimize temporary pressures on, or speculative surges against, individual currencies and to assure an adequate functioning of the international monetary system as a whole.

After 1949, exchange-rate adjustments have been used only sparingly. A much more intricate policy than in the day of the gold standard, or even in the uncertain inter-war years, evolved as most advanced countries found it necessary to seek new ways to cope with undesirable capital inflows, or to control outflows, by direct as well as indirect means. In more recent years, the use of credit lines for meeting temporary pressures and disequilibria—borrowing from the IMF, drawing on the currency swap network centered in the United States, or relying on other, mostly *ad hoc,* arrangements—became an important aspect of international monetary cooperation.

Greater central bank control over the management of foreign assets appears to have been more readily accepted by commercial banks than control over domestic credit flows, perhaps because of the widespread use of wartime exchange controls. Measures adopted by individual countries have included control over commercial bank borrowing abroad, regulation of their net positions in foreign exchange or in individual foreign currencies, and the establishment of limits on the volume of foreign currency claims or liabilities of banks (and, in some cases, of nonbanks as well). Forward exchange operations (Italy), variation of the rates at which the central bank is ready to provide foreign exchange cover (Germany), separate reserve requirements against foreign deposits (as already mentioned), and prohibition of payment of interest on foreign deposits (Switzerland) also have been used. Some central banks (like the German Bundesbank) have gone so far as to prescribe *where* foreign currency (dollars) that it supplies on favorable conditions to commercial banks and others should be invested.

In addition to regulating the foreign-exchange positions of domestic banks (or of the entire private sector), central banks have increasingly used active foreign-exchange operations to support domestic monetary controls. The scope of these activities has been widened by the development of the swap network and by the operations of some central banks in the Euro-dollar and other Euro-currency markets.

In recent years, with closer monetary cooperation growing out of economic interdependence, individual banks have sometimes acted in the interest of mutual accommodation. Indeed, central bank co-operation—together with other forms of economic coordination among advanced countries—has developed on an unprecedented scale. Bilateral and multilateral consultations have become more frequent, extensive, and in some respects also more informal than during the inter-war period. At the same time, such cooperation and the various institutions under whose aegis it has grown have provided frequent opportunities for analyzing and comparing the effectiveness of monetary measures taken by individual countries, be it to cope with domestic or international problems. Consultations and meetings sponsored by the IMF, the BIS, the OECD, the Group of Ten, and the Monetary Committee of the European Community, as well as less formal international contacts, spread knowledge of new techniques and processes and frequently permit a collective appraisal of their value and limitations. Sometimes such meetings also produce strong pressure for the adoption of new techniques in countries where they seem appropriate.

Developing Countries

In the newer countries, financing developmental expenditures is an important objective of monetary policy; central banking, from its inception in these countries, has played a leading role in the process of economic development. Central banks of the newly independent countries of Asia and Africa typically have fostered the development of an appropriate financial structure, encouraged savings, created new specialized credit institutions, and developed capital markets. Similar objectives have been pursued since World War II by the central banks in the former dominions of the British Commonwealth. The older central banks of Latin America, fashioned mostly in an earlier period and initially much imbued with more traditional central bank philosophy, have come to regard stimulation of savings and development of financial structures as a main objective of central bank policy. Endeavors to foster the development of capital and credit markets frequently led to capitalizing development banks and a variety of specialized institutions for medium- and long-term credit in specific sectors of the economy, such as agriculture.

The framework for central bank actions in developing countries has typically included irresistible social and political pressures to go faster than real resources, the institutional framework, available external finance, and the volume of foreign-exchange reserves permitted. In many of these countries, central banking laws have been fashioned after examples of countries with much more advanced economies. By and large, however, the developing countries have not been more successful than the older countries in applying traditional tools of monetary policy or in developing new tools suitable for their own problems.

Individual developing countries have used various combinations of general, selective, and direct monetary controls. Some techniques were patterned after the example of advanced countries; others have been developed to deal with these countries' specific problems (such as advance deposit schemes for imports, more recently also used by the United Kingdom). Frequently the temptation to find shortcuts through selective controls proved irresistible when attempting to meet sectoral problems, to speed up the pace of development, or to cope with recurring balance-of-payments difficulties. It is a melancholy observation that many of these central banks had to learn from bitter experience that no degree of sophistication in sharpening the most modern and complex tools of monetary controls could overcome chronic capital shortages, misuse of financial resources obtained from abroad, insufficiency of fiscal resources, political instability, and inadequacy not only of financial but also of legal and social institutions, aggravated in many countries by politically dictated misallocation of human, physical, and financial resources. To be sure, some countries have quite successfully preserved monetary equilibrium in the face of the inflationary forces generated by development. But such an outcome was more frequently than not achieved as a result of pressure from international organizations, such as the IMF and IBRD, and from aid-giving countries, rather than because of the skillful and timely use, at the initiative of the central bank, of controls available to it.

*   *   *   *   *   *   *

Post-World War II experience clearly shows that successful conduct of domestic and external monetary policy hinges not so much on the forging of new tools as on judgment and determination. Nor is explicit theorizing on means and processes of monetary policy a prerequisite for success. Even where monetary policy was provided with a fresh and original theoretical underpinning—as in The Netherlands under Dr. Holtrop's leadership—achieving growth without inflation and applying reason and quantitative guidelines were thwarted by explosive forces rooted in the struggle for distribution of the social product or in uncontrollable foreign influences.

Fifteen years ago, when discussing "Central Banking Objectives, Guides, and Measures," Karl Bopp wrote: "We have a responsibility to develop techniques best suited to our dynamic society."[11] In spite of the proliferation of techniques and instruments since World War II, his conclusion "that simple and direct methods may be effective, and that even the most ingenious central banking techniques will not be effective, unless they can and are permitted to influence the rate of interest, the availability of credit, or both" still stands unchallenged.

---

[11] *The Journal of Finance,* Vol. IX, No. 1, March 1954, p. 21.

MAKING PEACE WITH GOLD*

RALPH A. YOUNG

WHILE GOLD HAS PLAYED a role in monetary organization throughout the entire history of civilization, it was not until after the discovery of the New World that gold coinage acquired a parity with silver among the economic elite, i.e., merchants, traders, goldsmiths, bankers, and rulers. Even more recent was the use of gold as the basis for a money system. Great Britain was the innovator when, in a series of actions between 1816 and 1821, it adopted a weight of gold as its primary monetary unit; gave existing Bank of England notes full and ready convertibility into gold coin; and undertook to limit the supply of nongold money in order to assure that its ready convertibility into gold would be indefinitely maintained.

For 50 years thereafter, Great Britain stood alone in adhering to a relatively "pure" gold money system. In the 1870's, however, a gold money system also was established by Germany and France. By 1900, the system had been adopted by most countries of importance in the trading world, including the United States. Thus, it was not until the turn of the 20th century that an international gold-standard monetary system was fully launched and set on course.

This point is made to emphasize that what is known as an international gold standard is not a mechanism long imbedded in world monetary organization, as is widely believed. The notion of the sanctity of gold as an impersonal and nonfiduciary monetary standard is largely a product of recent times.

Moreover, the era of the international gold standard proper was short—barely 50 years. The disruptions of World War I gave it a shattering blow from which it was never to recover. Probably its life would have ended in a few decades in any case, for nongold money in the form of paper currency and bank checks was gradually displacing gold in domestic monetary usage. Gold was coming to serve primarily as a reserve base—and an increasingly slender base at that.

Why did the international gold standard hold undisputed reign for even as long as half a century? Why and how did the gold standard work? It worked because national governments accepted three neces-

---

* This essay originally appeared in *The Morgan Guaranty Survey* (New York: Morgan Guaranty Trust Company of New York, June 1968). It has since been revised and is reprinted here with permission.

sary conditions. First, the unit of national money was defined as a weight of gold, i.e., gold was given a fixed price in national money. Second, ready convertibility of nongold national money into gold was provided. Third, the price of gold in national money was so related to domestic price and interest levels that there was no incentive to convert nongold money into gold and to export it for profit.

The first condition called for a higher price of gold on world markets than would be fixed by the free play of market forces without a monetary demand—a price that would serve as an incentive to gold production and assure a continually growing supply of gold for monetary usage. Through most of the 19th and early 20th centuries this condition was sufficiently satisfied to keep prospectors searching for new gold fields, and capital quickly flowed to develop new finds. As a result, gold output was maintained well enough to permit a growth in monetary gold stock averaging just under 3 per cent a year from 1850 to 1914—about a fifth lower than the rate of growth in real gross national product.

Meeting the second condition of a gold-standard money system— namely, the requirement of convertibility for nongold money—furnished a basis for confidence in that money. Anyone who preferred the commodity to nongold money—mainly paper, check money, or silver coin—could, if he wished, convert; and gold could readily be obtained for payment in international transactions. Furthermore, the convertibility requirement had two further consequences. It acted to set a limit—to be sure, a very broad limit—on the creeping creation of nongold money for whatever purposes national governments deemed expedient or tolerated. Equally important, it effectively reduced the responsibility of the monetary authorities—in most cases, central banks—to a simple matter of providing a mechanism of convertibility. An aura of non-political objectivity in governmental administration of the monetary system was thus created. In the then prevalent view that the sovereign should provide a good money but not meddle with its usage or value, this consequence was both congenial and acceptable.

De facto debasement of the international gold standard by the faster creation of nongold money was so gradual during that standard's heyday as to be ignored for all practical purposes by the vast majority of people, and, accordingly, by governments. In fact, this faster growth of money in relation to the growth of tangible wealth and services is what kept the variation of the price level under the gold-standard reign within tolerable limits. And so long as international convertability of money could be counted on as a matter of high probability, confidence in the gold standard was maintained.

The third condition of a gold-standard monetary system—national gold prices equated internationally with what money could buy or earn domestically—had broad implications for world trade. It yielded a system of stable exchange rates for the continuing interconvertibility of national currencies and reduced money costs and risks in trade and investment among countries. It also furnished the world with an integrated price system as a guide to international output and commerce and fostered the development of specialization in accordance with the comparative advantages of regional resources.

During the ascendancy of the gold standard, world trade flourished; world markets for new national products emerged; industrial production was progressively concentrated in ever larger-units at lowered cost; and the fruits of industrial revolution became widely distributed over the face of the globe, and most widely over its gold-standard area.

This is not to say that the international gold standard was never threatened, economically and politically. On three occasions in the mid-19th century the Bank of England temporarily suspended the Bank Act of 1844 (thereby producing *de facto* inconvertibility of its notes), and a fourth suspension was narrowly avoided at the time of the Baring crisis in 1890. Likewise, the dominance of gold in United States monetary affairs was threatened severely by the populist wave culminating in William Jennings Bryan's grave warning that the people were in danger of being crucified on "a cross of gold."

But the domestic convertibility of gold and nongold money into goods and services varied little enough in any relatively short period that public indignation never reached a boiling point which could bring the standard's downfall. And always when the threats were most grievous, the bounty of nature came to the rescue. As one gold field became exhausted, another took its place: California, Australia, the Yukon, Western Canada, the Transvaal Rand, and (most recently) the Orange Free State. Gold output was enough, after satisfying industrial and hoarding demands, to sustain an increment in monetary stocks sufficient to frustrate the severest critics of the international gold standard.

Disruptions and devastations of World War I, together with the creation of money by governmental fiat to finance that war and economic reconstruction after it, spelled the doom of the international gold standard in its pristine form. The financial world was in a state of confusion as to what next to do. Future uncertainties and the pressure of events made action both necessary and inevitable.

Modifying the Gold Standard

Monetary beliefs, like other forms of social belief, tend to rest on a mixture of accepted tradition, experience, and myth. Hence it is not surprising that the responsible leaders in the monetary area finally reached a consensus after World War I favoring some kind of reconstructed gold standard. This consensus was not reached suddenly upon the termination of hostilities, but only in the face of widespread monetary disorder in Europe and dependent areas. It did not find formal expression until the International Economic Conference held at Genoa in 1922.

What governments were then advised to do was, first, to revalue their money realistically in terms of gold according to its current ability to purchase goods and services domestically. But in revaluing domestic money in terms of gold and in beginning once again to demand gold for monetary purposes, countries were further advised to reduce sharply the volume of gold coin in circulation and otherwise to economize on the use of gold by holding foreign exchange along with gold as monetary reserves to provide assured international convertibility. Thus, a subtle and critical change in the character of the traditional gold standard was to be introduced.

Lastly, governments were advised that their central banks—to whom responsibility for maintaining convertibility had previously been entrusted—might need henceforth to keep a closer eye on domestic money creation. The point also was made that central banks would find it desirable to cooperate actively with each other in keeping domestic monetary expansion in closer harmony among countries with a view to the overall as well as the domestic stability of money purchasing power. This advice gave recognition to a likelihood that the link between domestic money and monetary gold stocks might become looser than it had been.

By about the mid-1920's, a fixed exchange-rate system had been largely re-established among major trading countries, under the guise that it represented a legitimate and practicable return to an international gold standard. Countries did make every effort, and with success, to add to monetary reserves by reducing gold-coin circulation. And they did experiment fairly widely with the accumulation and use of foreign exchange—partly in sterling and partly in dollars—as a supplement to gold in maintaining external money convertibility, thus converting the gold standard into what came to be called a gold-exchange standard.

For a time, the reconstructed gold-exchange standard seemed to work commendably. World trade revived and grew; the output of goods expanded everywhere—with one ironic exception: gold itself. At the higher level of costs of exploration and costs of mining compared with prewar years, gold production languished.

That the world of that period should quite suddenly have become sucked into a maelstrom of industrial and commercial equity speculation, centering in New York, and that simultaneously a visible erosion of ethical standards and accounting practices in domestic banking and finance in major countries should have taken place, was more than a piece of very bad luck, for political and financial leadership should have been more alert and responsive. But it was not, and the world was plunged into a state of extreme distress by a catastrophic decline in equity prices, followed by an appalling collapse of urban and farm real-estate values and a precipitous drop in the prices of currently produced goods and services—in short, a near universal deflation without precedent in the history of capitalism.

The world was soon caught up in a vicious circle of money devaluations, including one for the United States dollar. This was followed by monetary reorganization in major countries that completed the banishment of gold coin from service as national money. The world's post-World War I gold standard—reconstructed as a gold-exchange standard—was in full collapse. In retrospect, that such disruption was permitted to happen seems incredible.

By the mid-1930's, world deflation bottomed out, but at very low levels. Thereafter national—and clearly nationalistic—recovery policies gradually began to take hold, accompanied by a slow commencement of world recovery. However, the shock of world recession, of widespread monetary devaluations, and of rampant nationalistic "beggar-thy-neighbor" policies was too much politically and economically, and soon forces threatening an outbreak of international conflict were in full control. International disorganization had gone so far as to defy any efforts by the leadership of major powers to re-establish world economic order. With the Far East in turmoil and with growing threats of conflict within Europe, the United States became the world's haven for refugee money and for gold. By the close of 1939, United States official vaults held more than three-fifths of the then existing monetary gold stock of the whole world.

Bretton Woods

This time wartime disruption and disorganization of production, trade, and finance, plus accompanying disintegration of the monetary mechanisms of many participants, was more than a repeat of World War I and its aftermath; it was much worse. But at least while the hostilities of World War II were going on, the best brains, monetary and financial, on the Allied side were concerning themselves profoundly and deeply with the problem of monetary reconstruction that seemed certain to present itself immediately after the war. Readers will recall the dramatic monetary conference held at Bretton Woods, New Hampshire, in July 1944, which negotiated a charter—known as the Articles of Agreement—for establishing the International Monetary Fund.

The concept underlying the Articles of Agreement of the International Monetary Fund represented radical innovation. For the first time in world history, all countries accepting and ratifying the Fund Agreement were called upon to surrender a measure of their independent monetary authority, in short, to share their monetary sovereignty. This they were to do by ceding to an international body the right to participate in determining the value of their respective national moneys in relation to the value of money in other countries and in relation to gold. Put more simply, all countries accepting the Fund Agreement consented to the fixing of a value for their money in consultation with the Fund, which, in turn, would have a responsibility for protecting the interests of other participating countries.

The Fund Articles of Agreement included critical supporting provisions, as well as a workable apparatus for cooperative monetary decisionmaking among members and for sustaining the viability of the new arrangement. Thus, each consenting country obligated itself: first, to maintain a monetary reserve position in gold or foreign exchange sufficient to support its spot exchange rate *vis-à-vis* the money of each other member within a range of 1 per cent of parity; second, to advise the Fund should any change in parity become necessary for reasons of fundamental disequilibrium in payments; and, third, not to change its parity for corrective purposes by more than 10 per cent without Fund concurrence.

To support the system of fixed exchange rates that was to be established upon the advent of peace, each Fund member was to contribute to a pool of resources, partly in gold (25 per cent) and more largely in its own currency with gold-value guarantee (75 per cent), in accordance with an assigned quota related to its production and trade importance in the world economy. With the Fund's consent, this pool could be drawn upon by individual members to cope with temporary imbalances in foreign payments. Ordinarily, such drawings were to be limited to 25 per cent of quota in any year and a total of 200 per cent of quota. But these limits might be waived by the Fund in the light of special circumstances and proper safeguards of the Fund's interest. Any drawing became subject to a charge graduated by the length of time outstanding. And each drawing was to be repayable in accordance with terms set by the Fund itself—presumably related to the payments problem occasioning the drawing.

The Fund Agreement contemplated that national policies regarding the expansion of domestic money supplies would be left to national determination. But they were to be subject to review and criticism by the Fund should they depart too far from requirements for sustained maintenance of external convertibility. Finally, to achieve good standing as full-fledged Fund members, nations electing to participate were to dismantle as rapidly as feasible all restrictions or controls on international payments that were a legacy of prewar nationalism or wartime needs.

Beyond these arrangements for the orderly administration of world monetary development, the Fund Agreement included one further radical innovation in international authority. It contemplated that Fund members as a group at different points in the future might want to make uniform changes in the par values of their currencies—in other words, to effect an increase or a decrease in the monetary price of gold by international fiat. With this provision, the framers of the Articles of Agreement presented what proved to be an almost insuperable roadblock to United States acceptance of membership.

A Managed Fiduciary Standard

At the time, the International Monetary Fund was thought of as a vehicle for re-establishing a form of international gold standard, or more accurately a form of gold-exchange standard. Such a conception, however, did less than justice to the revolutionary character of the accomplishment. For the new monetary arrangement was to be one in which:

1. The full faith and credit of member nations transcended gold in governing monetary relations between them;

2. National monetary management was "good" if it took reason-

able account of the interests of other nations, and transgressions of "good behavior" might be subject to monetary sanctions;

3. National monetary authority was to be elevated from a bureaucratic role of maintaining convertibility to a policymaking role within government establishments;

4. The interconvertibility of currencies was to be both a national responsibility and an international task to be worked on in cooperation with the Fund's membership;

5. Conditionally available monetary reserves—drawings on the Fund—were to be as legitimately usable in maintaining external convertibility as owned reserves.

If we need to type this new international arrangement in some shorthand way, we should probably call it a "managed fiduciary standard."

One year after the signing of the Bretton Woods Agreement and just a month and a half before the Japanese surrender, the United States Congress passed the Bretton Woods Act authorizing the President to accept membership in the International Monetary Fund, but with two highly important reservations. First, the act made it mandatory for the United States to advise the Fund that it would continue the existing gold parity of the dollar. Second, it prohibited the President or any person or agency on behalf of the United States to "propose or agree to any change in the par value of the . . . dollar . . ." or to "approve any general change in par values" under the Fund Agreement "unless Congress by law" should authorize such action.

Thus, in asserting its authority over the dollar price of gold via a general change in par values of money internationally, the United States Congress in effect indefinitely froze the monetary price of gold. For what change could there be if the United States could not go along without Congressional initiative? And if Congress were to debate at length the world price of gold, the whole international monetary system could disintegrate from uncertainty while the debate was going on. The world's monetary authorities could only tremble at the thought.

These reservations, however, were not so unacceptable as one might have thought to United States administration officials. Apparently they had concluded from the evidence at hand as to known gold resources, advances in the technology of gold extraction, and trends in gold-mining costs that the existing dollar price of gold of $35 an ounce was high enough to permit postwar gold mining and output to prosper and for ample supplies of new gold to become available for the world's monetary uses. And in addition, United States administration officials had to take into account other considerations that underlay the reservations of Congress.

For one thing, the 1934 devaluation of the dollar in terms of gold had come to be looked upon by many as a breach of faith with the domestic and foreign public, and as a serious blow to United States international prestige—an action not to be repeated again solely on Executive initiative and responsibility.

And a special fact making the reservations desirable to Congress and acceptable to United States officials was that existing United States gold reserves were much more than ample by modern standards of a sufficiency of monetary reserves. In addition, under the new arrangement, it would be possible and profitable for other monetary authorities to rely on dollar balances as a supplement to gold in monetary reserve usage.

Finally, the view that the future evolution of the world monetary system should be managed by the community of nations was gaining acceptance. Hence, should gold and dollar supplies prove inadequate for world reserve needs, the new institution—the International Monetary Fund—would provide a mechanism through which cooperative international effort might find a practicable remedy.

Whatever the real truth may have been about the United States reservations to the Bretton Woods charter for an International Monetary Fund, they were not so vital as to prevent the Fund's establishment. By late 1945, in fact, enough nations had accepted the Agreement's main provisions to make possible the Fund's establishment. A decade later, it had achieved a membership of 67 nations, including the principal industrial nations of the free world. Switzerland declined membership, preferring the role of neutral in economic as well as political matters. By the late 1960's, Fund membership totaled 113 nations in actual number. Of these, 34 were recognized as having attained full interconvertibility of their national money with other currencies at agreed parities.

Problems for the New Standard

What was to be the outcome of this new monetary arrangement? Could it and would it be sustainable and durable? Would it realize the vision of its conceivers? And what would be its effects on gold?

Actually, the new monetary arrangements met with remarkable success, and Fund members twice (in 1959 and 1966) joined in enlarging the Fund's resources appreciably. But its functioning was, for an extended period, greatly aided by the largesse of the American people in allowing their Government to extend huge amounts of post-war aid, economic and military, first to governments in areas devastated and disrupted by war and later to developing and less-developed countries.

Within a decade following World War II the "miracle" of European and Far Eastern recovery was there for the world to see. Production and trade flourished as never before; economic growth generally achieved unprecedented rates; and a new era of human enlightenment and welfare seemed to have opened up. If the new monetary system was not the cause of this almost unbelievable development, it palpably served to facilitate it.

Why then, by the closing years of the 1960's, was the free world faced with a fresh breakdown of its monetary arrangements?

Obviously, the causes of the new threats were complex—political as well as economic and financial. A critical legacy of World War II was an unsteady balance of world political and military power, with a continuing chill of Cold War. And a succession of localized conflicts at the margin of the power balance gave danger of spreading into wider conflict. In such an atmosphere, a pervasive undercurrent of inquietude could hardly help finding expression in widespread public unease—even distrust of ultimate power balance.

Economically, the recovery in Europe and the Far East had considerably altered the free world's economic power base. In the case of Europe, however, further strides in economic power had come to hinge heavily on further strides towards economic integration, and these further strides seemed temporarily blocked by insurmountable political obstacles. As for the Far East, its economic base of power rested too heavily on United States power and, further, continued to show vibrant strength partly in consequence of United States procurement there on behalf of the Vietnamese war. Naturally, observers hoping for steady progress toward a better or firmer distribution of world economic power viewed the overall situation with misgivings which were contagious.

Financially, the free world's monetary-reserve growth had taken too largely the form of dollar and sterling balances and too little the form of gold, at least in the sight of private financial communities. Moreover, when reserve growth took the form of gold, it was too largely drawn from the monetary-reserve stocks of the two countries whose money had been earlier regarded as satisfactory foreign exchange for the monetary reserves of other countries. And when the growth of monetary reserves took the form of foreign-exchange balances in dollars or sterling, the dollars or sterling largely constituted payments deficits of the parent countries.

At long last, the monetary authorities of major European countries reached a consensus that the quantity of dollars and sterling in the world's monetary-reserve base had attained, if not exceeded, a desirable ceiling, and that the United States and the United Kingdom should take decisive steps to correct their excessive international-payments deficits. These views were formally communicated to the representatives of these two countries through the facilities of various agencies of international economic cooperation, including the International Monetary Fund. In due course, the substance of the confidential discussions among officials inevitably became known to the private financial communities and subsequently to the world public.

In this moment of embarrassment, Soviet Russia saw fit to discontinue sales of gold on world markets. Concurrently, growing public concern found expression in a spreading purchase of gold coin, fractional gold bars, gold wafers, and gold leaf. And those who could afford it began to acquire standard gold bars, while the more speculative saw in the gold market an opportunity seldom presented—a one-sided speculation, at some cost to be sure, but with no risk of substantial loss. Before long, private demands far exceeded new gold supplies available for purchase. A worldwide run on gold was in the making.

What was happening in the meantime to the world's output of and demand for gold? In the years just preceding World War II, gold output had spurted, reflecting in part the increase in its real value during world deflation and in part the stimulus of the 1934 increase in its dollar price from $20.67 to $35.00 an ounce. For a decade after World War II gold output was well below immediate prewar levels. By the late 1950's, however, it had regained these levels and then exceeded them. At about this stage, Soviet Russia began to release to the market part of its rising gold production.

All told, from 1950 through the early months of 1968, some $23.8 billion in additional gold became available from output and from Russian sales. Of this large sum, industrial uses, objects of adornment, and the arts took only an estimated $5 billion and net additions to official monetary gold stocks roughly an equal sum. Thus the amount going into private hoards and speculative holdings aggregated something like $13.8 billion, of which as much as $3 billion apparently vanished into private holdings during 1967 and the early months of 1968.

Clearly, if this amount of hoarded gold had been available for monetary-reserve uses, along with the amount actually added to monetary-gold stocks, the world's monetary system would have had quite enough, perhaps more than enough, to "make peace with gold." The aggregate of new gold for monetary-reserve uses, however, was not that abundant, and there is little point now in deploring that fact.

Response to Disturbances

But it would have been deplorable if the world's monetary authorities had not become sharply aware of developing threats to its monetary arrangements. Actually, every government received due warning at the turn of the 1960's by four events. One, occurring just before President Kennedy's election, was a sudden surge of demand for gold on the London gold market which raised its price there from $35.20 (its normal limit) to $40.00 an ounce. Only the joint efforts of United States and United Kingdom monetary authorities brought this splurge under control. But the traumatic impact on the newly elected President Kennedy was such that, shortly after his inauguration, he pledged the entire United States gold stock to defense of the dollar.

The second event was the 5 per cent upward revaluation in terms of gold of the German mark and the Dutch guilder in the early spring of 1961 to correct their presumed undervaluation *vis-à-vis* sterling and the dollar.

The third event was a heavy run against sterling in the spring of 1961, which gave rise to a sizable package of emergency credits from European central banks and the United States authorities to help the Bank of England until it could arrange an International Monetary Fund drawing adequate to defend sterling.

The fourth was not strictly an event but the succession of three large and alarming deficits in United States international payments. Their occurrence prompted the International Monetary Fund, under United States urging, to negotiate an agreement with its ten leading members (the so-called Group of Ten countries) establishing special borrowing facilities that would complement the regular facilities that then existed. Under the agreement—formally known as the General Arrangements to Borrow—participants committed themselves to provide enough of their respective currencies, upon due consultation, to finance concurrently, if necessary, maximum permissible drawings from the Fund by two or three larger member countries.

With these portentous warnings of rough international financial waters ahead, three further developments of major import took place. The monetary authorities of the United States and the United Kingdom, together with those of six other major trading nations, organized a pool to support the London gold price within the market's parity with the United States Treasury's gold price.

Next, the United States Federal Reserve System launched a program of foreign-currency operations for the defense of the external convertibility of the dollar. And to facilitate the execution of any such operations, it established a network of standby credit (currency-swap) arrangements with the principal central banks abroad.

Lastly, the ministers of finance of the principal trading nations that were members of the International Monetary Fund plus Switzerland joined in authorizing their deputies to engage in a study of the world's future needs for monetary reserves and of ways to assure their steady growth. Significantly, the finance ministers instructed their deputies to proceed with the study on the premise that a world price of gold of $35 an ounce would be indefinitely adhered to.

Of these three developments, the first, the gold-pool arrangement, was brought to an end by the "gold rush" of 1967 and early 1968. The second, the central-bank reciprocal credit network, continues to prove useful and has indeed expanded from a modest beginning in 1962 of $700 million of potential temporary credits between participating central banks (including the Bank for International Settlements) and the Federal Reserve System to today's impressive total of nearly $10.5 billion. This expanded sum bears testimony to the concern among monetary authorities that resources in ample supply be promptly available to cushion large temporary flows of funds internationally and thus to help assure the maintenance of orderly exchange-market conditions. The third development—the product of four years of arduous international study, debate, and negotiation—was a concrete proposal for the creation of a new international asset to supplement gold in meeting the world's future needs for growth in national monetary reserves.

A New Kind of Reserve Asset

Of these three revolutionary developments, the third is the most far-reaching in its implications for future world prosperity and optimum freedom for international trade and payments. In September 1967, a plan for a new reserve asset was put before the annual meeting of the Board of Governors of the International Monetary Fund.

That body approved the plan and instructed the Fund's Executive Directors to reformulate it as an amendment to the Fund's Articles of Agreement. Completion of this technical task required more than a year, and thereafter a number of months had to elapse before member governments could process the proposed amendment and transmit to the Fund their formal acceptance. By midsummer 1969, an amended Fund Agreement was an accomplished fact. At the annual meeting of the Fund's Board of Governors in Washington in September 1969, that Board took the further historic step of approving activation of the new plan on January 1, 1970, a step described by the Fund's Managing Director, Pierre-Paul Schweitzer, as ". . . a momentous innovation, a landmark in international monetary cooperation."

The amended Fund Agreement provides for the annual issuance to participating member countries over stated periods of a quantum of Special Drawing Rights. Normally, the duration of such periods is five years, but the Fund, with reason, may modify the "normal" duration. Any Fund member is eligible to participate in an allocation of Special Drawing Rights provided it has formally accepted explicit obligations to a Special Drawing Account of the Fund, established to administer the Rights. Even if it has accepted these obligations, a participant country may decide not to share in an approved allocation of Special Drawing Rights.

The Special Drawing Rights are exchangeable on demand into equivalent value of any currency held or issued by other participating countries. Also, they are fully usable in transactions with the Fund to repurchase excess Fund holdings of a country's currency or in meeting assessments and charges of the Special Drawing Account.

Decisionmaking as to a creation of Special Drawing Rights is by elaborate formal process. It begins with informal consultation of the Fund Managing Director with participant members; is followed by his recommendation for Rights creation to the Fund Board of Governors, with justification in terms of world needs for supplementary monetary reserves; and concludes in formal action on his recommendation by that body. Protection against excessive Rights creation rests in the requirement of approval by 85 per cent of the Fund's voting power. Once created, unless or until extinguished by Fund decision, the Special Drawing Rights will have a continuing life of their own apart from the ordinary drawing rights Fund member countries have available by virtue of membership.

Upon authorization for creation, annual allocation among participating countries accords with each country's Fund quota. Members are free to use their Special Drawing Rights without condition as to their own monetary and fiscal policies. Expected uses, however, are to meet a country's balance-of-payments needs or to cushion adverse changes in a country's monetary-reserve position (though not for the sole purpose of altering the composition of its reserves). A further legitimate use of Special Drawing Rights is to help another country cope with its balance-of-payments or monetary-reserve problems.

A transfer between participants of Special Drawing Rights can only be effected through the Fund's facilities. Fundamentally, their value in use rests on the obligation of every participant to accept them in these uses, when properly transferred through the Fund, subject only to the qualification that no member is required to hold Special Drawing Rights in excess of 300 per cent of its cumulative allocation. In addition, each Special Drawing Right unit has the same gold value as the dollar, a feature consistent with existing arrangements under the Fund Agreement and providing technical or legalistic support to acceptability in use.

Each participant country is obligated by Fund Agreement to maintain holdings of Special Drawing Rights equal on the average to at least 30 per cent of its cumulative allocation. That is to say, if its uses of Special Drawing Rights cause its holdings to fall below a moving average of 30 per cent, it is obligated, within a specified period, to reconstitute them to equal that average. Reliance on transfer of ownership through Fund facilities has in part the purpose of assuring all participants that a minimum average holding will be adhered to by each participant and that, as a group, member monetary systems will sustain a reasonable balance between holdings of Special Drawing Rights.

These features of the recently adopted plan for a new reserve asset plainly represent a sensible compound of contemporary financial wisdom. Furthermore, prompt decision to activate the plan beginning in 1970, with a $9.5 billion issuance and allocation of Special Drawing Rights over the three years 1970-1972, expresses tangibly the confidence of world monetary leaders in that wisdom. While press headlines greeted the action as a "vote for 'paper gold'," this label failed to convey the true importance of the innovation. For the first time in civilization's history, the world is incorporating an international fiduciary money unit into its exchange mechanism—in other words, a money unit backed by the full faith and credit of all the national governments that voluntarily join together in its creation.

Termination of the Gold Pool

Let us next shift our focus to the dissolution over a mid-March weekend of 1968 of the international gold pool and the decision made on that occasion to allow the market price of gold to fend for itself, while continuing to have gold transactions among central banks themselves at the official price of $35 an ounce.

This decision by the central bankers of the seven major trading nations then participating in the gold pool was in effect one made "looking down the barrel of a shotgun." It had to be taken for the all-important reason that the world public's gold buying fever had to be allayed. And as the principal monetary officials of leading governments—charged with carrying out a public trust to keep solid the interconvertibility of their respective money units—these central bankers simply had to buy time for deliberation and decision as to further steps.

Was it, however, just a case of buying time? The gold panic had been months in forming. The participating central bankers must surely have discussed among themselves the possibility of an ultimate contingency and considered strategy alternatives for dealing with it. But one can only speculate about what transpired before the action and about its implications for the future.

As for the two-tier scheme for the price of gold—a market price independent of an official price—one might surmise that the central bankers concerned went through a planning process somewhat as follows. With the help of their experts, they individually looked at the long-term record of new-gold availability, at the best private and governmental estimates of gold-taking for industrial purposes, and at the record of annual increments in the world's monetary gold stock. Simple subtraction of the latter two sources of gold absorption from gold availability would have provided them a reasonable record of private gold-taking for hoarding, temporary investment, and speculation. If the central bankers had then weighed the private takings of gold in the past 18 months, they could have arrived at the inference that world gold markets faced a large overhang of gold in private hands which might, in the face of gold-price uncertainty, become actual market supply. From this conclusion, it would follow that the risk was minimal that the "free market price" for gold would soar to the skies, while the chance that the price would settle at a level close to or even somewhat below the official price was good.

But the action taken by these important central bankers on that fateful mid-March weekend seemed to go much further than mere technical consideration of what might happen to the market price of gold. In their published communique, they stated: "The Governors believe that henceforth officially-held gold should be used only to effect transfers among monetary authorities and, therefore, they decided no longer to supply gold to the London gold market or any other gold market. Moreover, as the existing stock of monetary gold is sufficient in view of the prospective establishment of the facility for Special Drawing Rights, they no longer feel it necessary to buy gold from the market. Finally, they agreed that henceforth they will not sell gold to monetary authorities to replace gold sold in private markets."

Such a communique wording suggested decision of far-reaching portent. It implied that monetary demand for gold might be permanently withdrawn from the market. It further intimated a potential severance of national monetary systems from any further dependence on an ever-expanding supply of new gold. And it also hinted that the central bankers present might be willing to accept the new international money unit as a displacement of future available gold in monetary-reserve usage. These interpretations may be stretching the intent of the communique, but, if legitimate, dethronement of gold as a monetary reserve asset was possibly a realized fact.

Political Leavening

Central bankers are experts in the techniques of money management but not necessarily in politics. When, a fortnight after their action, they accompanied their ministers of finance to the Group of Ten meeting in Stockholm to discuss the proposed amendment to the Fund's Articles of Agreement that would authorize the creation of Special Drawing Rights literally by the stroke of a pen, they found their superiors in a mood to compromise with political realities. While the ministers were prepared ". . . to cooperate in the maintenance of exchange arrangements of the world based on the present official price of gold . . . ," they considered only that the Special Drawing Rights would ". . . make a very substantial contribution to strengthening the monetary system . . . ," but ". . . not provide a solution to all international monetary problems . . . ."

Thus we are led to the judgment that "making peace with gold" remains an objective for the future. If so, the private financial community as well as the managers of national monetary systems must determine whether they are prepared to live indefinitely with a two-tier pricing of gold. And if they are not so prepared, they must decide upon an arrangement that will reconcile prevailing psychology about gold with practical necessities in a setting in which the community of nations may no longer be willing to leave the expansion of its combined monetary reserves to the vagaries either of gold production or of the public's caprice in hoarding gold. In addition to this adjustment, the two giants of international finance must prove that they can at least approach an equilibrium in their international payment flows, if not a firmly lasting balance. Perhaps, if each of these important steps can be accomplished, the way to "peace with gold" will simply be one of leaving gold alone—some of it to repose comfortably in private vaults and mattresses.

And, we may further infer that, as long as the community of nations has it within its power to supplement new-gold availability for monetary uses by creating, when needed, a supplementary reserve asset voluntarily acceptable in settlement of world commerce, the international monetary system can get along with present gold holdings and with whatever additional gold authorities choose to acquire. Perhaps a logical next step in extending the temporary truce with gold would be a pooling of the free world's monetary gold stock in an international agency. But probably for our time, it would be unduly optimistic to expect the modern state's reliance on gold as a symbol of independent sovereignty entirely to "wither away."

In closing, one may conclude that the thinking of leading monetary authorities has now reached a stage where the trappings of the gold standard are largely irrelevant. From such a standpoint, the sooner the international monetary mechanism is rid of the remaining vestiges of the traditional ties with gold the better.

At the same time, the world's statesmen in the monetary area— that is, its finance ministers—know that the myths surrounding gold remain a political reality with which they must deal. Persistence of lip service to a gold standard and retention of its symbols have merit to them for it provides continuity with society's past. Indeed, with the world yet to establish firmly a monetary system rooted in the full faith and credit of the community of nations acting jointly, the ministers would appear to find unconvincing an argument that respectful deference to the symbolism of gold as a monetary heritage is harmful.

It can be agreed that democracies today are trying, perhaps in a cumbersome way, to recognize their ever-closer monetary interdependence through a variety of procedures, intergovernmental arrangements, and ingenious institutional innovations such as the International Monetary Fund. The urgent incentive to these innovations has grown out of the long struggle to accommodate the use of a commodity—as unreliable in monetary supply as gold—as the base for an international monetary system in an ever-shrinking planet. As a matter of survival, world economic society is having to conclude: "If we can't make do with it, we'll have to learn to make do with as little reliance on it as we can."

As far as the general public is concerned, most of this struggle has had a very low visibility as compared with more obvious diplomatic and political activity; it is too complex, and too remote from everyday concerns. In this respect, it resembles international cooperation in scientific fields. Compared with these scientific fields, however, the area of money and finance is closer to politics and diplomacy, even if its visibility is low. Because of this, and because the social utility of money is so palpably relevant to human progress, cooperation in the monetary field is of immense and urgent importance.

The monetary authorities have been trying to "make their peace with gold" by persistently challenging its indispensability—and as time has passed, with mounting success. Eventually—perhaps none now living will see it—the world's statesmen will be found following in their wake.

CAPITAL MOVEMENTS
AND
BALANCE-OF-PAYMENTS ADJUSTMENT

ROBERT V. ROOSA

INTRODUCTION AND SUMMARY

WHEN KARL BOPP was giving me some of my early instruction in central banking, he once stunned me with this thought: no policymaker ever has enough theoretical analysis available for the job he is doing; look out for the one who thinks he has. Now, some twenty-odd years later, as a testimonial to the persisting validity of that thought, I venture to suggest that much of the conventional analysis of imbalances in payments flows among nations rests on a distressingly incomplete theoretical base. While neither I nor anyone else to my knowledge can offer a more inclusive and satisfactory theory of balance-of-payments adjustment, there may be some gain in floodlighting the gaps.

My own conviction is that the classical conception of the causes of imbalance in a nation's external accounts—on which so many assured prescriptions have been written—presumes an unrealistically simple structure of the determinants of international payments. Although discreetly avoiding explicit articulation of their premises, the traditionalists (including many in that fraternity of international bankers to which I belong) imply that the bulk of international transactions consists of trade in goods, and that such trade in turn represents a sizable proportion of each country's domestic product. That is why they can urge with assured conviction repetitively similar designs for the balance-of-payments programs of any countries, large or small, developed or developing, regimented or free. In essence, the formula has been: when in deficit, deflate until equilibrium is reached; for countries in surplus, do nothing. Appropriate action by the deficit countries, it has been thought, will in time restore a more nearly even balance in the accounts of the surplus countries as well. My concern is not that this formula is altogther wrong, indeed much that it implied may still be relevant, but for the decade of the 70's and beyond, I fear, it is woefully incomplete.

The more significant missing elements in this simple structure are, of course, capital flows, debt servicing, and governmental transfers. They have not been ignored in the customary balance-of-payments diagnosis, but they have generally been pushed aside as residuals, fitting into whatever place the trade accounts would allow. And quite consistently, many countries have long maintained controls over their capital accounts to assure that they would be accommodated to the flows of trade. Indeed, the Articles of the International Monetary Fund were designed in 1944 to recognize this position. The convertibility to be sought for currencies was only for current-account transactions (Article VIII), and paralleling this objective the IMF was to encourage unrestricted freedom for the movement of goods in international trade (as it has done through the General Agreement on Tariffs and Trade). Restrictions on capital movements were condoned as long as they did not become direct impediments to trade.

Under the Bretton Woods system after 1944, it was only the United States, the country whose currency was treated interchangeably with gold as an international unit of account, which undertook an implied obligation to avoid capital controls. Even that role for the United States was, at the beginning, self-imposed; it did not represent an agreed requisite for the functioning of the new system. Yet by the end of the decade of the 50's there was also a spreading belief among the newly convertible (Article VIII) countries that freedom for capital movements was also an appropriate objective for other countries, particularly larger ones, whenever they reached a suitable stage of economic maturity. Their balance-of-payments programs, it was frequently suggested, should be judged not only by their effect on trade but also by the impetus such programs gave toward greater freedom for inbound and outbound capital flows. This change of attitude was a by-product of the exhilaration accompanying the achievement of Article VIII convertibility by most leading countries in 1959. But underneath, the old premise was unchanged; for the unstated assumption still was that only trade really mattered. The emphasis was on free trade, to be sure, but the criterion of balance-of-payments policy was still to promote trade surpluses. Once successful in that, countries would then find, it was suggested, that they could also allow capital to flow freely.

This was a doctrine for the more developed countries, and perhaps only for some of the larger among them, but the less developed were not to be left out. With strong trade surpluses and freedom for capital outflow in several of the developed countries, private investment and Government aid could provide for the excess of imports that less advanced countries would need for their development.

The misfortune is that this simple, indeed elegantly symmetrical, system—which has been the conceptual basis for so many resolute proposals—has not existed in even the crudest approximation since the early postwar years when the United States stood alone on the one side as a net capital exporter and the rest of the world was on the other. Through the decade of the 60's, as some of the more developed countries edged closer, at least in potentiality, to the older pattern (though not the dimensions) of the United States, the United States in turn seemed to be edging into a new pattern as well.[1] Net transfers of capital from the industrialized countries to less developed countries, while rising modestly in absolute amounts, actually declined as a proportion of the capital formation occurring either in the developed countries or in the developing countries.

Despite these underlying changes, the prescriptions for national action, whenever one country or another slipped out of economic viability with the rest of the world, were still for the most part the same. Moreover, because of the continuing heavy emphasis on goods in trade as the primary moving force in balance-of-payments adjustment, a disconcerting tendency to resort to direct limitations on imports or to unusual subsidies for exports—albeit with protestations of temporary expediency—began to appear alongside the classical emphasis on deflation by the deficit countries. Meanwhile, there was almost universal dismay when the United States began gingerly placing limitations on the free outflow of capital, even though it did make suitable obeisance to the "temporary" nature of its succession of new measures.

Having participated in the early phases of the United States' fall from grace, and having anguished over each new step with diligent concern for the need to return promptly to the conditions of freedom for flows of goods and capital, I am beginning now to wonder whether I fully grasped the significance of what we were doing, at the time, and of the causes for the action we were initiating. Indeed I wonder now whether anyone's understanding of the complex of forces at work is yet sufficient to warrant the kind of assurance many of us have as to the proper pattern of policy to be pursued and of the objectives toward which we should return. Most of my questions seem to come

---

[1] Cf. my article "The American Share in the Stream of International Payments," *The Annals,* July, 1969, p. 21: "The United States position in the world economy has been changing fundamentally over recent years. The traditional large surplus accumulated through foreign trade disappeared in 1968. Gross capital inflows became as large as the proceeds of exports in that year. And the dollar declined in use as a reserve currency among central banks while its use expanded in private transactions outside the United States."

back to a central theme: that capital movements—including both short and long maturities, and direct investment as well as portfolio purchases and sales—may no longer be considered mere residuals of the trade accounts, but instead may often have an independent propelling force of their own. Debt servicing and Government expenditures abroad are in a way subsets of this generalization concerning capital movements, but they also have become independent rather than dependent variables.

Along with this apparent change have come other critical changes in the admissible scope for variation in the domestic economic policies of nations. Neither recession, nor unemployment, nor price declines can be permitted on any substantial scale. The result is that variations in economic policy to achieve domestic stability and external viability, country by country, can for the most part effect only differences in the pace of advance in economic activity, or in its composition, not a substantial or sustained decline. Thus the range for deliberate influences upon the outflow or inflow of resources through generalized policies working in a deflationary direction to spur exports and check imports, must necessarily be much narrower than was implied by conventional theories of balance-of-payments adjustment.

The outcome then, it seems to me, can be summed up in this dilemma: at the same time that capital movements (and their subsets) are becoming more nearly independently determined, and thus cannot be regarded as passive offsets to the major swings occurring in a nation's trade position, the traditional methods for adjusting the trade accounts themselves are becoming weaker and more circumscribed. The traditional conception of balance-of-payments equilibrium, and of the path toward restoring it, once a country has moved into deficit or surplus, has come apart. Is it little wonder then, in the face of such momentous change in the entire structure of international flows, that the international payments system which serves such flows should itself have been going through a series of convulsions during most of the decade of the 60's?

Without pretending to have a theory for knitting all of these disparate pieces together, I can perhaps help in clearing the way for others, who may attempt that task, by identifying a number of the problems which seem to me to have been created. And for those not content to wait for the theory, perhaps I can suggest a few of the approaches that may, after further critical analysis by others, prove helpful in meeting some of these problems or in modifying some of their more disturbing effects. The following pages will, then, be divided between "New Problems" and "New Approaches." And I hasten to interject that, of course, nothing is ever totally "new," and that my intention is to stress new emphasis rather than a new incarnation.

NEW PROBLEMS

The new problems which arise outside the boundaries of the old theory all have their roots in major institutional changes that have occurred since World War II. They can best be catalogued as changes related to long-term capital flows, to short-term flows, to Governmental transfers, and to debt servicing. Running across these four kinds of changes, two other ways of singling out the principal problems may also be helpful: the changing function and behavior of interest rates as a part of the adjustment process, and the still changing but special position of the United States.

Long-Term Capital Flows

The remarkable increase in capital requirements and capital formation over the two decades from 1947 to 1967 has not only produced a virtual mutation in the scale of worldwide economic activity, it has also generated flows of long-term capital among nations on an unprecedented scale. Direct investment through the multinational corporation, and portfolio investment across frontiers through a host of new instruments—debentures, convertibles, and equities, denominated in Euro-dollars, or units of account, or other Euro-currencies—have, both in multiplicity of directions and in total size, completely dwarfed anything experienced before World War II. As capital has sought every open doorway to free movement, the possibility for a neat and natural balancing of any country's capital outflows with its own trading position has become more and more remote.

In earlier times, when the typical pattern was for long-term capital to flow from the more developed countries to countries in a dependent or colonial status, there was, in the nature of the relationship, a built-in link between the flows of capital and of goods and services. In turn, the receiving countries, whether these were the United States in the early 19th century or Brazil or India later on, paid a return to the long-term outside investor which could be largely reinvested in the host country. Consequently, the chances were rather slight that a serious divergence would develop for the capital-exporting countries between the flow of goods across their frontiers and the actual export of long-term capital.

In the world of the latter half of the 20th century, however, autonomously generated outflows of longer-term capital are becoming a larger and larger element in the balance of payments of many of the developed countries. Moreover, the volume of this capital flowing to other developed countries is at least as large as that flowing to the less developed countries. It thus becomes almost inevitable that this segment of the balance-of-payments accounts will no longer passively adapt itself to a dominating pattern imposed by the flow of goods in trade.

Short-Term Capital Flows

As current-account transactions were being freed and payments on current account were becoming fully convertible during the later 1950's, a parallel development was introducing a comparable degree of internationalization in the flows of short-term capital among nations. To be sure, most countries, including many of the most fully developed in Europe, still maintained relatively tight control over identifiable long-term capital movements as a buttress for their effort to restore current-account convertibility. But the mere necessity to assure ready short-term financing for a growing volume of current-account transactions, dispersed among a larger variety of trading countries, created an urgent demand for the use of a single currency as an international transactions vehicle. The dollar met much of that demand. As this need expanded during the 60's it was, in the best spirit of energetic enterprise, paralleled by a rapid spreading of branches of American banks overseas.

Under competitive influences, not only the branches of American banks but also the offices of most of the leading banks in other countries began to accept and service dollar-denominated deposits, regardless of where the branch or bank might be domiciled. And almost as if fatalistically determined, the Federal Reserve's Regulation Q, by placing a relatively low ceiling on the rates of interest payable on time deposits in the United States, encouraged American banks to develop their dollar-denominated deposit business abroad. At the same time, these American branches were being called upon increasingly to finance the working capital requirements of overseas corporations, particularly the multinational corporations headquartered in the United States which wanted to rely upon the banking techniques with which they were familiar.

Out of all this emerged the Euro-dollar market—a market which by 1969 could be variously estimated at $25 billion to $35 billion in magnitude, depending upon the extent to which any statistician felt able to remove certain elements of double counting from sequences of deposits pyramided upon a single underlying account. The resulting market was highly sensitive to marginal shifts in demand or supply and was truly international in character, though buffeted at times by those whims of the foreign exchange markets that might create doubts concerning the established parity of a weaker currency, or create hopes concerning the prospects for possible revaluation of a stronger currency.

In this setting, reliance on traditional methods for promoting balance-of-payments adjustment became almost inevitably self-defeating. When Germany, for example, with a strong economy, relatively stable prices, and a somewhat undervalued exchange rate, began to fear internal inflation, the indicated response was to tighten modestly on credit availability. Yet in the presence of a large and volatile Eurodollar market, the initial effect of an increase in German interest rates was to draw additional funds into Germany, enlarging the credit base and providing an additional problem for monetary authorities aiming to assure some degree of overall restraint. In time, of course, this situation degenerated further. Interest rates were raised; in the absence of other adequate control limitations, additional funds flowed in; and expectations became greater that Germany would find it necessary, in order to maintain the desired degree of domestic price stability, to adjust the parity of the Deutsche mark upward.

In different circumstances, the United Kingdom had to undergo in quite another way the effects of the contradictory influences of trade flows and short-term capital movements. While much of the explanation for persistent British deficits, as I have argued elsewhere,[2] was attributable to the maintenance of enormous Governmental expenditures overseas as an inheritance of the obligations of pre-World War II empire, the simple position as seen on traditional lines was that of insufficient exports in relation to the rising volume of imports. For this situation, the prescription should have been, as in fact intermittently it proved to be, that of severe domestic restraint in order to limit price increases at home, check the rise of incomes, release home production for export, and reduce import demand.

What happened instead was that from time to time, as domestic interest rates rose higher and higher in the United Kingdom under the

---

[2] "Where is Britain Heading?" *Foreign Affairs*, April, 1968, especially pp. 505-506.

pressures of internal credit restraint, funds were attracted temporarily from abroad. Their arrival seemed both to lessen the pinch of restraint at home and to improve the British reserves, with the result of temporarily lulling British opinion until additional reserve losses on trade and Government account revived doubts again. And then, as fears of exchange-rate devaluation became predominant, the same short-term funds, and more, found ways—despite the continuance of exchange controls and a very high premium for transfers into securities purchases abroad—to flow out again, thereby making the later position of the British balance of payments even worse on an overall basis. To be sure, throughout this period there was also essential validity in the implications of the conventional view that Britain should readjust by restraining. But because this had to occur in an environment characterized by large flows of volatile short-term funds, even the appropriate implementation of a traditional action program was disrupted.

Government Flows

The world before World War II had seen, of course, large and varied overseas commitments by many of the governments of leading countries, but there was no precedent for the scale of international aid—both military and economic—undertaken by the United States (and in time by several other countries) in the post-World War II period. Through most of the decade of the 50's, as the bulk of these international transfers on Government account were either effected by the United States, or cleared without substantial balance-of-payments distortions by means of the European Payments Union, there was no challenge to the traditional concept of balance-of-payments adjustment. But by the end of the 1950's both the United States and the United Kingdom—which had by then become the leading deficit countries and remained so throughout the 1960's—were sending abroad through economic and military aid, and through expenditures in support of their troops overseas, amounts which annually far exceeded the size of their own balance-of-payments deficits. And there were good reasons, defensible in terms of world order and security, for maintaining such overseas expenditures.

One early reaction, as the deficits themselves continued, was to attempt to "tie" more and more of these overseas disbursements to direct shipments of goods by the donor country. The record of that tying, and of the many ways through which its intention was frustrated while its spirit was criticized, has been too often reported to need repetition here.[3] The record of various "offset" agreements to cover in part the balance-of-payments costs of British and American troops stationed in Western Germany is probably equally well-known. Moreover, in the face of persisting deficits, there was an intuitive validity in the arguments advanced for forcing the amount of these overseas aid and military commitments to conform to whatever magnitudes could be permitted by the principal elements, in combination, of a donor country's balance of payments. Without arguing over the principles, or the costs, however, the mere citing of this record is enough to emphasize the nature of the new dilemma. All leading countries must, almost regardless of the current status of the other elements of their balance of payments, if they are not to abdicate the responsibility of leadership, undertake some commitments to assist the economic advance, even if not the military defense, of many of the less developed areas of the world And those commitments, however they may be trimmed from time to time to reflect long-run changes in a donor country's basic economic position, will have to be determined at least in part from year to year by independent considerations. By their nature, and because of their critical importance for other prime objectives, they cannot be left to vary purely as balancing residuals of the trade accounts of leading countries.

Debt Servicing

While the leading countries have, both directly and through various multilateral agencies, been extending Government assistance to many of the developing countries, and while the great multinational corporations have been adding impressively to their own direct investments in these countries, the recipient countries have been encountering new problems of their own. The magnitude of their requirements for outside resources, as they have attempted to telescope into decades a scale of progress that had earlier required centuries, has involved imports of capital on a tremendous scale. Not only has much of this capital come on terms requiring regular amortization after an initial period, but much of it has also carried sizable rates of interest.

As a result, by the later 1960's, the annual requirements for external debt service in most of the less developed countries were about as large as the total volume of new capital arriving. Indeed, because of the debt-servicing obligation, many of the less developed countries

---

[3] Compare the conclusions in the report of the Pearson Commission, *Partners in Development* (Praeger, New York, 1969), pp. 172-177.

were able only to earn with their enlarged capital base enough to pay the interest and amortization due on that capital.[4] This was a circular flow that could eventually spell virtual stagnation as far as the advance of domestic living standards was concerned.

The expedient of interest subsidies or a moratorium on repayments did not offer a fully satisfactory way out. For measures of this kind, understandably proposed in order to reduce the transfer burden across the frontiers of the developing countries, could also seriously misguide the patterns of capital and resource allocation for the future. The alternative of attempting to apply the traditional analysis to these less developed countries, by expecting them to deflate in order to increase the attractiveness of exports while reducing imports, was on its face unacceptable except for brief periods of temporary correction.

Interest Rates

As each of the problem areas just described was coming into clearer visibility, some of its effects were also being etched across the experience of many countries in another way. For it began to appear that with prices often free to vary up and down only from an upward trend line, and with employment to be kept virtually full, the rates of interest paid for short- or long-term funds in various countries would have to become a much more important variable for implementing overall economic policy.

In terms of the balance of payments, given the narrow range within which adjustments could occur in the trade position even if traditional prescriptions were followed, greater reliance for policy purposes might have to be placed on changes in underlying domestic credit availability and thus on variations in rates of interest. Ways might have to be found to increase the size and flexibility of offsetting shifts in capital flows, to take the place of what had been larger swings in the trade balance or to compensate for what had now become an intractable minimum of disbursements abroad by governments. Particularly during the decade of the 60's, the potentialities for relying on variations in credit availability and interest rates to influence capital flows among nations have had to be much more extensively explored.

Statistical verification is extremely hazardous in matters of this kind. In attempting to make some check on my own marketplace observations, however, one of my colleagues has tried several different

---

[4] Cf. *Partners in Development, op. cit.*, pp. 74 ff.

measures. One approach, mentioned here only as an illustration, has been to examine the relative impact of exports and of interest-rate differentials on the outflow of short-term capital from the United States over these years. His results thus far, always conditioned by the fact that correlation does not mean causation, are quite striking. The difference between the two periods 1961-1964 and 1965-1968, is so great that, even after appropriate allowance is made for vagaries and variations in the data representing the underlying phenomena being measured, one general conclusion can scarcely be avoided. The correlation between exports and outflows of short-term funds declined sharply, to become almost trivial in the latter period. At the same time, the correlation between the United States-United Kingdom interest-rate spread and variations in the outflows of short-term funds from the United States increased significantly by every test attempted.[5]

Yet it has begun to appear that even interest-rate flexibility, and the underlying variations of credit availability which induce rate changes, have limits. In part this comes from the perverse pattern indicated by the references to Germany and the United Kingdom above. In part it also comes because the impact of sizable changes in current interest rates to effect external flows may have gravely distorting effects upon domestic capital flows in national economies whose institutions are geared to relatively slow changing rates of return. Moreover, the existence of the nonnational Euro-dollar market has provided a vehicle through which an intensification of credit restraint, for domestic as well as for external reasons, will, in a market as large as that of the United States, be speedily transmitted into the markets of many other countries whether or not their own immediate external position requires reserve drains (or reserve gains) of the dimensions that result.

No doubt many countries affected by the tightening of the Euro-dollar market during the later half of the 1960's have overstated the seriousness of the impact, partly because they have not yet experienced the impact long enough to develop the techniques for offsetting that impact through appropriate central bank action. Nonetheless, after recognizing all of these qualifications, the fact remains that the international transmission of short-term capital movements has become a highly volatile influence upon the foreign exchange reserves

---

[5] The supporting analysis by Richard Fischer would require all of the space allotted to this paper for adequate presentation. His findings, after further testing, will be published separately.

and the external overall balance-of-payments position of most of the leading countries, and indeed on that of many others. Because these flows cannot be presumed to fit comfortably into place as mere residuals in the complex balance-of-payments adjustment among nations —since they do not simply run parallel with trade—something more is needed, in theoretical analysis and in operating techniques, if the adjustment process is to function effectively.

The Special Position of the United States

Throughout the decade of the 60's, there has been an ambivalence among the critics of the United States balance-of-payments performance. Our deficits have been continually criticized; our efforts to correct them, particularly when the traditional formulae of deflation were being applied, have brought anguished complaints. Yet these two approaches need not be either surprising or inconsistent. They flow from four major aspects of the United States position which, in their combined effect, distinguish us from all other countries—and distinguish us enough to require a separate addendum to, if not a completely separate version of, any comprehensive theoretical formulation of an appropriate process of balance-of-payments adjustment within the world economy.

First, the United States is large, accounting for nearly one-third of all production and capital formation in the world, although for much less than one-sixth of all trade. Second, the United States dollar is far and away the most widely used transactions currency in international commerce, and it now provides the principal common medium for the Euro-currency market. Third, the United States has spawned a widely diversified complex of multinational corporations that is unique in scale and performance across the world. Fourth, as political leader of the free world, the United States has undertaken external commitments, both miltary and economic, that together far exceed the external expenditures for these purposes of any other nation, not only in gross amounts but also as a proportion of gross national product.

How can the balance of payments of such a country be expected to conform to the same pattern, and correct its aberrations by resort to the same measures, as those indicated by the traditional norms? Such an attempt was made, nonetheless, during the early years of the 60's. Even though the United States was already running a sizable trade and current-account surplus at that time, dollar outflows to the Euro-currency markets, capital outflows on portfolio as well as direct investment account, and seemingly intractable Government outlays overseas brought about a net deficit position. The United States reacted by trying to raise productivity more rapidly, in turn holding prices relatively steady as domestic incomes and employment rose. The result, up through 1964, was a resounding rise in the surplus on trade and current account; but as capital outflows and Government payments continued rising, the net deficit shrank only slowly.

After 1965, with the stepping-up of Government expenditure at home and abroad to meet the Vietnam commitment, a price and income inflation got under way. Imports rose much more rapidly than exports. By 1968 the trade surplus was gone; the current-account surplus was reduced by three-quarters; and only a sequence of tightening controls over net capital outflows made possible some further reduction of the overall deficit. In 1969, a severely restrictive (deflationary) monetary and fiscal policy came into play, and perverse though it seems, the deficit skyrocketed. But just as paradoxically, because the domestic restraint made Euro-dollars even more attractive to banks in the United States than to holders abroad, the dollar was in greater overall demand, and its current technical position in the foreign exchange markets was stronger, than at almost any other time in the decade.

Such, in stark oversimplification, is the strange record of the United States balance of payments and the dollar through the 60's. Toward the close, a classical tight money policy, aiming at deflation, brought a massive inflow of short-term funds. Statistically, the deficit zoomed; in the markets, the dollar was strong; yet the balance of trade did nothing. Moreover, fragmentary evidence, too tentative for presentation here, was beginning to suggest that the trade balance might not be capable of substantial improvement. Data suggested that as long as incomes rose, the United States economy, in its present form, would continue to draw in a more-than-proportional rise of imports— that the relevant elasticity determining purchases of goods abroad was income change in the United States, and that even if relative price stability could be attained, imports would go on rising at about the same pace.[6] Since no economic policy for the United States could contemplate static incomes over time, the chances of regaining a trade surplus sufficient to carry most of the other United States overseas

---

[6] H. S. Houthakker and Stephen P. Magee, "Income and Price Elasticities in World Trade," *Review of Economics and Statistics*, May 1969, pp. 111-125.

disbursements on capital and Government account were beginning to seem remote indeed.

Some way would have to be found, it would appear, for the United States at least, if not for other countries, to effect changes in overall capital and Government outflows, in net terms, as a response to general measures of economic policy, if our external accounts were ever really to balance. Perhaps by conventional standards the United States would have to become a habitual renegade, able barely to keep its trade accounts in balance, with a modest surplus on current account, with an *entrepot* role for vast flows of capital both in and out, with a more or less regular increase in the short-term dollar liabilities used for transactions purposes around the world, and with Government disbursements tailored to fit whatever proved to be the residual of all these other elements, after some allowance for increases over time in monetary reserves.

NEW APPROACHES

The arresting challenge presented by the array of "new problems" just described is to find a comprehensive new theory that can envelop all of them. Until that challenge is met—and I will insist here, without pausing for the argument, that the theoretical structure of a "floating" exchange-rate system is no answer—the approaches taken will have to be eclectic. Perhaps as they are followed through, a new and comprehensive theory will emerge. Meanwhile, there is one proposition, it seems to me, that cannot be avoided under any approach: in the aggregate the accounts of any solvent country must balance, on the basis of transactions willingly undertaken and of balances willingly held, in accordance with generally accepted standards of performance. The search now should be for those additional parts of an equilibrating mechanism that will enable each country to achieve its own viability with less interruption or strain in its all-round economic performance.

What is needed, then, if the new problems have to be confronted individually, rather than in one new all-embracing system, is an airing of various possible approaches to each of the problem areas. The hope can be that wider discussion and debate will produce a consensus of reasonable acceptability, at least for improved handling of some of them. The beginning of such an effort will be sketched here for six possible approaches, not with any pretense at completeness, not with the conviction of advocacy, but in the hope of stimulating critical elaboration. The six are: (1) general influences on long-term capital flows, (2) specific influences on long flows, (3) short-term money flows, (4) Government flows, (5) interrelations between interest rates and exchange rates, and (6) the United States potential as an *entrepot* for world capital mobility. In all six, of course, attention should be directed to gross flows, both inward and outward, and not merely to the critical net position.

General Influences on Long-Term Capital Flows

Ordinarily, the prerequisite for sustained and substantial outflows of long-term capital from a country is the continuation of a surplus on trade and current account. Yet for decades, even centuries, a by-product of this emphasis on surpluses has been the development of a mercantilist mentality, with emphasis focusing on the accumulation of reserves. To the extent that an overriding desire for additional reserves has been a deterrent to the massive outflow of long-term capital, the recent completion of arrangements for Special Drawing Rights in the International Monetary Fund should serve as a major corrective influence.

During the course of the debate preceding agreement on the SDR's, there was spreading recognition of the inherent risks in rivalry for acquisition of a severely limited aggregate of usable monetary reserves. A built-in deflationary bias was beginning to distort the functioning of the international payments system and drive individual nations, large and small, into undesirable protective or restrictive measures aimed at improving the current-account position in order to acquire a larger share of a relatively constant total of primary reserves. From 1970 onward, however, substantial annual increments to the supply of primary reserves will become available in the form of SDR's.

Henceforth, with each country receiving an annual increment to its reserves through direct allocation of SDR's, the pressures of reserve accumulation will be somewhat lessened. Many individual countries will still seek to earn more, but the strain imposed by this effort will not be so great when the total of reserves is continually growing. In turn, countries may find it easier to use some part of their resources, and their external earnings, in the normal extending of longer-term capital commitments. The SDR's may thus provide lubrication for a system that had been "seizing up." Indeed it is through the release of other resources, much more than through any direct siphoning of additional SDR's themselves into the less developed countries, that the system may be "freed up" for much more meaningful flows of

long-term capital from the developed to the developing countries
over the years ahead.

Thus what may prove to be one of the most significant "new approaches" for encouraging equilibrating capital flows during the next
decade, particularly long-term flows from developed countries in surplus to the developing countries, is already under way. To be sure,
the potential which the SDR's may represent, in terms of greater
freedom for the exporting of long-term capital, is only a prerequisite
for such flows and not an assurance that the flows will occur. However, by reducing the preoccupation of developed countries with reserve accumulations, the new arrangements should greatly encourage
capital flows from surplus countries to developing countries in deficit.

Direct Influences on Long-Term Flows

Most countries, recently including the United States, have had to
resort, at least at times, to specific governmental controls over one or
more components of their long-term capital outflows. Despite the
undoubted advantage of widespread freedom for the optimum diffu-
sion of direct investment around the globe, for example, or for the
uninhibited investment of funds in various types of portfolio assets
anywhere, complications have developed. As the scale and diversity
of these capital flows have grown, almost unavoidably a bunching of
excesses has occurred in one country or another, threatening to push
its immediate balance of payments into deficit, or actually doing so.

So far as direct investment is concerned, the installation of operating facilities in other countries cannot practicably be varied from
year to year in response to current changes in the balance-of-payments
position of the country in which the head office is domiciled. Moreover, attempts to control the aggregate of direct investment flows from
the home country are likely to be frustrated, if they continue very
long, by the ability of established international corporations to pursue
most of their objectives by reinvesting earnings that arise abroad, instead of repatriating them.

Without disturbing the orderly evolution of a firm's foreign investment program, however, there is a short-run potential for regulatory
devices to induce the multinational corporation to raise some part of
its funds in the countries whose balance-of-payments position is currently strong. One of the fortunate results of the rapid growth of the
Euro-dollar market has been the emergence of a truly European-wide,
in fact almost free-world-wide, international money and capital market to which such demands can be diverted. Paralleling this develop-

ment, partly for reasons of imitation and partly under the pressure of growing competition, more active markets have also begun to emerge within several of the other leading countries. The problem is how to direct some of the capital requirements of the multinational corporations toward the savings available in surplus countries, without also exceeding the aggregate of the surpluses available in these countries themselves.

No single technique, nor combination of several, can do more than help toward achieving more evenly distributed results. One approach, of some limited usefulness, can be to work with the host countries to space out direct investment inflows. Most of them, both developed and developing, already maintain controls over investment within their borders by firms domiciled or headquartered outside. To fit in, by agreement with other countries, some consideration for the sources of outside funds should not, as a temporary approach at times, be out of the question.

Another approach, particularly for instances in which the capital inflow depends in part upon insurance facilities of various kinds, is to effect a degree of variation in the initiation of investment projects by using the leverage available to the creditor nation (or international agency) which extends the guarantees. Regrettably, but perhaps inescapably, there has been an increasing propensity on the part of less developed countries for nationalization of concerns owned outside their borders. Investment in many of the less developed parts of the world is thus becoming increasingly dependent upon the obtaining of some kind of insurance guarantee from the home country, and as a result the potential for purposive variation from year to year to reflect variations in balance-of-payments availabilities has become considerable.

Resort by the home country to compulsory controls over capital exports, or earnings repatriation, on the part of international corporations may also from time to time prove inescapable and, at least on a temporary basis, may be moderately effective in shielding some countries from an unbearably heavy concentration of long-term capital outflows.

With respect to curbing outflows to acquire portfolio investments, preference should, one would think, be for those types of limitation that most nearly reflect the functioning of market processes. That was the intention of the designers of the interest-equalization tax in the United States. To be sure, for a number of years, that tax was regarded simply as an absolute prohibition and very little business was transacted on the basis of payment of the tax. However, with the passage of time, more and more investors in the United States have discovered that fruitful opportunities for portfolio investment can be found abroad, even after payment of the tax, though to be sure the magnitude of these opportunities has been much smaller than it would have been without the tax. The success of several mutual funds in the equity market in Japan late in the 1960's illustrates, moreover, the potential that remains for purely market considerations within the framework of the tax. Therefore, it may be reasonable to conclude that the variable use of instruments such as the interest-equalization tax by one country or another, at particular times, may be a helpful method of regulating, without totally interrupting, the outflow of funds for portfolio investment.

United States experience since 1965 illustrates still another dimension of potential influence, in this case, upon inflows of capital. The Foreign Investors Tax Act, as mentioned again shortly, opened up the possibility of not only improving, but also varying, the inducements for long-term capital to flow into the United States or to remain here.

Still another possibility is suggested by the more or less *ad hoc* approach that the United States has used in screening the borrowing of various international financial institutions in the United States market. As the scale of lending activity by the IBRD, or the various regional development banks, becomes greater—as it undoubtedly should and will—the scope of their borrowing operations becomes correspondingly larger. The potential which these borrowings contain for variation from year to year, in the extent to which one market or another is tapped, offers another meaningful method for distributing over time the balance-of-payments burden of the transfers likely to follow the placing of such securities in any given country.

Indeed a case can be made for extending this approach from an *ad hoc* to a systematic arrangement. One such possibility would be for a group of leading countries to make a firm commitment to one or more of the international lending institutions, undertaking to provide a fixed amount of resources each year for a period of, say, five years. By agreement the initial distribution of shares among the participating countries could be established on some independent criterion, such as the gross national products of each, possibly modified in some measure by the proportion of gross national product devoted to international trade or represented by some other grouping of international transactions. With a quota for each country's contribution over the five-year period agreed upon, the group of countries could then provide for variation from year to year in the actual contribution made by each within its quota. Recognition could in this way be given to the recent balance-of-payments position of each of the participating contributors—perhaps that of a year of two earlier in order to allow for the lag in reliable statistical data.

Provision would no doubt have to be made that every country must fulfill its quota within the five-year period. However, it might also be understood that any country in sustained balance-of-payments deficit, or suffering a series of unpredictable misfortunes, could satisfy its requirement by borrowing from others before the end of the five-year agreed interval. In this way, it would simply carry over into the next five-year period a somewhat larger charge against its own resources, to be met across its own exchanges.

Short Money Flows

The most conspicuous causes of aggravation in balance-of-payments difficulties, or of foreign exchange strains, through the decade of the 60's was the volatile movement of short-term funds in large amounts. For the most part these movements were motivated by rumors or expectations concerning possible changes in exchange rates.

With the completion of the French franc and Deutsche mark currency changes in 1969, one might have hoped that sufficient realignment had occurred to provide a reasonable assurance of continuity in most exchange-rate parities for some time in the future. Unfortunately, that would be an illusory point of view. The economic progress of nations cannot be in lock-step unison, neither in the performance of their domestic economies nor in their changing relative capabilities to expand exports or imports, of goods or of capital. As these differential rates of change are reflected in performance, some changes in exchange rates will from time to time be almost inevitable. That is why the discussion of exchange-rate questions became so fervent and widespread as the 60's were drawing to a close.

Whether or not any major change may ultimately be introduced into the currency parity system under the aegis of the International Monetary Fund, one possibility which has attracted particular attention could be pursued further without requiring any change in IMF procedures. This is the suggestion that exchange-rate changes, when the need for them becomes reasonably clear, should be made with somewhat greater frequency, and in somewhat smaller amounts, than was considered customary or appropriate during the first decade of convertibility, beginning in 1959. Should that approach become accepted, neither the potentialities for gain, nor the uncertainties of prolonged delay, could be so great, nor could they have as much impact on movements of short-term funds, as they did during the decade of the 60's.

In addition, following the United States initiative in developing its own $10 billion "ring of swaps" during the 60's, many of the leading countries have developed arrangements for making short-term transfers of sudden inflows of reserves back to the country from which they had flowed. For conditions in which the normal reversal of swap lines within one year could not be readily fulfilled, additional techniques have been developed. These provide for the debtor country to extend the credit for two or three or more years by issuing to the creditor a security denominated in the creditor's currency. Varying provisions for redeemability, in order to assure central banking liquidity, have been introduced.

In some instances this intermediate-term instrument was used, in effect, as a transferable means of shifting reserves as an offset to short-term capital flows from one country to another outside the United States. A country holding such claims on the United States might, when losing reserves, redeem the claims; the United States at the same time could issue a corresponding amount of similar securities to the country receiving much of the money in transit, denominated in that country's currency. The net effect would be a return of dollars from the country receiving them to the country losing them. This occurred, for example, when there were heavy movements of funds from Italy to Germany late in 1963 and early in 1964. Italy redeemed United States bonds, denominated in lire, and the United States in turn issued new bonds to the Bundesbank, denominated in Deutsche mark.

While neither the swaps nor the foreign currency bonds provides a totally adequate offset to the impact of speculative flows of short-term funds, they have served an essential purpose and should occupy an important, perhaps an increasing, place alongside the facilities of the IMF itself in the roster of routine instruments available for use in minimizing the balance-of-payments disruption related to short-term money flows. But, of course, expectations concerning exchange-rate changes were not the only factor in such "hot money" flows. Another factor has been the influence of interest-rate differentials among the short-term markets of leading countries. These will be discussed further below.

Government Flows

As already suggested, perhaps the most important single area for deliberate variation in flows across the exchanges lies in the transactions carried out by governments themselves. The hope would be that governments could develop within their regular overseas payments a capability comparable to that of the so-called "built in" or automatic stabilizers that help to promote stability in the domestic economy.

The general format of one such approach has already been suggested in outlining the possibility for variation among countries in the contributions that each might make toward an agreed annual collective contribution of resources to the international development banks. Similar arrangements might very well be considered for consortia arranged among leading countries for the extending of other kinds of direct aid. Clearly, to the extent that aid, whether through loans or through grants, can be extended on a multilateral basis, the potentialities become much greater for variation from year to year in the burden placed upon one contributing country or another.

There are still two other ways in which, preferably through multilateral forms of agreement, some more or less automatic variation in balance-of-payments burden could be accomplished. One would follow from a more general recognition that individual governments, even of developed countries, can appropriately borrow abroad to accomplish particular purposes at times when the need for continuity in a program conflicts with the immediate balance-of-payments position of the particular country. Or in cases in which government accounts themselves are not involved, there would also be a possibility, at times of balance-of-payments strain at home, of extending guarantees or inducements to private concerns engaged in investment abroad, in order to encourage borrowing in other markets, possibly denominated in other currencies.

Perhaps the zone of greatest interest, however, is also that which, from the point of view of the less developed countries, is that of greatest need. This is the question of debt servicing emphasized earlier in the outline of "new problems." A considerable part of the receipts of many of the leading countries in any given year now comes from the return of amortization payments (and in many instances the receipt of very high interest payments) from loans made earlier to many of the less developed countries. To some extent, through consultation among the leading countries, there would seem to be scope for outright renegotiation of some of these terms in order to minimize the future burden of past indebtedness. Even where this is not practicable, the possibility for postponing such payments for several years at a time offers an important opportunity for extending balance-of-payments relief to the less developed countries, while spacing out the inflow of hard currency in the accounts of creditor countries during periods when they are already enjoying balance-of-payments gains. To the extent that postponement would be contemplated by private lenders domiciled in strong creditor countries, the postponement might have to be paralled by either guarantees or actual government "takeouts," with recourse as to ultimate credit risk. For any of these approaches, the most promising procedure would seem to be for a multilateral undertaking, worked out under the aegis, for example, of the Development Assistance Committee of the OECD, or of the IBRD.

Interrelations between Interest Rates and Exchange Rates

As indicated earlier, interest-rate comparisons among financial markets, and between the Euro-dollar market and any other given market, seem to have become much more important factors in causing short-term money flows during the late 60's than the characteristic patterns of trade financing. Indeed, we have seen that at times a perverse relationship developed between domestic interest rates and the balance-of-payments results intended by the authorities when introducing either a restrictive or an easing monetary policy. The same experience has also suggested, however, that as long as some uncertainty remains concerning the actual exchange rate likely to be in effect in the marketplace when foreign short-term investment is unwound, another dimension can be at work to help minimize any unwanted effects of interest-rate spreads. That is, the gain from an interest-rate differential must be adjusted for the cost of forward cover.

The possibility consequently exists at times to induce or deter short-term money flows by narrowing or by widening the margin of forward discount or premium on the currency in question. To be sure, the scope is not unlimited for variation in such forward rates, but the Articles of the International Monetary Fund do not lay down any mandatory limits. Consequently, there have been times when, even though no imminent crisis was threatening, the discount in one direction or the premium in another might rise to as much as 3 or 4 per cent in the forward market. Just as a discount would offset some of the attraction of higher interest rates, and probably diminish the flow of funds into a currency, so a forward premium might encourage flows in the other direction.

For some time, a number of central banks have been reluctant to nudge forward rates upward or downward as a conscious instrument of policy. However, as one experiment after another was attempted during the decade of the 60's, the practice began to acquire some degree of acceptability. To be sure, heavy forward purchases of sterling by the Bank of England for many months before the devaluation of November 1967 did eventually prove rather costly when the parity was in fact changed, but this experience might well turn out to be the "exception to prove the rule." Particularly if parity changes are to be made in smaller amounts and somewhat more frequently, the potential burden on central banks or their governments can be reduced, while the scope for meaningful variation in cost of forward cover, over the 3 or 4 per cent range, for example, would still exist.

One other important possibility has been discussed in recent months. That would be to provide for a widening of the band around the exchange parity. While some have suggested a widening on both sides of parity, the case may perhaps be stronger for a widening on the up side. Surely, as far as reluctance to change parity is concerned, it is readily demonstrable that revaluations occur less readily than devaluations. Out of the last one hundred changes in exchange-rate parities, only three had been appreciations prior to the German move near the end of 1969. Yet possibly the greatest distorting influence upon short-term money flows, particularly when a mixture of interest-rate and exchange-rate uncertainties were involved, has occurred because of the pull of funds into a currency which was clearly undervalued. If there were a range, with a wider band, above parity, for the spot rate to move up as much as 2 or 3 per cent, while the forward might move correspondingly above that, the potential for deterring speculative inflows could be very great. Many of the more extreme swings of short-term money flows of the 1960's might have been averted, or held to much smaller figures, if this approach could have been followed.

The United States as an *Entrepot* for Capital Mobility

If some of the questions already raised concerning the United States should prove to be valid, then the prospects for this powerful nation to go on contributing directly to development in other nations primarily by means of a substantial trade surplus appear doubtful. There should, of course, be room for other kinds of contributions through other elements in the current account, perhaps notably through the deferral or forgiveness of some debt service. Moreover, interest and royalty and other "invisible" earnings derived from other developed countries should provide considerable support for this country's external commitments. Nonetheless, taking all these together, the scope for United States activity overseas would appear severely limited in relation to the aspirations and demands likely to arise.

One very important additional source of future capital outflows may come through attracting more capital inflows, through a greater development of the United States role as an *entrepot* capital market There is little doubt that the highly developed facilities of this country's capital markets, and the skills of its many participants who now operate actively abroad through the Euro-currency markets, can effectively place much larger amounts of funds than can be raised in the domestic United States market. Conversely, one of the greatest shortcomings, even now, among most of the other rapidly advancing developed nations is that they do not have the capital market facilities for effectively putting their own savings to use outside their own economies. The opportunity still exists, consequently, despite all that has already been accomplished during the 60's, for the United States to move more aggressively into the role of intermediary, drawing in nearly as much capital from outside as it distributes. That was a part of the philosophy underlying the Foreign Investors Tax Act of 1966. Although not intended as a variable influence on inflows of foreign capital to the American markets, its role in increasing the volume of these inflows can be of immeasurable help toward achieving, over the years, a closer approach to balance in the United States external accounts.

*   *   *   *   *   *   *

There is much more to be said, of course, on this approach, as on all of the others so briefly touched upon in these comments. But my aim has not been to present a fully detailed brief. Instead, in the spirit of open inquiry that has been the epitome of Karl Bopp's career, my hope has been to present enough circumstantial evidence to raise a presumption of doubt concerning the traditional identification between the trade balance and the total balance of payments. Having raised the doubt, and indicated that capital flows and government transfers have become critically important, independent influences on the balance-of-payments positions of many countries, I have gone on to suggest some approaches for coping with these influences, alongside the flows of goods in trade, as part of a comprehensive process of balance-of-payments adjustment. From all of this at least one conclusion seems to emerge, in confirmation of the counsel that Karl Bopp gave me years ago—there are still many more problems than answers in the formulation of appropriate adjustment policies.

CURRENCY CRISES:
THE RECORD AND THE REMEDY

FREDERICK L. DEMING

IN JUST TWO HOURS of the morning of Monday, September 29, 1969 some $250 million flowed into Germany in anticipation of a revaluation of the D mark. The German authorities re-closed the German exchange markets which had just been re-opened after being closed the previous Thursday and Friday to avoid speculative runs into the D mark prior to the German elections. The authorities announced that when the markets were opened again, as they were on Tuesday, there would for a time be no official intervention to hold the official parity, as is required under IMF rules. Thus the D mark was allowed to float temporarily, as an answer to the latest questioning of the international monetary system. Late in October it was officially revalued to a new and higher fixed parity.

In November, 1968 and again in May, 1969 the world had questioned seriously the viability of the then current D mark parity. In the first instance some $3 billion, and in the second some $4 billion had run into the D mark in the belief that it was a prime candidate for revaluation. Despite heavy capital export which more than offset a strong current account surplus, German reserves gained sharply in the first nine months of 1969, reflecting the short-term capital inflow.

Neither the November nor the May runs brought a D mark revaluation. The Bundesbank managed to "recycle" a significant portion of the inflows, and general international monetary cooperation worked to make relatively tolerable the impact on reserves of weak currency nations. But it is noteworthy that it was not only the so-called speculators who believed the D mark was a candidate for revaluation. In November the Ministers and Governors of the Group of Ten countries, the most powerful financial nations in the world, believed that revaluation was both necessary and desirable and urged that course on Germany. The argument made good economic sense but apparently no political sense in Germany. In May, both the Bundesbank and the Economics Ministry strongly backed revaluation, and many industrial leaders in Germany were prepared to accept a higher parity; but the government rejected that course again and in doing so declared the then current parity was "for eternity"—a period which turned out to be five months.

In May, 1968 riots and strikes in France brought the (up to then) highly regarded franc into a weak position. For more than a year, with massive foreign assistance, France fought off capital outflow, balance-of-payments deficits and heavy reserve losses. In basic economic terms a reasonable case could be made as to the viability of the then current franc parity. France herself evidently regarded that case as convincing, for she forewent devaluation in November, 1968 when all of her Group of Ten partners were prepared to accept a modest downward movement in the franc parity. Then, despite large reserves, large foreign credits, a program of austerity and fairly strong exchange controls, France was finally forced to devalue in August, 1969, and by the same amount regarded as acceptable (even though in French eyes unnecessary) in November, 1968. According to Finance Minister Giscard d'Estaing, French reserve losses were very heavy and the drain showed no sign of abating significantly, so that France had no choice but devaluation.

In March, 1968, the Gold Pool, operated by seven of the key financial powers in the world, gave up its fight to hold the free market price of gold equal to the monetary price. The London market was closed for a short period and the link between monetary and nonmonetary gold was broken by stopping supply of the residual demand in the London market. This move was regarded widely as desirable on its own merit; there was a considerable body of opinion that held that a two-tier gold system was both feasible and desirable. That opinion has proved to be correct. But the move also might be regarded as making a virtue out of a necessity. The run into gold really reflected in large part a run out of currencies and a broad lack of confidence in the international monetary system.

That, in turn, was a partial product of the fall of sterling in November, 1967. The struggle to preserve the $2.80 sterling parity began in earnest three years earlier, in November, 1964, when a massive credit package for Britain was put together by the leading financial powers of the world. Britain took a series of restrictive actions designed to improve her external position. Results were disappointing and sterling remained weak. In September, 1965 another credit package and further international monetary cooperation repelled a major bear raid on sterling. A year later the same thing happened again. Yet, by the spring of 1967 Britain had repaid all her short-term debts and was in process of repaying her IMF advances. It looked as though the struggle had been won. But then came the Arab-Israeli war, which led to heavy British reserve losses, and there were some bad trade results during the summer and fall. By November, Britain had lost so much in reserves (almost $1.5 billion alone on the day before devaluation) that the parity change could be resisted no longer. In this instance, also, a case could be made that on economic grounds the old parity was viable, but that case could not be made credible to holders of short-term funds, both British and foreign, for any sustained period. And even after devaluation and still more austerity, the pound stayed basically weak and suspect for some two years.

In March, 1964 a large balance-of-payments deficit in Italy brought a massive run on the lira. Much opinion of the time was that the lira should and would be devalued. But a large credit package and a savagely restrictive economic policy combined to break the speculative attack and restore the external position of Italy. While the broad economic cost to Italy, and perhaps the world, of the strongly restrictive policy was fairly high, the Italian current account position has remained strong since that time. But even with a substantial current account surplus the lira suffered from capital outflow in 1969 when the impact of the French and German currency situations plus the unsettled political situations in Italy led to some loss of confidence in the lira.

In the spring of 1962 the Canadian dollar faced a major speculative attack. It had had no fixed parity for a number of years but during a large part of that period it had an effective rate of more than par with the United States dollar. By 1962, however, it seemed evident that the parity, effective or fixed, would be sharply reduced. The Canadians finally settled on a fixed parity of 92.5 cents but had to defend it fiercely at the time, and could do so only with large financial help from the United States. And, even with a fairly solid economy, Canada suffered another period of heavy reserve losses in early 1968, following announcement of a new and stronger United States balance-of-payments program. That drain was arrested only after Canada was effectively and publicly insulated from the impact of the United States program.

In March, 1961 the D mark and the Dutch guilder were revalued. The revaluation was mild—only 5 per cent—but it was the result of and triggered what at the time was regarded as major flows of speculative funds. It is noteworthy that comment from the Federal Reserve Bank of New York on this development was:

However effective these moves may ultimately prove to be as a contribution to international balance-of-payments equilibrium, their immediate effect was a shattering blow to market confidence in a system of fixed currency parities. All major currencies immediately became labeled as candidates for either revaluation or devaluation, and an unparalleled flood of speculative funds swept across the exchanges.[1]

In late 1960 and early 1961 there was an earlier rush into gold. This run reflected two factors: three years of very large American balance-of-payments deficits, and widespread uncertainties about continuation of the American policy of converting dollars held by monetary authorities into gold at the fixed price of $35 an ounce. In a real sense the run was the result of a crisis of confidence in the dollar, and involved not only a sharp rise in the price of gold in the private markets but large conversions of dollars into gold from the United States Treasury. This crisis was overcome following a strong public statement from President Kennedy that the United States would continue to convert dollars into gold at the $35 price. But from that time forward the United States has been constrained to adopt a number of restrictive programs designed to improve her international payments position and maintain confidence in the dollar.

The above record adds up to 15 major currency crises since late 1960. Except for those directly concerning the Canadian dollar in 1962 and 1968 and the lira crisis of 1964, all of the crises produced severe strains in the entire international monetary system. The system has become ever more closely interlinked so that either excessive strength or weakness in one major currency has tended to produce repercussions on other major currencies and to have serious impact on the host of minor currencies. That excessive strength or weakness may occur solely as a result of growth or failure of confidence without a clear economic basis for the confidence change.

Interdependence of Currencies

The 1969 Annual Report of the International Monetary Fund observes that since most major currencies became convertible some ten years ago there has been a great growth in the volume of short-term funds that can flow from one currency into another. "In this respect the framework within which countries can conduct policy differs

---

[1] "Treasury and Federal Reserve Foreign Exchange Operations," reprint from the *Federal Reserve Bulletin,* September, 1962, p. 1140. It is an interesting historical note that the "unparalleled flood" of early 1961 was less than one-tenth the size of the May, 1969 flows into the D mark and just a bit larger than the two-hour flow of September 29, 1969.

importantly from that envisaged at the time of Bretton Woods . . . .
The drafters were well aware that a country might have to alter its
exchange rate in response to relative changes in its real economic
position. But they did not envisage that a country would have to be
so much concerned about the public's changing views on the strength
of its currency. Speculative capital movements were expected to be
suppressed rather than financed . . . ."[2]

It is important to recognize that the growing interlinkage in the
monetary system makes today's currency crises dangerous for the entire system. It might be expected that a crisis for the dollar would
have widespread impact. The dollar is the world's great reserve and
trading currency; the United States is the greatest economic power in
the world and stands at the very core of the Bretton Woods system.
Practically speaking, the parity of the dollar cannot be changed relative to other currencies; they peg against the dollar which is convertible
into gold at the fixed price of $35 an ounce for monetary authorities.
Even should the dollar price of gold be changed, it would be highly
unlikely that the parities of other countries relative to the dollar would
be changed. That is not to say that another currency cannot appreciate against the dollar, but it is not practical nor would it be desirable
to change the dollar parity against the system as a whole or any significant portion of it.

Nevertheless, there can be a crisis of confidence in the dollar, as
there was in late 1960-early 1961. In a sense the gold crisis of late
1967-early 1968 was a crisis of the dollar also, but only in a sense.
That reflected, as noted, more lack of confidence in currencies as a
whole rather than in the dollar itself even though much of the impact
fell on the United States gold stock.

Still, since 1960 the United States has had to struggle to maintain
confidence in the dollar; the United States balance-of-payments program of January 1, 1968 itself was designed in part to moderate a
gold crisis. And because of the economic size of the United States, its
various balance-of-payments programs, particularly the 1968 program, had adverse impact on other currencies—notably the Canadian
dollar and probably sterling. So weakness or strength in the dollar
affects many other currencies.

But strength or weakness in other major currencies also has major
impact on the system. The chronic weakness of sterling before devaluation kept the whole monetary system in a state of nervousness,

---

[2] *1969 Annual Report,* International Monetary Fund, p. 31.

and the immediate post-devaluation effect was a massive run into gold. The excessive strength of the D mark had serious adverse effect on the system, and particularly on the French franc and on sterling. It also brought heavy reserve losses to Denmark and Belgium, led to capital outflow from Italy, and produced speculative upward pressure on the guilder and the Swiss franc. From May, 1968 to the present the French franc has been a destabilizing factor in itself but has also had severe impact on Belgium, adversely affected Italy and at times added to sterling's problems.

Different Positions

Because of the triple fact of crisis frequency, the heavy flows of short-term funds that move at times without real economic reasons, and the strong interlinkage of the system, a number of people have raised questions about the viability of the system itself. Given the facts that the world has prospered greatly and that world trade has expanded markedly under the Bretton Woods system, is there not some better way to achieve these desirable ends—a way that would at least cut down on the frequency and fierceness of currency crises?

Relatively few people contend that the system should go on unchanged; the basic differences lie between those who would make radical changes and create, in effect, a new system and those who believe that modest change, essentially within the present system's framework, would meet the need.

In part, the differences reflect differing economic philosophies but in part they reflect differing economic analyses of the causes of crises. While there is no general agreement as to the causes of crises among those who would make only modest changes within the present framework, the following points are usually made in support of that position: (1) The basic weakness lies in the failure of countries to follow sensible economic policies; they know better than they act. The balance-of-payments adjustment process would be made to work smoothly if countries had the political courage to take appropriate economic action; (2) a particular version of this argument, widely accepted in Europe, is that the persistent weaknesses in the international payments positions of the United States and the United Kingdom have been the major factors of instability. If the reserve currency countries, with their especial responsibilities, followed better economic policies the crises would be both less frequent and susceptible of easier containment; (3) the system could be made to work far better than it has if it operated in the manner envisaged by the

Bretton Woods founders. That system was designed to accommodate parity changes when they were indicated. Obtuse resistance to desirable changes in parities is a major factor in crises; (4) at least part of the instability of recent years has reflected nervousness about needed reserve-growth sources for the future. A few have believed that this should be accomplished by an upward change in the monetary price of gold. The great majority sought other means and this has led to the new fiduciary reserves, the Special Drawing Rights.

Many of those who wish to work within the present framework of a fixed parity system seemingly would be willing to accept changes in the system that even a short time ago would have been regarded as radical: a modestly wider band above and below parity, a modest crawling peg, or a combination of these two. But these remedies do not satisfy those who believe that the system needs really radical change, by which they mean a major breakaway from a system of fixed parities usually accompanied by a demonitization of gold. Basically they hold a fixed parity system is destabilizing in itself, that it leads to bad economic policies both internally and externally, that it is absurd for countries to follow restrictive economic policies which hurt growth in those countries and in the world, that the adjustment process should rest essentially in the exchange rate, and that the rate should be allowed to fluctuate widely.

E. M. Bernstein has written that the objective at Bretton Woods was to retain the fixed parity aspect of the gold standard while abandoning the rigidities imposed by the traditional gold standard. Article IV, Section 5, of the Fund's Articles of Agreement says in part that a change in the par value of a member's currency may be made only on the member's proposal and after consultation with the Fund, but that the Fund shall concur if it is satisfied that the change is necessary to correct a fundamental disequilibrium in the balance of payments.[3]

The 1969 Annual Report of the Fund states:

> *This system was intended to provide a stable environment which, by encouraging international transactions, would stimulate the growth and sharpen the efficiency of the world economy. Stability, as the Fund has stressed in the past, does not mean rigidity . . . changes in par values were contemplated as one of the means of adjustment . . . ex-*

---

[3] "Flexible Exchange Rates and Balance-of-Payments Adjustment," *E M B* (*Ltd.*), December 11, 1968.

*change rates that are no longer appropriate . . . contribute
to the persistence of payments disequilibria, the encouragement of speculation, and crises in the exchange markets . . . .*[4]

The Report, on this subject, concludes by noting that the Fund
Board has been discussing extensively the mechanism by which exchange rates can be changed. No conclusions have yet been reached
and the study will continue. But the Executive Directors stressed
that:

> *. . . any changes that might be made should preserve the
> essential characteristics of the par value system, which re-
> main as beneficial for the world as they were when written
> into the Fund's Articles of Agreement 25 years ago: that the
> stability of exchange rates at realistic levels is a key con-
> tribution to the balanced expansion of international trade,
> and that the determination of the rate of exchange for each
> currency is a matter of international concern.*[5]

The Thesis: A More Flexible Approach to Parity Changes

The thesis of this paper may be expressed in three propositions:

1. The international monetary system of fixed parities has proved
   highly beneficial to the world and should be preserved essentially in its present form. No basic structural changes are necessary or desirable.
2. The workings of the system can be improved significantly, and
   the frequency and intensity of currency crises can be moderated
   by some relatively simple procedural changes that would involve
   only the big financial and industrial countries.
3. A generalized system with more flexibility would not be particularly useful but a more flexible approach to necessary or
   desirable parity changes for the big countries would be helpful
   and should be adopted.

The thesis rests on six major premises:

a. The smooth working of the international monetary system
   depends primarily on the conduct of the big industrial and
   financial powers. A currency crisis that involves a major
   country almost always has the potential to shake the entire
   system. This is not true of a minor country, nor is it true of
   a big country which has a relatively minor currency.

---

[4] *1969 Annual Report,* International Monetary Fund, p. 31.
[5] *Ibid.,* p. 32.

b. Necessary and desirable changes in parities of the big countries are likely to be infrequent. In the past ten years there have been only six parity changes among the major currencies—three up and three down. While the manner, timing, and magnitude of some of these changes may be subject to criticism, it is highly doubtful that there should have been more changes.

c. No system of fixed parities, and probably no system of floating rates, can be made to work without a reasonable degree of agreement among the big countries on a set of principles concerning broad economic policies and responsibilities for the workings of the adjustment process and a reasonable degree of assurance from each of them that the principles will be implemented by appropriate action.

d. There is no need to amend the Articles of Agreement of the Fund. The present Articles are sufficiently broad to permit the Fund to pursue a more flexible approach to any necessary or desirable parity change for either a big or a small country.

e. A workable and acceptable procedure of meaningful consultation and discussion at a high political level and in confidence prior to a parity change by any big country can be developed.

f. Adequate credit facilities, both outside and inside the Fund, will remain available to aid in a smooth adjustment process and to repel speculative attack on a currency. It should be possible to enlarge and improve such credit facilities, especially those designed to "recycle" funds received from speculative currency flows.

Problems of Parity Changes

Before proceeding to discussion of the simple procedural changes and the more flexible approach to parity changes, it is useful to delineate three basic problems with respect to parity changes by big countries. First is the problem of frequency and timing. With appropriate policies, changes in parity should not be required frequently; it was noted above that there were only six changes in the past ten years and that probably no others were needed or desirable. But certainly questions can be raised about the timeliness of some of the changes. The big countries have tended to regard a parity change as an indication of failure of policy and consequently to utilize such only as a last resort. One consequence of this approach is that change

almost automatically is the product of crisis and may well be instru-
mental in producing a crisis. It would be well for the big countries to
regard parity change as a useful but infrequently used part of the
adjustment process, to be employed with care and sparingly but not
to be completely foresworn except in case of a catastrophe. The big
countries have the right to expect that their trading partners will not
depend on parity change simply to avoid other hard policy choices and
thereby shift the burden of adjustment to others. But maintenance
of a nonviable parity carries costs of its own and parity change may
be the best course of action in certain cases.

Second is the problem of magnitude of change. Unfortunately, the
art of economics cannot yet determine with any precision just what
is a viable exchange rate. And particularly in recent years, as the
1969 Fund report notes, pressures can develop on an exchange rate
almost apart from basic and real economic factors. Any exchange
rate change has to be "credible" to the market itself as well as viable
in an economic sense. The tendency, therefore, is to err on the side
of safety and make the change relatively large, particularly when a
devaluation is involved. That tendency in itself raises additional problems—e.g., the "domino effect" both for self-protection and because
of shifting market pressures.

Third is the problem of confidentiality. It is self-evident that governments cannot publicly discuss parity changes without inviting
major market movements of short-term capital. But some people have
to know about prospects for change if any change is to be carried out
successfully, and it is of key importance for a government contemplating change to reach a judgment as to the response of its major
trading partners. In addition there is the stated requirement in the
Fund's Articles of Agreement that parity changes should take place
only after consultation with the Fund.

All of these difficulties might be muted if devaluations and revaluations were the product of full international discussion and understanding and if the approach to a parity change were made more
flexible. A change stemming from full international discussion would
carry the real endorsement of the country's big trading partners and
the explicit pledge of no counteraction. It would carry with it pledges
of necessary credits. And perhaps most importantly, it might be made
in more timely fashion and in a way that would enhance credibility.
Probably that would mean that the change could be kept smaller and
would be regarded as a real part of the adjustment process to be
accompanied by other appropriate policies.

In this connection there is much to commend the recent German method of finally revaluing the D mark. Germany could not gain the formal approval of the Fund to float but she gained Fund acquiescence, and the final parity fixing was really a reflection of market judgment as well as political judgment.

Procedure for Changing Parity

The procedural changes which would improve the workings of the international monetary system relate to premises (c) and (e). With respect to premise (c) it probably is more correct to suggest that further evolution of present procedure is what is needed rather than a change in procedure.

In 1966 the Organization for Economic Cooperation and Development issued a report on the adjustment process[6] which had been prepared in Working Party Three of its Economic Policy Committee and was agreed to by the countries represented in the Working Party, basically the big financial and industrial countries. It spelled out in fairly explicit terms the responsibilities of both surplus and deficit countries and laid down a series of policy actions which might be taken to smooth the adjustment process. Thus there is in essence an agreed set of principles already in being. The Fund's Articles of Agreement also constitute an agreed set of principles.

The regular meetings of the Economic Policy Committee, Working Party Three, the Group of Ten, and the central bank governors at Basle provide discussion forums for analysis and policy recommendations in an international setting. The Fund's consultations with individual countries can supplement these multilateral discussions. Participants in these meetings are sophisticated and have a high level of understanding of the political, economic, and social facts of life. In these groups it should be possible to foster implementation of the principles agreed to, and produce the necessary assurances and international support for sound economic policies.

It would be politically naive to expect a single and agreed set of economic policies among the big countries; there are significant differences among them in political, economic, and social structures and goals, and in the available mix of policy instruments. Furthermore, it is unlikely that there will ever be absolute agreement on the trade-offs between domestic goals and international responsibilities. Nor, with

---

[6] *The Balance-of-Payments Adjustment Process,* Report by Working Party Three of the Economic Policy Committee of the O E C D, August, 1966.

the best of intentions, is it likely that any government can give absolute assurances that it will follow a given set of policies and achieve a particular goal. But it is possible for the big countries to assure each other that, insofar as is possible, they will act responsibly to make the adjustment process work and that in their formulations of policy they will pay due regard to the prospective impact of their policies upon their trading partners.

The key points on which agreement should be reached and assurances given are that no country will, either by action or lack of action, deliberately shift an undue portion of the adjustment burden to its trading partners; and that it will use changes in the exchange rate responsibly when needed as part of the adjustment process but will not regard changes, particularly depreciations, as the sole method of adjustment.

It is not unduly optimistic to expect the reasonable degree of agreement and assurance required. There already has been considerable progress and it should continue. And with growing understanding there also should be improved political performance.

With respect to premise (e) it is instructive to examine the Bonn meeting of the Ministers and Governors of the Group of Ten in November, 1968. That meeting was a real international consultation at a high and responsible political level where firm commitments could be made. It was designed to discuss fully and in advance of any announced action possible parity changes by one or more important countries. It was called in haste, was by necessity not well planned, and was conducted in the white heat of worldwide publicity. Since no parity changes followed the meeting it was widely criticized as a bad example of financial diplomacy.

While much of the criticism was justified, the critics seem to have overlooked the positive features of the Bonn meeting. The basic objective of the meeting was multilateral consultation in advance of parity change. It underlined the point that parity changes are a matter of international concern, and that essentially unilateral action and *pro forma* consultation and approval are unsatisfactory expressions of that principle.

The substantive achievements of the meeting were not trivial. It was called and conducted in the midst of a great currency crisis, and with its conclusion the crisis was resolved for the time being. There were three specific results. First, the conferees urged Germany to revalue the D mark. Basically for domestic political reasons Germany rejected that course but did agree to take certain actions aimed at reducing her large current account surplus and at repelling speculative flows. The fact that these actions proved inadequate is a principal reason for criticizing the meeting. Second, the meeting was designed to insure that any prospective French devaluation would be contained within moderate and acceptable magnitude and that the other big countries would not follow a modest French move. France made two points quite clear: there might be no devaluation, a course most of the conferees favored; if there were, it would be no more than 11 per cent. The other countries committed to hold their parities and to participate in additional credits for France.

In sum, there are both positive and negative lessons to be learned from the Bonn meeting. There are also lessons to be learned from normal Fund procedures in dealing with parity changes.

When big country parity changes are involved the Fund's role has tended to be mainly passive. As noted earlier, Article IV of the Fund's Articles of Agreement states that a change in a member's parity may be made only on the member's proposal after consultation with the Fund, which shall concur if it is satisfied the change is necessary to correct a fundamental disequilibrium. Partly because big countries are important and jealous of their sovereignty, partly because a big country parity change may have severe market impact and shake the entire system, partly because such changes have been infrequent in recent years, and partly because in the case of revaluation the Fund has no effective financial leverage to employ, the process of consultation for the big countries has tended to be not much more than very short-term advance notification, and Fund concurrence by necessity has been almost *pro forma*. Even in cases of devaluation where the Fund will have some financial leverage the big country knows that it can count on support for a drawing from the Fund, if necessary. In many of those cases the Fund can impose some conditions, but they tend to be drawn up *post hoc* and are not really part of the consultation process.

The important point to note here is that the consultative process in the sense of a full discussion and negotiation simply does not exist. The Fund, of course, will have background staff papers; when a major currency is under pressure that fact is known and preparatory work will have been done. But the time framework is such that there can be no meaningful international discussion. Usually the country concerned will have announced its intention after market closing for the weekend with effective action before market opening after the weekend. With the possibility of very large currency flows no country can afford a protracted discussion that would carry past the weekend, once an intention is announced. And there is no practical way to reject the proposal—the currency would be suspect. Thus the Fund Board is forced to concur willy-nilly; it faces a *fait accompli.*

The Fund's role in situations concerning countries of lesser economic and financial importance, whether developed or developing, is considerably less passive. Both the consultative and admonitory policies and procedures are handled with greater efficacy and acceptability than those with major countries. That is not to say that the correct policies are easy to formulate, that they necessarily are implemented well, or that they always lead to the desired results. But the simple fact is that Fund management, board, and staff have carried more weight and worked more effectively with the smaller countries than with the bigger ones. Usually more time is available to discuss timing and magnitude of parity changes and programs to accompany them; there is less speculative pressure and less prospect of untimely publicity. The latter point may reflect partly the fact that parity changes come with more frequency in the minor countries and are more acceptable because they rarely strain the whole monetary system.

It should be possible to devise a procedure under which the Fund will play a more active role in big country parity changes and one under which meaningful international consultation can take place without the glare of publicity. Two possible methods suggest themselves and, in an emergency, a third might be followed.

One key requirement for the success of any approach is a more activist role for the Fund management in connection with big country parity changes. The Fund management might well take the lead in pressing for parity changes it regards as desirable. This role would be perfectly consonant with the provisions of Article IV. There is nothing to prevent the Fund management from discussion with and making suggestions to a country; it does so with many of its smaller members. The country concerned, of course, makes the formal proposal. The Fund management should assume a more positive role in ascertaining a country's views on a possible parity change and undertake to participate actively to ascertain the positions of the other big countries toward any change. Finally, the Fund management could make specific suggestions as to the approach taken in reaching a new parity.

The other key requirement is security, which means essentially that very few people should be privy to the discussions. Practically, that requirement means that there should be no formal meetings attended by full-scale delegations and staff. The discussions simply have to be kept confidential in every respect. One way to proceed would be to follow the pattern that developed in connection with the devaluation of sterling. Sterling was under periodic pressures over a long period. Every big country treasury and central bank was fully aware that the fight to preserve the sterling parity might be unsuccessful. As the situation developed there were many quiet conversations, largely bilateral but some multilateral, and from them it became reasonably clear that a devaluation of no more than 15 per cent would be acceptable to the big countries and that none of them would be likely to take retaliatory action, either by changing its own parity or by other measures. In the actual event, no major country followed sterling down. Actually very few countries outside the sterling bloc made parity changes.

The above should not be taken to mean that the timing, magnitude, or method chosen for sterling devaluation was optimum. The central point is that there were meaningful consultations of a sort and reasonably clear understandings reached without publicity and in a confidential atmosphere. These, however, were mostly outside the Fund; its management, board, and staff did not participate very actively.

There is no reason why the Fund management should not play a more active role and follow this kind of pattern. Senior Fund management and staff travel extensively. Quiet conversations with high-level political and technical officials can be arranged easily. Either by positive Fund suggestion, made in utter confidence, or by secret advance notification by the country contemplating a parity change, the consultation process could be started; and it could be carried out in confidence and with reasonable speed.

This approach basically involves a set of bilateral consultations with heavy engagement of Fund management and very senior staff. Another approach might be employed which would be more multilateral and in which Fund management and staff would play a smaller role in the consultative process. This approach would not preclude a more activist part for the Fund management in its discussions with the country or countries making the actual parity change.

The deputies of the Ministers and Governors of the Group of Ten are essentially the same people who head the country delegations in Working Party Three, and the countries represented are essentially the big countries. Furthermore, the Group of Ten might be enlarged to bring in the three or four countries which are not now members but which are of importance in a financial or industrial sense. It has become a standard habit for the heads of the delegations to meet for dinner and discussion on the occasion of any meeting of the Ten or the Working Party, and a meeting can be called quickly if necessary. The schedule is periodic but not necessarily regular. These people are very high-level officials with sophisticated understanding and with virtually instant access to their principals, who themselves are political leaders in their governments. Certainly, quiet and confidential consultations could take place within this group of delegation chiefs, and both technical and political decisions could be taken. Since a senior Fund official normally attends both the meetings and the dinners, Fund representation would be assured; and since the countries' representatives on the Executive Board of the Fund normally get instructions from the same people who are the deputies, the actual and formal final consultation in the Fund board would have more meaning.

The third, or emergency, approach would be to convene the Ministers and/or Governors of the Ten—hopefully with no public notice. This is possible. A meeting of central bank governors in Frankfurt late in November, 1967 was convened on a Sunday with virtually no publicity. It dealt with a most sensitive subject, the policy of the Gold Pool, and was kept quiet until its conclusion when a communique was issued. The specifics of the Bonn meeting pattern should not be repeated but the basic objectives of the Bonn meeting—real international consultation at a high political and decisionmaking level—should be susceptible of attainment in a better way.

Greater Flexibility Possible Now

The last point for discussion is the suggestion that the Fund follow a more flexible approach to methods for making parity changes in big countries; that this would be more satisfactory and useful than to seek to modify modestly and generalize the modest change within the present fixed parity system.

It has already been stated under premise (c) that the present Articles of Agreement seem sufficiently broad to permit the Fund to pursue a more flexible approach, and the belief that there is no need to amend the Articles. That belief, of course, requires underpinning in a legal sense by an opinion of the Fund's counsel. As expressed here, it rests on the following points.

First, with the possible exception of an automatic crawling-peg system, a crawling-peg approach to parity change is well within both the spirit and letter of the Articles. A crawling peg that is publicly announced as a policy action by a government and expressed in terms of specific amount and with specific timing can be viewed as either a discrete change in parity to be made effective in a series of steps, or a series of discrete changes in parities. In either case the Fund should have no legal or procedural difficulties in approving such an approach if a country requests it.

Second, as a matter of practice the Fund has condoned, without giving formal approval to, or in certain instances has found the legal authority to approve, a whole variety of parity arrangements that can be regarded as conforming to a fixed parity system only in a highly technical sense. In particular, the Fund permitted the Canadian dollar to float, albeit that float was an effectively controlled one, for years. Quite recently, as noted, it condoned a float for the D mark—although that move was a very short-time one. The German float was a fairly free one with minimum market intervention by the Bundesbank. The operation was carried out most successfully and certainly should be regarded as a step toward strengthening the international monetary system.

Third, it does not seem legally possible without amendment of the Articles for the Fund to permit a generalized system of operation within a wider parity band. Whether such a system would be useful or not may be open to question and is not considered here on its merits. But, if the Fund can condone a temporary float as a means of reaching a more viable parity there would seem to be little logic in opposing a wider band for temporary use by a particular country. In practical effect, a wider band would merely be a definitively limited float in one direction. Surely a currency would not be likely to vary widely on both sides of par in a short time period unless the central bank were deliberately avoiding any offset to seasonal forces, or unless market appraisal of the currency fluctuated violently, or unless the underlying economic situation changed radically. In either of the last two instances, the situation which had suggested use of the temporary wider band would require reappraisal. The first case would seem highly unlikely.

There would seem to be little or no reason why the Fund in practice could not condone any of these methods as a means of reaching a more viable fixed parity in the future. And equally, there would seem to be little or no reason to opt for a generalized system of modestly greater flexibility which probably could encompass only one or perhaps two of the above-noted approaches, particularly if that generalized system would require legislative amendment of the Articles. The more flexible approach outlined does not foreclose any of the options.

The point might be carried one step further. If the Fund management is to play a more activist role, there is no reason why it should not suggest methods to a particular country concerned with reaching a new and more viable parity. Particularly if the departure from the formal rules of the Fund is to be relatively short-term, it would seem the course of wisdom to suggest temporary breaching of the letter of the rules, if the alternative is a struggle to maintain a nonviable parity and possible major disturbance to the whole system. This does not mean that Fund management should publicly advocate breaking Fund rules. It does mean that Fund management could give reasonable assurances to a country that temporary breaching of the letter of the rules would not invoke automatically any sanctions, because in practice such violations do not bring retaliatory action anyway.

It is important to stress that the above approach is not an approach geared to expediency alone. The whole thrust of the argument has been that no big country should take unilateral action but that action should come only after full consultation and discussion among its international partners, with the Fund management playing a leading and active role in analysis, consultation, and decision.

If the big countries are agreed on the wisdom of a course of action for one of them, if the country concerned follows a course in good faith and does not attempt to shift an undue portion of the necessary adjustment process to its trading partners, and if it keeps in close consultation with them and the Fund, the procedure and program outlined would be positively useful for the international monetary system. Such a program and procedure should help meet the problems noted with respect to big country parity changes and should help moderate both the frequency and intensity of currency crises.

ECONOMISTS AND PUBLIC POLICY

CHARLS E. WALKER

> . . . *the ideas of economists and political philosophers, both*
> *when they are right and when they are wrong, are more*
> *powerful than is commonly understood. Indeed the world*
> *is ruled by little else.*
> *Practical men, who believe themselves to be quite exempt*
> *from any intellectual influences, are usually the slaves of*
> *some defunct economist.*
> . . . *the power of vested interests is vastly exaggerated com-*
> *pared with the gradual encroachment of ideas. Not, indeed,*
> *immediately, but after a certain interval . . .*
> . . . *soon or late, it is ideas, not vested interests, which are*
> *dangerous for good or evil.*

So Spoke John Maynard Keynes in the concluding paragraphs of his *General Theory* in 1935. Have these observations stood the test of time?

Indeed they have. As we enter the 1970's, the influence of ideas on events, particularly in economic policy, seems even more powerful than when Keynes wrote. And the wide acceptance of Keynesian analysis among policymakers justifies Keynes's optimistic remarks, which were made in response to his own query as to whether the policy actions implicit in the *General Theory* represented anything more than a visionary hope.

If anything, Keynes was overly modest, if not for the 1930's then certainly for the 1960's and 1970's. "Defunct" economists, especially Keynes himself, do indeed influence the actions of "practical" men. But so do the ideas of the hale and hearty. I also believe that the time lag between the inception of ideas and their impact on policy has decreased as the number and influence of economists in Government have grown.

The support for the view that "live" economists are increasingly influential in Government is easy to find. The Council of Economic Advisers may be small in terms of staff and *de minimis* in terms of budget, but it makes up in prestige and clout for what it lacks in numbers. Dangerously close to extinction in 1953, the Council was saved by Gabriel Hauge and Arthur F. Burns. Its stature increased significantly during the first half of the 1960's, when expansive fiscal and monetary policies appropriately moved the economy back close to full employment without inflation.

The role of economists in the Executive departments and in Congress has also expanded greatly. In the Cabinet departments, the influence of economists has grown as more and more policy-level positions have been filled by men with professional economic training or experience. In the Congress, professional economists work on the staffs of the banking, taxation, and Joint Economic committees.

The influence of the Joint Economic Committee deserves special emphasis. Although lacking the power to initiate legislation, the Committee more than makes up for this deficiency by the depth and breadth of its studies.

The beneficial effects are twofold. First, the conclusions of the studies have been very useful in pointing the way to appropriate Federal economic policies. (I am not referring to the Committee's annual comments on the President's *Economic Report,* which unfortunately in recent years have acquired a highly partisan color, but to the careful studies carried out by the Committee's subcommittees and staff, and by outside economists.)

Second, the studies and hearings conducted by the Committee have provided a valuable education process for the Committee members and, through them, for other members of Congress. Several members who had only a smattering of economic knowledge when they joined the Committee have since developed a high degree of sophistication.

The size and quality of the economic staffs of several of the independent agencies, including the Federal Reserve Board, have also been strengthened considerably. I shall have more to say about the importance of the economic function in the Federal Reserve, along with Karl Bopp's contribution to that function, later.

The influence of professional economists in Washington has not been confined to economic policies. The pervasiveness of economists in the Federal establishment assures that the economic aspects of all domestic and foreign policies will be carefully considered. In addition, the methods of the economic analyst have been adopted in handling other problems. In the Kennedy Administration, professional economists applied systems analysis to problems of national security. Later, these techniques, under the leadership of the Bureau of the Budget, spread to other departments. At this writing, the top leadership of the Bureau is dominated by professional economists.

And it should not go without notice that during the first year of the Nixon Administration the top White House staff position was held by

Dr. Arthur F. Burns, an outstanding professional economist and a past president of the American Economic Association.

Clearly, the day of the economist in Government has arrived. The influence of the "living" economist on policy is great indeed.

Thus it is not at all surprising that the time lag between the inception of ideas and their impact on policy has decreased. Keynes laid the modern base for compensatory fiscal policies, including intentional Government deficits, in the *General Theory*. His disciples refined these ideas and instilled them into college students, including men such as John F. Kennedy, in the late 30's and in the 1940's and 50's.

But it was not until 1964, almost thirty years after publication of the *General Theory,* that the United States Congress could bring itself to approve an income tax cut in the face of a Federal deficit—and then only after more than a year of debate.

In contrast, the lag between the rebirth of money supply theory and its impact on policy has been only a decade or so. To be sure, the acceptance of Milton Friedman's basic thesis does not require a flouting of the "Puritan ethic"—the term that Walter Heller applied to the reluctance of the American people to cut taxes in the face of a Federal deficit. It is probably also true that the simplicity of the Friedman theory has its own special appeal to many policymakers.

But the fact remains that in a relatively short period of time a large number of analysts and policymakers have swung to the view that money does indeed matter, and that it matters a great deal more than Keynes and his disciples were willing to admit.

Noteworthy examples of the rapid transmission of ideas into policy can also be found in the international monetary field. A case in point is the willingness of finance ministers, central bankers and international civil servants to discuss, if not yet embrace, the concept of exchange-rate flexibility—at least, greater flexibility than was envisaged at Bretton Woods.

Even more striking is the relatively short period of time from drawing board to adoption of the SDR's. The importance of this step in diminishing the significance of gold in the international monetary system should not be underestimated. One reason for the rapidity of its design and adoption was the fact that the group of deputy finance ministers who designed the SDR were also highly qualified professional economists.

The factors that account for the rising importance of economists in Government—thus helping to free "practical men" from the ideas of "defunct economists"—are manifold and complex. The rising level of economic understanding on the part of both the public and their leaders in Government is undoubtedly one of the more important factors. This is not meant to imply that the goal of widespread economic understanding among the American people has by any means been reached. But progress has been made, and this progress has in turn contributed to the rising influence of economists in Government.

The success of post-World War II economic policies has also reinforced the role of economists in Government and raised their prestige. The recessions of the late 40's and the 1950's were mild and short-lived compared with those of earlier years. The inflation that occurred in those years was not excessive in comparison with the liquidity stored up in financing the war.

Even more important, the success of the "New Economists" in promoting growth without inflation in the first half of the 1960's— resulting in an unprecedented period of economic expansion—convinced many skeptics that the business cycle could indeed be stabilized and that growth without inflation was a real possibility. The disappointments of economic policy during the last half of the decade are, as they should be, recognized by thoughtful men as errors of politics rather than errors of economic analysis.

The Federal Reserve System has played an important institutional role in elevating economists in public policy. This has resulted in part from the Federal Reserve Board's heavy emphasis on high-quality research and a willingness to give largely a free rein to the district Reserve Banks in their research efforts.

It was not always thus. Except for the New York Bank, the research departments of the district Banks in the 20's and 30's were relatively small. Their studies were largely confined to regional economics.

Today things are different. Regional economic matters still receive heavy and appropriate attention in the district Banks. But their expertly staffed research departments now range far and wide; some even go as far as to challenge the very assumptions that underlie the System's monetary policies.

Karl Bopp played a leading role in widening the research activities of the district Banks. Before the end of World War II he was publishing a monthly *Business Review* that not only treated matters of national economic importance (the Philadelphia *Review* was in the select minority that forecasted inflation, not recession, for the post-World War II period), but one with articles that the intelligent layman could enjoy and understand.

These efforts of Karl Bopp and the other district research directors served the cause of economic policy in two ways. The widely read district economic reviews have helped raise the level of economic understanding throughout the country, thus facilitating sound but sometimes unpopular policies, such as the surtax actions in 1968 and 1969. Second, the analytical inputs of the district experts, directly and through their principals on the Federal Open Market Committee, help make for better national economic policies. Gusts of fresh air from the hinterland can be more than a tonic—they help immensely in fighting the parochialism that often prevails both in Washington and on Wall Street.

Karl Bopp has therefore played a meaningful role in reducing the influence of Keynes's mythical "defunct economist" and cutting down the lag between inception of ideas and their use in public economic policy. Although by no means his only contribution to the world in which he has lived (the strength of his personal friendship and loyalty will always be remembered by those, such as myself, who were privileged to study and work with him), I suspect that it might well be the contribution of which he himself is most proud.

For from the start of his career until today Karl Bopp has been a teacher, regardless of the title he has held at any given time. And he knows full well that not all of the teaching takes place in classrooms—when it comes to economic policy, much of it of necessity occurs in the very halls where such policies are made.

CENTRAL BANK LEADERS AND CENTRAL BANK CREDIBILITY

C. R. WHITTLESEY

A NOTABLE FEATURE of central banking in the twentieth century has been the extent to which the current scene, here and abroad, has been dominated by a few outstanding personalities. Norman in England, Schacht in Germany, Strong, Eccles, and Martin in this country—all of these were giants in their time. The influence of the personal element in the early history of the Federal Reserve was commented upon by Karl Bopp in his *Agencies of Federal Reserve Policy*. One wishes that after more than a quarter century of viewing central banking from within, much of the time from a lofty seat among the policymakers, he would tell us what his evaluation now is of the role of the individual in policymaking. Would he conclude as he did then that "rivalry, jealousy, etc. may be more important in conditioning policy than are matters of high principle"?[1]

Whatever human frailties may exist at those levels or elsewhere, there has been a succession of outstanding figures among central bankers. Is it to be conjectured that they have influenced the course of central banking development to a degree corresponding to their contemporary prominence? Or might central banking have progressed in much the way that it did if they had been men of milder stamp? Influential as these men were for varying periods of time, how lasting has been their influence? Of significant changes that have taken place in the art of central banking, what proportion can be traced to them? Did great leaders make for great events or is the reverse nearer the truth, namely, that great events tended to make the leaders great?

Background of Central Bank Leaders

There is another line of questioning, different from the first but not unrelated to it. It has to do with the sources of the exceptional

---

[1] Karl R. Bopp, "Agencies of Federal Reserve Policy," *The University of Missouri Studies,* a Quarterly of Research, Vol. X, No. 4 (Columbia, Missouri: University of Missouri Press, 1935), p. 80. Insiders have access to much knowledge to which outsiders obviously do not. But it is likewise true that they are bound by constraints from which others are free. The two factors partially offset one another. Considerations of official responsibility, loyalty, and personal propriety can be expected to seal lips in many situations where closeness of association has opened eyes.

power and status held by these few individuals during their terms of office. Why did they overshadow others about them, as well as others who preceded or followed? They were clearly superior in administrative influence whether or not they were of superior talents; from what did their superiority derive? Do similarities of background, personality, or character offer clues as to why they came to hold positions of exceptional authority and influence?

The latter set of questions, bearing as it does on the sources of their power as central bankers, is more easily disposed of than the first, which bears on the durability of their influence. In both cases, however, one must rely more on general impression than on conclusive evidence. Contrary to normal expectation, high academic achievement was not a requirement for high position as a central banker. Honorary degrees were fairly generously distributed among those mentioned but the same cannot be said for earned degrees. Two were college graduates, each with an advanced degree. Another was a dropout and two did not attend college, one because of straitened family finances and the other for just the opposite reason, i.e., to share in managing the family's burgeoning business enterprises.

That all were intelligent is certain; that they were highly intellectual, as we know the term, is not. Nor were their qualifications as economists or experts in their field particularly high. Norman's conception of the role of an economist is said to have been to explain to him why he decided as he did, after a particular action had been taken. Another felt obliged on one occasion to call on a staff economist to identify the terms of the Quantity Theory equation to a Congressional interrogator rather than do it himself.

If outstanding academic accomplishment was not a precondition of success in central banking, the same cannot be said of success in business. All had demonstrated extraordinary ability as businessmen before being chosen as heads of central banks. As an imaginative and vigorous younger man in New York banking circles, Benjamin Strong early came to the attention of the city's financial leaders. Norman had achieved prominence on both sides of the Atlantic as a leading investment banker. Schacht, the man who stabilized the Reichsmark; Eccles, the Mormon banking tycoon; Martin, the boy prodigy as investment banker, head of the New York Stock Exchange, and draftee made colonel in three years—all of them had demonstrated ability in ways that established their prestige in business circles and provided solid credentials in places where those credentials mattered most for appointment to governing posts in central banking. There can be no doubt that past success in business also counted with the public and with political leaders in the weight their opinions subsequently carried. Equally important, in all probability, was the assurance which success of this sort gives the individual himself when it comes to dealing with others.

That they came from families with the right connections was surely no disadvantage. But it is not unreasonable to believe that this did little more than set their steps in promising directions. They had within themselves qualities of mind and personality that furnished the drive to carry them forward, rapidly and far. These qualities included a high degree of self-confidence and self-assertiveness. To say this is not to overlook evidences of introversion and personal doubt which, in the case of Norman at least, sometimes reached pathological proportions. (That such qualms became more acute in later years when his influence was on the decline suggests a sequence of interaction that helps confirm the original hypothesis as to the bearing of self-confidence on effectiveness as central banker.)

Combined with all this was deep devotion to the cause of public service in general and to central banking in particular, a devotion more profound in some than in others but lacking in none. In the case of Norman this attitude fell little short of a religion. In the case of Martin, whose father had been a central banker before him, it was to become a way of life. It is reasonable to suppose that without this devotion neither Norman nor Martin would have remained in central banking as long as he did or been half so effective.

Sources of Influence as Central Bankers

All of the men were conspicuously skillful, each in his own way, in handling other men. Martin in particular became a master in dealing with Presidents and with Congress, though there is little doubt that the time and effort which this required was often extremely burdensome to him. Mere length of time in office can become a source of strength, as the experience of Norman and Martin clearly demonstrated. Situations may come to exist where the Government of the day would hardly dare to dismiss a particular central banker because of the alarm which that might cause among businessmen and the public. This is most likely to be the case, of course, where the official has acquired a reputation for caution and dependability in financial matters, especially if the Government in power is less esteemed for these virtues.[2]

There have been other sources of central banker power aside from those mentioned. During the period of the New Deal and then of World War II, Eccles derived strength from the confidence reposed in him by President Roosevelt. After the Presidency changed, Presidential support declined and so did the influence of Mr. Eccles. Not to be overlooked, also, are the exigencies of problems arising out of depression and war as contributing to the influence exercised by central bankers of the day. This was true of Schacht, Norman, and, notably, Eccles. But war or no war, a man of Eccles's temperament would have tended to dominate the scene of which he was a part.

A central banker who has achieved a reputation for responsible leadership acquires significant personal power just because of that fact. This was unquestionably an important element in the strength of the position held by Mr. Martin on Capitol Hill. It is widely believed to have deterred President Kennedy—who later became a staunch ally of Martin—from replacing Martin early in his Administration. The same consideration contributed to the influence, in their day and respective countries, of Hjalmar Schacht and Montagu Norman. At the same time, it is a factor that could conceivably cause an official to remain on after he had outlived his greatest usefulness.

Behind the influence that derives from past service lies the weight of public opinion. The basis of popular support for Schacht was not the length of his service but his reputation as the man who stabilized the Reichsmark. There is little doubt that Schacht and Hitler held each other in profound disregard. Hitler apparently would have liked to appoint a favorite, a little-known economist named Feder, to head the Reichsbank (risking the opportunity this would give critics to exploit the term "Federgeld" which translates as "feather money"). But Schacht enjoyed enormous prestige in financial circles abroad. His name was certain to contribute to the strength of the mark in foreign exchange markets. And so he and not Feder was placed at the head of the Reichsbank.

Without much question, the respect accorded Benjamin Strong by other central bankers and by students of central banking over the years

---

[2] The same point was made in the popular saying that Chairman Martin was worth $5 billion (or whatever the figure) in gold reserves. On the other hand, at a time when his conservative policies were said to be holding back the stock market, it was likewise said that Martin was costing 50 points on the Dow Jones!

has exceeded that accorded any of the others. The early years of the Federal Reserve System were a period when the prevailing point of view shifted only gradually from the micro-orientation appropriate to a member bank to the macro-orientation consistent with the status of a central bank. That the Governors of the Reserve Banks, who were mainly drawn from the ranks of experienced bankers, should have shared the narrower view is less surprising than that members of the Board, for whom this was not the case, also did so. Strong was one of the first to adopt the wider conception.

While the possible effect of open market operations on credit conditions was early recognized,[3] such operations continued to be thought of as primarily a means of providing income for the Reserve Banks. Strong was the most persistent in advocating the use of open market operations as a policy instrument. He did so initially as an offset to gold imports and later as a means of regulating credit conditions.[4] Either way, it was a repudiation of the narrow, micro point of view.

What we regard as the broader and therefore more truly central banking approach would ultimately have come to prevail in any case. But Strong was the leader in bringing it about. His intimate knowledge of banking and the money market meant that he was familiar with the mechanics of open market operations. Where he was most distinctly ahead of his colleagues and his times, however, was in basing open market policies on the state of the economy without regard to the effect on earnings of the Federal Reserve Banks. Chief opposition, curiously enough, came from A. C. Miller, who, despite his credentials as the most highly qualified professional economist on the Board if not in the System, continued into the late 1920's to urge their use solely as a means of providing earnings for the Banks.

Strong look a leading part in facilitating a return to the international gold standard after World War I. Accordingly, he attempted to respond to gold movements in ways that would make them less disturbing to internal economic conditions in this country. At the time and subsequently, he was criticized for the particular measures which he espoused. The principal objection was that by interfering with adjustment processes his methods impaired the long-run viability of the international gold standard. It was further charged that the

---

[3] Lester V. Chandler, *Benjamin Strong, Central Banker* (Washington: Brookings Institution, 1958), p. 76.

[4] *Ibid.*, pp. 220, 228.

resulting credit expansion contributed to the financial crash of 1929 and events that followed. The criticisms may well be valid. Yet the fact remains that he, more than anyone else, helped to shift the focus of central banking in this country from the point of view of an individual bank to that, not only of the nation, but of the nation within a community of nations.

The ideological orientation of central bankers may be expected to play a part in the position they come to occupy. None of the five men was notably conservative but all would readily be classified as safe. Mr. Eccles is the only one who stood out among contemporary businessmen as a liberal. His right to be regarded as liberal stemmed from his early endorsement of policies for expanding employment and his close association with Franklin D. Roosevelt. He came to the attention of the Roosevelt Administration because of speeches indicating a point of view sympathetic to New Deal philosophy, an attitude which, among successful businessmen of the day, marked him as an anomaly. Following his appointment to the Federal Reserve Board, his personal drives quickly carried him to a position of extraordinary influence. It was a time when the System in general and the New York Federal Reserve Bank in particular were signally lacking in strong leadership. Conditions were ripe for reorientation and rejuvenation of the entire Federal Reserve System. He, the New Deal, and the war and its aftermath all contributed to that end.

That Eccles carried off the role of leader at the highest Governmental levels forcefully and effectively is not to be denied. But that it was the times of crisis that lifted him from a position of relative obscurity is likewise true. Eccles served the System well—as did the System, Eccles. His experience contrasts with that of the other outstanding central bankers, all of whom tended to be identified with relatively conservative causes: Strong, Norman, and Schacht with monetary stabilization in terms of gold, and Martin with the prevention of inflation. Schacht and Norman specifically disavowed responsibility for attempting to combat unemployment.

It must, of course, be remembered that in the earlier period, before the publication of Keynes's *General Theory*, it was easier than it is now to overlook the relief of unemployment as a policy objective. Moreover, prevailing attitudes tend to reflect recent experience. Events of the early years after World War I had dramatized the evils of inflation, as depression was to dramatize the evils of mass unemployment a decade later.[5] Perhaps it would be fair to say that the central bankers were as conservative as it was necessary to be in order to be chosen for the position in the first place and, in the second place, to command that degree of popular trust and respect thereafter that was the precondition of their continuing effectiveness.

Role in International Affairs

It is significant that of the five individuals mentioned as most outstanding during their time of service three are especially noteworthy because of their international interests and activities. Montagu Norman, like Strong, was actively involved in the monetary reconstrution that followed World War I. The leadership of Winston Churchill in bringing about Britain's return to the gold standard was largely based on advice from Norman. Churchill is said to have blamed Norman for the unfortunate economic results that followed, with a resulting rift between the two men.

Norman's internationalism was carried to the extreme of lending Bank of England support, and even pledging its resources, to economic reconstruction abroad. A far cry, this, from the parochialism evident at the same time in the United States where monetary policy was based on the protection of central bank earnings. The objective of Bank of England policy, far from concentrating on the state of the Bank, had reached beyond the state of the economy all the way to the state of national economies abroad. The extension was presumably based on enlightened self-interest: as a trading nation Britain's prosperity was thought to depend upon the recovery of countries that constituted her natural markets. Norman sought "to save Britain by saving the world."[6] But at times indirect benefits to England seemed to take second place in Norman's thinking; he refused to accept mass

---

[5] Concern for stable prices rather than employment is not to be regarded as a dependable index of a central banker's conservatism. It is not only that fashions change with the times, even in central banking. More important is the fact that the priority of objectives varies with changing conditions. In particular, it depends on the degree to which current economic trends deviate from accepted norms. At a time when the price level is rising and employment is relatively full, price stability takes precedence over full employment as a policy objective. At a time when prices are stable and unemployment is rising, on the other hand, employment becomes the prime objective. A better measure of central banker conservatism might be the length of time it takes him to accept a change in conditions and adjust his thinking accordingly. The fact that conservatives tend to be thought of as being more concerned with price stability than full employment may only reflect the fact that for a longer time stable prices have been a recognized aim of central bank policy.

[6] E. R. Wicker, *Federal Reserve Monetary Policy*, 1917-1933 (New York: Random House, 1966), p. 139.

unemployment as his official concern or to admit that depression might be aggravated by the international orientation of his policies.[7]

Hjalmar Schacht was also involved in monetary reconstruction after World War I, though in quite different ways. But for his reputation at home and abroad as the man who finally succeeded in stabilizing the Reichsmark, he would never have been placed at the helm of German financial fortunes and given almost unlimited authority. He claimed to have been responsible for the establishment of the Bank for International Settlements, though that honor is more commonly ascribed to Montagu Norman. Perhaps his principal claim to fame is as the man who shaped exchange control into a major instrument of policy. He is reputed to have found the uses to which it was put highly distasteful; but it was undeniably effective in accomplishing political as well as economic and financial ends. In milder forms exchange control has remained in use in different parts of the world ever since, without significant advance over the techniques which Schacht developed.

Monetary reconstruction and exchange control are essentially special situations, even when the situations become chronic. Of greater continuing interest and importance is central bank cooperation. The beginnings of such cooperation could doubtless be traced to whenever it was that there was another central bank with which to cooperate. The exchange of substantial financial assistance between the Bank of England and the Bank of France throughout the nineteenth century is well-known. Central bank cooperation was commented upon explicitly by Walter Bagehot, R. G. Hawtrey, and others long before it became a commonplace in recent years. Cooperation among the central banks of countries which are allies is a natural concomitant of war finance. In the decade after World War I there was close cooperation between Strong and Norman, as has already been mentioned.

A notable step in the development of central bank cooperation was the establishment of the B.I.S. in 1930. Almost immediately it became a meeting place—a private club—of central bankers. So effectively did it serve this function that central bankers of the belligerent countries continued to meet there, though somewhat less frequently, throughout World War II. Its role, however, is primarily that of a forum for discussion where central bankers meet face to face, rather than a channel through which cooperative undertakings are mainly carried out.

---

[7] *Op. cit.*, pp. 194, 282.

All this is preliminary to saying that the years after World War II were a period of increasing central bank cooperation. Starting at Bretton Woods or before, a host of central bankers and Treasury officials had a share in this development. The name of no individual central banker stands out conspicuously above the others in bringing it about. Thirty or forty years earlier that was not the case.

Concrete manifestations of international central bank cooperation took the form of organizing financial assistance for central banks under pressure, swap agreements, and so-called re-cycling arrangements, to name only the most familiar. These innovations and many others took place in the term of office of Chairman Martin. They may be presumed to have met with his approval. But they are in no way identified with him personally either as originator or as sponsor. Staff members, officials outside the System, and central bankers abroad had as much to do with their development as he did, or more.

In Martin's case, then, fame as a central banker rests less on activities in the international field than was the case with Strong, Norman, or Schacht. This is not because changes of an international character have been less important than those made earlier; the opposite is quite certainly true. One of the reasons is that, in the United States at least, Treasury officials now have more influence than they once did on international monetary policies, and more, quite probably, than their central banking colleagues. Another reason may be that the entire structure of international financial institutions has become more integrated. We now have a relatively close-knit international financial system. Innovation and development are a normal output of the system and no longer depend to the extent that they once did on the inspiration and initiative of any one person.[8]

Contribution to Internal Organization

Matters of internal structure and organization received little conscious consideration throughout the earlier history of central banking. The Bank of England apart, central banks were typically given their form at the time they were established and from then on simply proceeded to grow. After World War I and even more after World War II, the situation was quite different. Mention has already been made of the changes introduced as part of the sweeping banking reform following the Banking Holiday which, along with suspension of the gold standard, ushered in the New Deal. The intensive re-

---

[8] Measures of centralization introduced in the 1930's probably mean that the head of the New York Bank could never again exert the influence in international affairs that Benjamin Strong did in the 1920's.

examination of the financial structure of Great Britain by the Macmillan and Radcliffe Committees, culminating in famous reports published in 1931 and 1959, had their counterpart in Congressional investigations in the United States under Senator Douglas and Representative Patman, respectively, with publication of their reports in 1950 and 1952.

Strong, Eccles, and Martin each made distinctive contributions to the process of internal reorganization of the Federal Reserve. Strong was involved in what at times resembled power struggles turning on the role which the New York Federal Reserve Bank would play relative to the Board on the one hand and to the remaining Federal Reserve Banks on the other. No one can say how the conflict would have come out if Strong had lived and the depression had not intervened.

A few years later Eccles's influence was decisive in settling the structural issues in favor of greatly increased centralization. Important changes toward that end were embodied in the Banking Act of 1935. And, by force of personality more than of law, Eccles helped to determine that thenceforth the Chairman of the Board of Governors would be the dominant figure not only on the Board but in the System.

Martin succeeded to this central position in 1951, and during his long tenure did much to enhance it. His unique contribution, however, was in the direction not of centralization but of unification. The principal means of bringing this about was through vitalization of the Federal Open Market Committee. Meetings were put on a regular three-week schedule with attendance by the presidents of all twelve Banks, accompanied by a senior economist from each. The result was to provide a forum in which all governors and presidents participated and which at the same time became an avenue for the exchange of information and a channel for influencing policy. Practices were introduced which extended the lines of communications further down within the staff in both Board and Banks. At sessions of the Committee, Martin proved supremely successful in deriving a consensus from among diverse and sometimes divergent points of view.

The results were as noteworthy in terms of morale as of current operating procedure. *Esprit de corps* was enormously strengthened. A sense of participation and of being abreast of what was going on came to prevail throughout the System. All this was accomplished without the necessity of adding an elaborate bureaucratic superstructure. A significant by-product of bringing all parts of the System into the stream of policymaking was to generate an extraordinary degree of respect and personal loyalty for Chairman Martin.

There is something peculiarly fitting in the thought that the most apparent contribution of the more outstanding of the central bankers should have been in the area of internal organization. All of them had been highly successful businessmen, and organization is essentially a management problem. The qualities of a business executive no less than a background of experience in business should, in all logic, provide the expertise required for dealing with it. And that appears to have been the case.

Contributions by Others

To stop at this point would be to leave out of consideration by far the largest number of those who occupy positions at the center of power and influence in the Federal Reserve System.[9] It is pertinent to ask whether persons whose hierarchical position is less high, or whose conduct brings them less into the public eye, may nonetheless exert a greater, and perhaps a most lasting, influence on central banking. These would include staff members who may have originated the innovative ideas for which their chiefs received credit. There can be no doubt that significant contributions to central banking have come from outside the charmed circle at the top. The nature and extent of such contributions are exceedingly difficult to identify in terms of individuals and are likely to remain largely unrecognized.

In the nature of things, unsung heroes are destined to remain unsung. Only within a limited coterie inside the organization are the signal contributions of subordinates likely to be known, even if they exist. In most cases significant advances are the product, first, of evolution and, second, of combined efforts where no individual's contribution stands out markedly from that of others. This is not to disparage the importance of group efforts by staff members or of germinal minds undoubtedly to be counted among them. It is to amplify, rather, what was said earlier to the effect that the prominence of a

---

[9] That nexus was explored briefly a number of years ago in an analysis which undertook to rank the holders of power within the Federal Reserve in order of the influence exerted (C. R. Whittlesey, "Power and Influence in the Federal Reserve System," *Economica*, February 1963). The substance of what was said there may be regarded as still applicable. An insider comment, undoubtedly correct, was that the attempted ranking failed to bring out the great degree to which the influence of the Chairman of the Board of Governors, Mr. Martin, exceeded that of any of the others.

few outstanding central bankers seems traceable more to feats of action than of intellect.

Discussion of the influence of particular individuals on the development of central banking would be incomplete without recognizing the part played by persons outside the circle of central bankers. Without much question the most important influence was that exerted by Walter Bagehot, the author of *Lombard Street*. And Bagehot was never a central banker. Another such case was Ricardo. The influence of Keynes was likewise very great; while membership on the court of the Bank of England made him technically a central banker, that role was entirely secondary to his academic status. In our own times, Milton Friedman must be accorded credit, if that is the correct term, for considerable influence on monetary policy.

Conclusions: The Credibility of Monetary Policy

We arrive in the end at the conclusion that enduring contributions to the art of central banking by the few most outstanding central bankers were hardly proportional to the prominence they occupied during their terms of office. By talents and by training they were far better equipped to apply and to lead than to invent or innovate. But what they undoubtedly did bring to the conduct of central banking was an invaluable element of credibility and conviction. Their presence at the summit of the central banking establishment added immeasurably to a belief that the policies they advocated had merit and would succeed. It was primarily the weight they were able to bring to bear through prestige and personality that made this possible.

To find in the contribution which they made to the credibility of monetary policy the secret of the success of this handful of outstanding central bankers is not to disparage the importance either of monetary policy or of outstanding leadership. For it is in the nature of economic policy in general and of monetary policy in particular that the priceless ingredient of success lies in being believed. The reason why this is so is very simple: *in situations where a conviction prevails that stabilization policies will succeed, market forces are set in motion which assist powerfully to that end. To the extent that doubt as to final success exists, on the other hand, resulting market responses operate to impede and defeat a successful outcome.*

We are left with a crucial question. Can ways be found to establish more securely the credibility of central bank policy? Or must we continue to rely on chance to supply us spontaneously and at the right time with uniquely prestigious central bankers? It is of comfort to be able to say that, in a democracy, times of crisis help to call forth qualities of leadership suited to coping with them, as the history of the American Presidency clearly demonstrates. Nevertheless, a policy of drift fails to commend itself. Rational man must aspire to mastery of his destiny, even in the face of evidence reminding him of its dependence on fortuitous elements.

Two courses of action suggest themselves for lessening our reliance on the emergence of an occasional preeminent leader to bolster the credibility of monetary policy. One is to strengthen the processes whereby capable leadership is developed from within the System. (Progress in that direction may prove to have been Chairman Martin's finest achievement!) The other is to strengthen the tools which central bankers have at their disposal. It may seem presumptuous to suggest adding to Federal Reserve powers at a time when the authorities are under criticism for the manner in which they have exercised the powers they have. But inadequacy is no less a cause of failure than ineptitude. And it may well be that the only route to achieving credibility of stabilization policy and the benefits that would flow therefrom is by assigning to the central authorities—monetary, fiscal, and Presidential—powers so complete as to leave no doubt that announced goals can and will be achieved.

The credibility gap that plagues monetary policy today could be closed, as has been said, by elevating central banking powers to the level of existing goals. Or it could be closed by admitting defeat and lowering aims to the level of existing powers. The worst of all worlds is where goals demanded are kept high while authorities are starved for powers adequate to assure the attainment of those goals; the effect can only be to defeat policy and discredit policymakers. Yet that is the world in which we have lived for, lo, these many years. We have reaped the harvest of such a course in the form of mounting skepticism as to the effectiveness of monetary policy and an insistent belief in the inevitability of inflation, a state of mind that has consistently confounded efforts to stabilize prices while maintaining employment and growth.

To urge the granting of a greater panoply of economic powers is not to favor increased intervention in economic activity by the central authorities. The intended inference, in fact, is just the opposite. The aim should be first and foremost to diminish the credibility gap by fostering the conviction that announced goals will be realized. We can then expect that market responses will be induced that will promote those ends with a minimum of Governmental intervention.

There is an analogy with the enforcement of law and order. The effectiveness of a police force is measured not by the number of arrests that are made but by the encouragement given to the sort of behavior that makes arrest unnecessary. The same holds true, in a free society, of an ideally functioning central bank within a larger structure of stabilization authority.

No lesson stands out more clearly from over a half century of Federal Reserve experience than the importance to the success of stabilization policy of being believed. We have witnessed the sudden crippling effect of fear of devaluation and the long-drawn-out frustration of a belief that inflation is inevitable. For brief periods outstanding leadership, coupled, perhaps, with strong measures to meet the emergency of war or other crisis, has helped to replace doubt with credence. We have seen that we approach the goals of economic stabilization only to the degree that we succeed in establishing the conviction that those goals can and will be achieved.

"Government of laws or of men" takes on whatever meaning it has according to the laws and the men we have in mind. Safeguards designed as protection against the acts of the inexperienced or incompetent when a central bank is in its infancy inhibit the talented when that bank has assumed professional status. The same applies to all other areas of government by agency where power, even autocratic power, is delegated by democratic processes.

The shortcomings of monetary policy are not to be laid solely at the door of central bankers. It is not just they who fail the cause of stabilization. It is, rather, the legislators, and behind the legislators the public, who demand stability but fail to provide the means that would make stability sure. To succeed, monetary policy must be credible, and credibility involves us all.

CENTRAL BANKERS:
THEIR ATTRIBUTES AND DEVELOPMENT

C. C. BALDERSTON

THE FINANCIAL HUSBANDRY of a nation centers in the soundness of its money. The monetary unit pervades the economy so completely that its stability is a matter of daily concern to investors and borrowers alike. It is at the heart of the calculations of businessmen. Hence it influences their willingness to venture by borrowing. Conversely, it affects the willingness of savers to incur the risks of lending.

The wide concern with such matters need not be labored here. Politicians are torn between pressures for public spending and fears about the impact of rising prices upon savings and upon living costs.

In achieving financial husbandry of a high order, a country's central banking plays a key role. But a central bank consists essentially of human beings, hopefully endowed with objectivity, knowledge, skill, and dedication. What are the attributes of a central banker? How may their possessors be found? How may their talents and knowledge be developed? These are the questions treated herein.

The central banker's responsibility is to keep changes in the money supply in tune with the needs of the economy. Since the latter has an ever-changing pace, either up in expansion or down in contraction, its needs fluctuate faster than they can be reflected in current data. The reported data lag the actual transactions. Conversely, the decisionmaking of entrepreneurs, to the extent events leave them free to exercise choice, takes place long before the event in the case of capital investment. Expectations govern decisions to buy or not to buy, to invest or to save, to "go long" or to "stay short." Knowledge of the trend of these expectations is hard to come by. Even if up-to-date news becomes known to a central banker, the sampling is often so small as to mislead.

Then, too, the central banker works within limitations imposed by fiscal policy. The spending of governmental units is superimposed upon private spending and must be taken into account in regulating the pool of credit. The power to spend governmental funds, however, is beyond the reach of the central banker, except as the cost and availability of funds reflect credit restraint. Nor can central bankers influence the taxes levied and the size of the spending above tax receipts for which governments must resort to the capital markets. In short, fiscal policy is beyond the reach of central bankers, but creates the milieu within which they operate.

But central bankers perform functions within that milieu which are vital to the nation's economic well-being. The steady hand of Nicholas Biddle was a beneficent force for good in our own country and the aftermath of his removal by President Jackson from a position of power and influence bears testimony to the value of his service. Whatever his diplomatic shortcomings, he kept, through the Second Bank of the United States, a money climate in which the country could make steady progress.

Or, take the careers of such central bankers as Lord Norman of the Bank of England, as Sir Henry Clay has described it, or of Benjamin Strong of the Federal Reserve Bank of New York, as Professor Lester Chandler has portrayed it. In Italy's crisis of the late 1940's, Einaudi turned raging inflation into relative price stability. Those who have met similar crises in Italy and other countries since that date are a small, little-publicized corps of central bankers who have demonstrated their prowess as problem solvers. Little does the general public know or appreciate the crises that have been avoided by their imaginative devices, supported by faith in the integrity of their colleagues.

It would be premature for me to single out any of the current group of stalwarts for comment. The list of distinguished bank governors is long, indeed. Eventually their struggles, policies employed, successes, and failures will be worthy subjects for competent biographers.

It was as a historian of central banking that I first met Karl Bopp. He had been granted a year's leave-of-absence by the University of Missouri where he was a faculty member and had received his college education. The year was to have been spent in the same sort of intensive study of the Bank of England that he had already made of Hjalmar Schacht, Central Banker, and of the German Reichsbank.

The outbreak of World War II, however, made that period inauspicious for research, and so he returned to the United States just when needed for a 1940 survey desired by the Chairmen of the twelve Federal Reserve Banks. They appointed a committee consisting of Thomas B. McCabe (Philadelphia), Owen D. Young (New York), and General Robert E. Wood (Chicago) to oversee an investigation of the official compensation paid by the Federal Reserve Banks and their branches.

To carry out this mission, a team of Karl R. Bopp, who had a special interest in central banking, William H. Newman, now Samuel Bronfman Professor of democratic business enterprise at Columbia University, and I devoted the summer to visiting all twelve Banks. At each one we met with the board chairman, other directors, the president, and his fellow officers. Our purpose was to describe the duties and responsibilities of each officer, appraise his relative importance to the conduct of the Bank's affairs, and suggest compensation in relation to commercial bank salaries in the area.

In the following year the same team of three was asked to study the problems of executive development in the Federal Reserve System. Again there was a round of summer visiting (and a very pleasant round it was!) to find out how each of the Banks discovered and developed those with the talents needed for their top posts. Although there was some attention to aids to improve selection, the bulk of the inquiry centered in methods of broadening and grooming those who appeared to have potential capacity for officers. A greater stress was laid upon policymaking positions rather than upon the more routine supervision of daily activities.

These two studies, to which Karl Bopp contributed so significantly, led inevitably to the question: What is a central banker, and how do his functions differ from those of a commercial banker? The distinction lies at the heart of the questions posed for us. One obvious difference is that a top commercial banker must be able to "get business." He must have the ideas, contacts, and drive to increase the loans and deposits of his institution. He must withstand the rigors of formal dinner courses and of golf courses where business is to be found. All the while he must understand the essentials of solvency and of running a sound, safe bank. "No loan looks bad at the time it is made," as a late Philadelphia banker used to observe, and so the commercial banker, if prudent, will look to the liquidity of his institution as setting limits to his urge for it to grow in size and in earnings.

Within the limitations of such soundness, that the confidence of depositors and other customers may be preserved, present-day commercial bankers are bursting the traditional bounds of their industry. This new aggressiveness results in extensive competition as distinct from the intensive cultivation of previous markets. As David P. Eastburn stresses in his introduction to *The Federal Reserve on Record,* "Modern society is undergoing a process of rapid and accelerating change." Bankers share the urge to mechanize, computerize, and devise. In addition, they broaden their offerings, partly by innovations like the credit card, and partly by "poaching" on territory that other industries had considered their own. They lease equipment, they share computer time, they service mortgages and sell insurance, they make travel arrangements, they increase their lendable funds by capital debentures, certificates of deposit, and short-term promissory notes. They own and lease offices. Through their foreign branches, they help corporations finance new operations abroad, and in addition tap the Euro-dollar market when funds are scarce at home. By now, hundreds of banks have changed their corporate attire and dressed as one-bank holding companies.

The harder part of the distinction between commercial and central banking is to portray the latter. The function varies from country to country and from time to time. How the function is administered depends upon the economic philosophy, understanding, business sense, and political astuteness of the central banker.

On this point, Professor Newman and I prudently leaned upon Karl Bopp who had studied Schacht in depth and looked, too, at other central banks including the Federal Reserve System. Hence, I quote from the chapter of our 1940 report that dealt with "The Role of the Reserve Banks in a Balanced System."

"The role actually played by the Reserve Banks in the economic structure has varied materially since the establishment of the System and, more particularly, since the depression. For convenience these variations may be grouped under these heads:

    a. The power of monetary instruments—whoever employed them—has fluctuated widely from time to time.

    b. The agencies which control these instruments have changed.

        (1) The power of the Reserve System has decreased relatively as that of other agencies has increased.

        (2) Within the System itself, the power of the Board of Governors has increased relative to that of the Reserve Banks.

    c. The technical services performed by the Reserve Banks have increased greatly.

    d. The provision of leadership in crises continues to be an important function of the System.

"The history of money demonstrates the difficulty which men have to distinguish the permanent from the temporary. In the 1920's only a few skeptics doubted that America had entered a new era of permanent prosperity or that the wise exercise of great monetary powers was responsible in considerable degree for that prosperity. In the 1930's, on the other hand, the pendulum swung to the opposite extreme. The notion of permanent prosperity was replaced by the notion of a matured economy with a large amount of permanent unemployment. At the same time the idea became widespread that monetary policy could not accomplish *anything,* and that it would *never* be able to do so.

"If one adopts the longer view, it appears that monetary powers vary in importance from time to time, but that they are never either omnipotent or impotent. Consequently, whatever their importance may actually be or appear to be at the moment, the provision made for the exercise of monetary powers is never a matter of indifference. . . .

"When the Government determined in the early 1930's to use monetary instruments as an integral part of national policy, it no longer delegated their control exclusively to the Reserve System. In the first place, the Government instructed the Treasury to exercise some of its 'latent' monetary powers actively. For example, when the Government decided to vary the price of gold in 1933, it did not delegate the power to do so to the Reserve System, but retained it in the Treasury. Another illustration is variations in Treasury deposits at the Reserve Banks. Increases in these deposits have precisely the same monetary effect as an open market sale of securities, and decreases have the same effect as a purchase of securities by the Reserve Banks. The added importance of Treasury deposits has resulted from the *much larger variations* during the past seven years than formerly.

"The monetary powers of the Reserve System have been decreased still further because certain powers formerly exercised almost exclusively by the Reserve System have been delegated in part to other agencies. When the Government created new institutions, such as RFC, to deal with specific problems, it allocated both monetary and nonmonetary powers to them without distinction. At the same time, the Reserve System, cautious after the crash of 1929 and feeling that the use of at least some of the unconventional monetary instruments would aggravate rather than relieve the depression, was disinclined to be aggressive to secure control over them. For example, formerly the Reserve Banks were alone among public institutions which extended credit to banks. The Reserve Banks were active during the depression in lending on eligible and acceptable commercial paper or Government securities; but at the outset they were not empowered to extend credit on miscellaneous assets. Other agencies, such as the RFC and the FDIC were created and empowered to extend such credits.

*   *   *   *   *   *   *

"Indeed, the history of the major central banks of the world shows that it would be a mistake to suppose that the recent tendencies which have been described for the Federal Reserve System are permanent. In other countries and in other times, periods of extreme economic disturbance have witnessed similar tendencies to weaken the powers of central banks (e.g., England and France during Napoleonic Wars; France in 1870; England, France, and Germany during and after the War of 1914-1918). But the policies of weak central banks have frequently resulted in financial difficulties, and sooner or later monetary powers have been returned to the banks (e.g., England and France after the Napoleonic Wars; France in 1871; Germany in 1923-1924; England in 1925; France in 1926). This strength continues until the next period of extreme strain (such as the crisis of 1933) when the whole cycle starts anew."

The foregoing recital of the ebb and flow of central bank power and influence ends with World War II. Were Karl Bopp to up-date his narrative, what changes would he stress? Again he would note the destruction and inflationary aftermath of war. Hyperinflations in the defeated countries of Austria, France, Germany, and Italy were followed by the rebuilding of industry with capital supplied by the United States. The recovery was most rapid in the so-called defeated countries of Japan, Germany, and Italy and most sluggish in Britain, a victor.

To cope with all this, central bankers and their cohorts in their respective treasuries devised the International Monetary Fund and its twin, the World Bank. American loans supplied the badly needed capital and bridged the "dollar gap" so that United States exports could pass over and the corresponding export income cross back. The dollar became the leading reserve currency and, with sterling, helped to stretch the stock of gold available for central bank reserves in other countries.

Then came troubles that challenged the ingenuity and courage of central bankers as a group. Countries whose currencies were supposed by speculators to have weakened because of disequilibrium in their respective balance of payments were subjected to raids. Not only did speculators sell short, but these currencies were further hurt by the "leads and lags" of their foreign trade. To offset these speculative fevers, "swaps" were devised as a loss-free method of mutual assistance among developed, industrialized countries (originally referred to as the "ten"). These lines of credit have helped the United States to guard the dollar, but have given other currencies life-giving injections when sick and in crisis. The Canadian dollar, English pound, Italian lira and, more recently, the French franc all bear witness to the efficacy of an injection of adequate liquidity in time.

A central banker of these days has problems both domestic and foreign. He must seek effective support from fiscal policy so that monetary and fiscal policies may be in balance. He must persuade the government of the moment that delay in the making of unpopular decisions damages the country's money. A weakened and faithless currency rots the underpinnings of the economy. But these decisions that are so vital cannot be arrived at by formula or by book, though scientific research helps enormously. Rather, central banking is an art featuring the solving of endless problems both domestic and international.

Its scope and complexity suggest that a central bank should stress the finding and hiring of enough young people with real potential for development. A satisfactory product will not result from an officer-training program if the raw material is deficient. Consequently effective selection at appropriate age levels is an essential first step toward developing a stream of those with the requisite talent and experience for top positions.

But the process needs to be planned to avoid either an under-supply or oversupply at each age level who are thought to have exceptional promise. To have too few would waste the effort and expense of training. To have too many in relation to the job opportunities at higher echelons would cause those who are most aggressive to lose the hope of rapid recognition and larger responsibility. Stagnation would lead to loss of morale and departure of the best prospects.

The team of Bopp, Newman, and myself suggested that a guide to such planning should take the form of a pyramid with the presidency and first vice-presidency at the apex. On the echelon just below them, the board should plan to provide at least two, and perhaps three, officers ready to fill each of the two top posts. At a stage of development just below these, there should be four to six individuals, still younger by five to ten years, who might qualify for the top posts.

At a still younger age level there should be an additional eight to twelve "comers."

To plan such a pyramid of posts to be filled by those who are being watched and developed is a responsibility at the highest administrative level, i.e., the board of directors, because it relates to the long-run organizational strength of the Bank.

Although the team of three did not turn their backs completely upon the efficacy of aptitude testing to discover executive talent, they recommended that a practical selection method would certainly involve group judgment by means of a number of interviews. Those selected for hiring should then be watched closely and their performance judged on a series of jobs. Such an appraisal requires the systematic accumulation of comments by superiors close to the work being done.

On-the-job training is the oldest and most widely used method of executive development. Although it needs to be supplemented by continuing education off-the-job, it can never be eliminated or bypassed.

Positions that may prove to have special training value are those in bank examination and in research and statistics. The former does more than familiarize one with commercial bank operations and problems—it requires an aptitude for meeting and dealing with people in situations that may involve tension. Here, at least, one's judgment can be tested.

Research and statistics develops an understanding of the financial aspects of our complex economy. Not only does it keep the employee intimately acquainted with the ebb and flow of business, but with the myriad of forces that play upon the state of business. Insofar as factual analysis aids in policy decisionmaking, those engaged in research and in the reporting of trends that are significant get an admirable education. They will learn, if they are truly wise, that beyond the inferences to be drawn from factual data there is an area influenced by mass psychology and shifting expectations. In short, they learn the role of judgment in policymaking.

Not only has Karl Bopp been a student, but a practitioner of the art of central banking. First attracted to the field by an intellectual interest, he was drawn into the aforementioned investigation as to how to create a supply of central bankers. Then he himself became an outstanding example of the combination of talents, knowledge, and judgment that is the true central banker.

THE ROLE OF THE DIRECTOR: THE IDEAL AND THE REAL

WILLIS J. WINN

A NOMINATION TO BECOME A DIRECTOR of a Federal Reserve Bank is both flattering and puzzling. No call to public service, of course, is ever to be taken lightly by anyone concerned for the effective functioning of a democracy. And to citizens accustomed to viewing the central banking organization as the very apex of the vast financial structure that undergirds our capitalistic system, an invitation to join the board of a Reserve Bank is a signal honor indeed. That the honor and opportunity of directorship are well-recognized is attested by the generally strong boards that have been the rule at the various Reserve Banks throughout the history of the System.

On closer examination, however, it is hard to escape the conviction that the status of the director falls considerably short of what it ideally might be. Nor is this impression greatly altered by actual experience as a director. It is not that rewards in terms of remuneration, influence, prestige, and even of perspective on what is going on are circumscribed. It is the feeling, rather, that achievement is not always up to potential. The very fact that boards are strong exaggerates the anomaly—with boards of lesser competence, the loss from failure to use their talents fully would not matter so much. The boards have been quite conscious of this situation and have been the leaders in repeated questioning and self-appraisals of their role and function within the System. On more than one occasion such discussions have raised doubts as to the viability of the present organization and structure, and also as to the ability of the System to continue to attract strong leadership at the regional level. But the System survives, new directors join the boards, and the debates continue.

Centralization and the Plight of the Administrator

In all facets of our society, from schools and colleges to highest levels of government, we are witnessing serious questioning of highly centralized structures of organization. The discontent arises from the fact that organizational restraint, stemming from central control that is often inefficient, tends to limit the scope of human behavior. Not infrequently, problems confronting organizational structure are so large and complex that they seem to overwhelm the ability of administrators to solve them.

Even the ablest individuals equipped with all the known technical tools cannot hope to deal perfectly with the manifold complexities confronting centralized structures. The remoteness of central direction adds to the oppressiveness and discontent which breed in this environment. It becomes increasingly difficult to persuade individuals, faced by these complexities, frustrations, and potentialities for misunderstanding and personal abuse to participate as leaders of such organizations.

Increasingly, the need for decentralization is being discussed, in government and business circles, with a view to transferring power to smaller units and relating the decision process to the scale of problems to be solved. It is worth noting that these discussions do not envisage the removal of operating guidelines or centrally formulated general policies, rigorous general standards, or centralized supervision. The discussions do indicate, however, that by gaining the counsel of a greater number of individuals, improving two-way communication, and closer personal contact throughout the organization, institutions may become far more viable in our society by becoming more sensitive to the needs of their clientele and more efficient and effective in carrying out their mission.

The Federal Reserve System, unfortunately, is not immune to organizational pains and pressures. No high marks will be given the central bank simply on the basis of its mystique. If such marks are to be accorded they will have to be earned, and to be able to earn them the Federal Reserve System will have to strive continuously to develop the most effective organization possible. Among the major components of any such organization will be the boards of directors of the local Federal Reserve Banks. Directors can play a genuinely vital role only if they are permitted to reach their full potential within the System. Such a role, of course, will carry great responsibilities and challenges.

The Director in the Table of Organization

The Federal Reserve System has been criticized as outdated, archaic, and obsolete from the standpoint of its organizational structure. Nevertheless, with its division of powers among the Board of Governors, the Federal Reserve Banks, and various committees and councils, it may represent a possible forerunner of things to come in more and more business and governmental organizations. Far from perfect in theory and in fact, the organization of the System does contain a number of features sought in the further democratization of both governmental and business activities. Many of these features presently exist, however, only on paper, and the full potential of others remains to be fulfilled.

Banking legislation in 1935, which substantially cut the powers of the boards of directors of Reserve Banks, officially recognized and sanctioned the trend toward centralized control over the nation's central banking system. The trend which existed then continues today. It can be argued that much of the elaborate organization and ritual that has been maintained in the System is, in fact, a facade.

In view of the trend toward centralized control in the System, some observers have suggested that the district Banks should be operated solely as service facilities to clear checks and to provide currency and coin for community needs. Such a suggestion would signify abandonment of the remaining feature which has provided the real strength of the System, namely, the sharing of responsibilities for both policy and operations between the Board of Governors and the staffs of the Federal Reserve Banks. This elaborate check-and-balance organization with its procedures for joint decisionmaking has at times been as frustrating to the Chairman of the Board of Governors as it has been to a member of the board of directors of a Federal Reserve Bank. Nonetheless, it probably represents a unique source of strength for the System. Under greater centralized control within the Federal Reserve, the check-and-balance system would tend to disappear and mistakes, which are inevitable under any structure, could be that much bigger. This price could be too high even if the System organization were to become less costly to operate.

The challenge to the System is to make its still relatively decentralized structure function as effectively as is administratively possible. This does not necessarily involve any extensive transfer of power within the System from the Board of Governors to the Reserve Banks or vice versa, but it does call for a conscious effort by each part of the System to carry its full share of the burden while permitting other segments to carry their share.

Only in an appropriately decentralized organization can directors maximize their distinctive contributions to the System. Unlike all other officials within the System, directors of the Reserve Banks have no vested interest in their positions—in any sense of the term. Moreover, they are serving in the public interest to make whatever contributions they can to the effective functioning of our nation's monetary system. It is the obligation of the directors to make the System function as effectively as possible within the guidelines provided by Congress and the Board of Governors, or to get the guidelines changed if this would result in a more efficient monetary system. In fact, they are under obligation to seek changes in the System, as drastic as the possible elimination of the present role of the Federal Reserve Banks, if they feel that such changes would contribute to the better achievement of the nation's monetary goals. The director's place in the organizational structure is that of an independent monitor, counselor, advisor, interpreter—yes, even critic of their place as a regional component in the organizational structure of the Federal Reserve System.

Selection of Directors

The procedures for nomination, election or appointment, and rotation, as well as the personal qualifications of the directors of the Federal Reserve Banks, have been carefully spelled out both in statute and in regulations of the Board of Governors. In practice, these particulars are far more detailed than any description of or statement concerning the duties and functions of a director. The rigid selection process makes it impossible for any group to seize control or to dominate the policies of a Federal Reserve Bank. In addition, they are designed to accomplish certain purposes. Commercial banks which are members of the System elect six directors and the Board of Governors appoints three. Each bank has one vote irrespective of the number of shares it owns, and the member banks in each district are divided into three groups based on asset size. Each group selects two directors— one to represent the member banks on the board and one who is actively engaged in business in the District to represent the interest of business, agriculture, and commerce.

Member bank representatives (Class A directors) have responsibilities for communicating with their constituency. This is normally achieved simply by the selection of officers or directors of a member bank and assumes that in the course of their activities they will be engaged in two-way communication with their constituency. From the communication standpoint alone, it is essential that Class A directorships be filled by active leaders of the banking community. The directorates should not be used as a *pro forma* or honorific post for those who have the time to undertake public service or who are no longer in the mainstream of the operations of their own institutions. A Class B director, elected to represent the business interests of each member banking group, has the responsibility of sharing his expertise and knowledge with officials of the Federal Reserve Bank, but is in no way obligated to report back to the business community. The member banks, the banking system, and the business community are weakened by this gap in the communication feedback system. Class B directors are not selected from any particular size category nor are they necessarily even customers of any bank in the groups they are presumed to represent. Consequently, the size of the businesses represented by Class B directors is not so well-balanced as the member bank representation.

Both Class A and Class B directors are elected for a three-year term, but the latter may be reelected for a second term while the former may not. Each year one A and one B director must stand for election.

The three C directors who are appointed by the Board of Governors to represent the public interest cannot have any affiliation with a commercial bank. There are no other restrictions on them except a requirement of residency within the district and the general prohibition, applicable to all directors, against anyone holding political or public office or holding a major committee post in one of the political parties. In practice, a majority of the C directors have been businessmen. While this may have strengthened the information-gathering network of the System with respect to business developments, it is by no means clear that a somewhat broader representation of the public might not improve the overall information flow into the System and back into the community at large. In the Third District, a conscious effort has been made to assure geographical representation in all three groups of directors.

In spite of the very elaborate structuring of representation on the boards, all members operate as public members, in fact if not in theory. Promoting the general welfare of our society is the predominant objective of both policy and operational deliberations, and an unacquainted observer at the meetings of the board would be hard put to identify the particular constituency of individual directors from the discussion or voting records.

Existing procedures for selection of directors may, in fact, provide an inadequate representation of the banking and financial community on the boards. With only one representative permitted from the large banks and with little or no representation from other large financial institutions, absenteeism or limited knowledge can seriously restrict the informational input of directors in an area of primary concern to the Reserve Banks. Accordingly, provisions designed to avoid any undue influence by a particular group may, in practice, be an obstacle to the more effective functioning of the System.

The rigid tenure restrictions applicable to directors have merit for a number of reasons. For example, the more people who become involved in a responsible way with the Bank and the System, the greater the informational inflow to the System and the larger the number of semi-official representatives of the System in the community. But the tenure restrictions have major disadvantages as well. Limited terms keep the System from tapping most effectively the considerable talent represented on the boards. It takes time for any new director to become familiar with the personnel, operating practices, and problems of the organization. Moreover, time is also essential in order for people to become sufficiently acquainted with one another to work most effectively together and to develop an *esprit de corps* and an operating style. And because of complicated jurisdictional relationships and divided responsibilities between the Board of Governors and the individual Reserve Banks, it takes time for the directors to gain an understanding of their zone of action and to develop into an efficient and effective part of the System structure.

Finally, if the Banks are to attract to directorates the top leadership of the community, the directors must be given the maximum opportunity to use their talents. It is not clear that this objective is achieved if turnover is so rapid that the potential contributions of any board member are never fully tapped. On the other hand, the dangers inherent in relatively permanent boards which have become sterile provide all too pointed examples of the desirability of reasonably limited tenure. Whether present tenure rules are the proper ones is an open question.

Role of Directors

Every job or position has its rewards as well as its burdens and obligations, and a directorship of a Federal Reserve Bank is no exception. Directors who have served with the man who is being honored in this volume are quick to realize that their rewards are manifold and far exceed any obligation they may have incurred. Great teaching is a rare talent; thanks to Karl Bopp, every board meeting at the Philadelphia Reserve Bank became a rich learning experience for the directors and staff that was both exciting and real. The directors' understanding of central banking and economic analysis grew at each meeting, and their admiration for a warm, sensitive, human being whose every breath conveyed a concern for principle and truth, knows no bounds. While the classroom performance of the students may not have merited a Phi Beta Kappa designation, the shape of the learning curve was very real and will remain a prized possession of the group.

At the same time, a directorship does entail its frustrations. Ninety-five per cent of the personnel of the Reserve Bank are engaged in operational activities relating to the flow and storage of money and credit, with only 5 per cent or less concerned with issues of monetary and credit policy. Quite properly, deliberations of the Board of Governors fall into, roughly, the reverse proportions; yet in one sense, the board of directors has almost been divorced from the determination of monetary policy. With the heavy reliance on open market operations as a policy tool, the role of the local Federal Reserve Bank, and more particularly the role of the director, was substantially reduced. While all presidents of the Reserve Banks participate in deliberations of the Federal Open Market Committee, they participate as individuals and are not bound by instructions from their boards of directors. Moreover, they have no obligation to report on these deliberations to their boards. This gap in the flow of information makes some of the advice and guidance offered by directors on policy questions less useful than it might be. In view of the number of individuals currently privy to the deliberations of the Federal Open Market Committee, and in view of the leaks which have occurred within this group, one cannot but wonder if the added secrecy which the present policy affords is worth the sacrifice in terms of directors' morale and in the effectiveness and quality of their advice on policy issues. While board opinions undoubtedly influence the views of the presidents, it is recognized that board reactions are by no means unanimous and the president clearly has the right to his independent judgment. It is the information loop—input into the System from the board and the feedback to the board—which is missing.

Directors do participate in the discussions concerning discount-rate policy. In this role, directors make a unique contribution by presenting information regarding sectors of the economy with which they are familiar. Directors have a feeling for developments in their particular areas of competence, and they can often report those developments to bank officials before statistical evidence becomes available. Their collective input on underlying conditions and attitudes is by no means confined to questions related to the discount rate; it influences all monetary policy deliberations.

The importance of the directors' activities regarding the discount rate is often questioned. Although by law directors establish the discount rate at least every 14 days, any action regarding rates is subject to approval by the Board of Governors. Moreover, relatively little use is presently being made of the discount window by the member banks.

So it is difficult to make discount policies the major contribution of a director. Even if the System should modify the discount rules to encourage greater use of the window by member banks, it is by no means certain that the role of the director in this area would increase materially. It is nevertheless important to recognize the positive contribution that the director makes through his discussion of discount-rate policy, and that the directors' influence on the monetary policy is broader than this. For example, the directors may help in the evaluation of the weights to be assigned to different social or monetary goals at various stages in the political-economic cycle. It is recognized that many of these goals may be in conflict at any particular time. Society clearly needs all that the best minds available have to offer, not only in the resolution of these conflicts but also on the establishment of appropriate priorities.

All too often monetary policy issues focus too simplistic an objective. For example, much of the discussion of the goals of monetary policy treats full employment as an alternative to price stability. The possible conflict between the two goals under certain economic circumstances is recognized, but to accept this conflict as inevitable is to assume the availability of only limited solutions to the problem. The directors can influence policy and issues by asking for a thorough reexamination of underlying assumptions and by pointing up new policy tools both within and without the System to resolve such conflicts. The influence of a single director on policy decisions is miniscule; but the cumulative impact of the opinions of 108 directors of the 12 Reserve Banks can be a significant element in the decision process.

In the operating area, too, it is essential to recognize that freedom of action of each Bank is circumscribed because it is part of a larger System. In spite of each board's lack of autonomy, the directors can nonetheless exert considerable influence on operations. Moreover, these contributions may have real impact not only upon the individual Bank but also upon a wide range of institutions.

Directors play an important role by providing advice and guidance on the internal operations of the Bank. They bring a wide range of expertise and experience to considerations concerning labor relations, salary administration, financing policies, public relations, building maintenance, audit policies, and long-range planning for physical facility needs, to mention only a few. Because officers of Federal Reserve Banks are not permitted to hold outside directorships, Bank management may tend to lose touch with latest management techniques developed in the corporate world. The board of directors assures a considerable degree of protection against the development of institutional insularity by providing a link with the procedures, practices, and policies of other corporate institutions. This role is important not only in terms of the operations of the Reserve Bank; it is highly relevant also in terms of the role the Reserve Bank and its staff can play in improving the operational efficiency of member banks. The same applies to other financial institutions falling within its sphere of influence.

Primary responsibility for selection of bank management rests with the board of directors, and the achievements and success of the leadership exercised by officers depends in part upon the support and guidance they receive from the board. Restraints imposed by the necessity for the Bank officers to operate within restraints and rules of a larger System can be as frustrating as is realization that the director's role is not to direct in the traditional sense of the term. But a strong board of directors can provide the guidance and the balance which will channel these frustrations into useful influences both within and without the System. If the Reserve Banks are to play a constructive and innovative role within the region, and at the same time are to influence the formulation and execution of policy on both the national and international level, top caliber talent is a prerequisite.

As essential as the role of directors in management succession may be, the majority of directors serve out their terms without participation in this process, inasmuch as the turnover in top personnel in the Bank is so low. Even though periodic reviews of personnel planning are conducted by the board, this is hardly a *raison d'être* for a board. Thus the ability to attract strong board members must rest upon a considerably broader base than this.

All components of the System can profit greatly from the challenges and demands continually advanced by an active and imaginative board which not only reacts to the problems placed before it, but is constantly pushing and probing on its own initiative on all fronts.

The Challenge to Directors

Despite their restricted role within the organization of the Federal Reserve System, directors have challenging opportunities to make positive contributions to the System and, thus, to society.

In the operating areas, directors have great opportunities to exercise more initiative than they have evidenced in the past. For example, our understanding of the monetary system and its impact on the economy is far from complete. Under the leadership of their directors, staffs of individual Reserve Banks should be encouraged to attack particular segments of the unknown for concentrated study, e.g., consumer and corporate behavior, organizational structure, regionalism, institutional flows, and money substitutes. Such efforts would not only help to strengthen the research thrust of the Bank and the System in these areas; they also would make it easier to attract top personnel to the staffs and provide new and important bridges to many external interfaces between the Reserve Banks and the community. Innovations in Reserve Bank operations and management techniques can provide important means for establishing better communications and contacts with the banking and business community.

Directors are faced with challenges in the policy area—among them, the effectiveness of voluntary restraints. This challenge is more than just an informational function, important as that may be; it touches on the basic philosophy of *volunteerism* (to coin a clumsy term), i.e., obedience to verbal appeals to follow generally prescribed courses of action in pursuit of desired social and economic goals. There is evidence that wide variations exist in the degree of restraint exercised as a result of such appeals. Among possible causes of the inadequacies of volunteerism is insufficient knowledge, a difference of opinion on the relevance or the accuracy of the underlying conditions leading to these verbal appeals, a simple unwillingness to cooperate, or a cynical evaluation of the rewards from deliberate flouting of the request. The question arises as to what penalties, tangible or otherwise, should be applied when problems arise from failure to cooperate for whatever reason. Can the directors play a role in this milieu, or is volunteerism suspect and inherently weak as an appropriate policy tool?

Congress has the power stemming from the Constitution to issue money and regulate the value thereof. To transfer this power to private interests without adequate regulation or supervision is highly questionable, but abhorrence of centralized control has led to the development of a monetary mechanism which at best is an anachronism. Here again, directors are challenged to reexamine the structure and functioning of the monetary system from their particular vantage point, and to stimulate discussion regarding both strengths and weaknesses. The possible expansion of the type of institution permitted to issue demand deposits, the fragmented coverage of regulatory agencies of the monetizing institutions engaged in the process, and the ability of private institutions to change the structure of the Federal Reserve System more or less at will—all these pose very real problems of both equity and efficiency. Directors can take the initiative in expanding public understanding of the issues involved and in warning of the problems inherent in these conditions. While history provides little evidence of basic changes in our banking structure short of a major crisis, the latter may be closer than we realize. But it is to be hoped that greater public understanding of both issues and problems can provide a corrective mechanism short of the crisis stage.

Perhaps the greatest challenge to directors is to appraise the organization and operation of the Federal Reserve Banks within the context of the Federal Reserve System in order to assure that both attain their realistic potential. By word and deed, directors must play a major role in this appraisal. If they are content merely to follow the traditional ritual of board meetings developed through fifty years' experience, to exercise little or no initiative and to be passive in their actions, the role of a director will be little more than a walk-on part at best. But if they use their wisdom and experience to invigorate the System, they may serve as a critical catalytic agent in multiplying the effectiveness of the System and in demonstrating the strengths of a decentralized organization. Moreover, this can occur without any change in the responsibility, power, rights, or prerogatives of other components of the System.

THE FEDERAL RESERVE AS
A LIVING INSTITUTION:
A PRESCRIPTION FOR THE FUTURE

DAVID P. EASTBURN

To One Who Has been part of an organization for any length of time, observing and sharing its successes and failures, its manic and depressive moods, its victories and defeats, a question of enduring fascination is what keeps the thing alive and well. What are the ingredients of a living institution?

The Federal Reserve is now well into its second half century. It is a mere adolescent compared with the Bank of England, but has been around considerably longer than most central banks. In this time it has established a record and developed a personality which I propose to examine here—rather impressionistically, and, of course, non-objectively—as a sort of case example of a living institution.

In search of guidance, one tends to look for a general theory of the rise and fall of institutions. Many writers, in fact, have touched on various aspects of the problem. Bernstein has detected a kind of life cycle in regulatory commissions in the United States.[1] Kenneth Boulding has distinguished three ages of an institution, with varying effects upon what he calls its legitimacy.[2] John Gardner has offered much inspirational insight on self-renewal.[3] C. Northcote Parkinson has analyzed the decline of organizations, a phenomenon which he attrib-

---

[1] According to his analysis, the typical progression is from gestation, a phase stimulated by public pressure for reform; to youth, a chaotic period of conflict and enthusiasm; to maturity, a stage of high professionalism with policies and procedures well-established and adhered to; and finally to old age, a condition of passive conservatism and inefficiency. Marver H. Bernstein, *Regulating Business by Independent Commission* (Princeton: Princeton University Press, 1955), pp. 74-102.

[2] He points out that institutions build up legitimacy "just by sticking around," but that the function may be non-linear. "When things are new, they have the special legitimacy of babies, young people, or the new fashion. At a certain point they become middle-aged or old-fashioned and legitimacy declines sharply. Then as time goes on further they become antiques and legitimacy increases once again." Kenneth E. Boulding, "The Legitimacy of Central Banks," *Fundamental Reappraisal of the Discount Mechanism* (Washington, D. C.: Board of Governors of the Federal Reserve System, July 1969), pp. 4-5.

[3] John W. Gardner, *Self-Renewal: the Individual and the Innovative Society* (New York: Harper & Row, 1963).

utes to a disease—"injelititis."[4] These observations are helpful but, as far as I am aware, the definitive work on growth and decline of organizations remains to be written.

Observation of the Federal Reserve System leads me to believe that three factors go far to explain its past and, more importantly, could have a profound influence on its future. These are: (1) the values it holds; (2) the professionalism of its personnel; and (3) the nature of the decisionmaking process.

Values

Proposition 1: **The Federal Reserve System will be strong and effective in the long run to the extent that the values which govern its actions are in accord with the values held by the society which it serves.**

Although the concept of values often carries with it ethical connotations, and although moral purpose may be essential to the strength of an organization,[5] it is not necessary for my thesis to go this route. By values I have in mind simply the ". . . norms or principles which people apply in decision-making, that is, the criteria they use in choosing which of alternative courses of action to follow . . . ."[6]

In a very broad sense, however, the *basic* value, or criterion, governing decisions of Federal Reserve authorities *does* have strong

---

[4] This is "the disease of induced inferiority" caused by the fusing of incompetence and jealousy to produce a new substance, "injelitance." An infected individual can spread the disease to an entire organization, systematically eliminating all people of ability. The first phase of the disease is characterized by a too-low standard of achievement; the second by smugness as these aims are achieved; and the third by apathy. Cases of recovery are rare, but occasionally an organization recovers because some individuals have developed a natural immunity. "They conceal their ability under a mask of imbecile good humor. The result is that the operatives assigned to the task of ability-elimination fail (through stupidity) to recognize ability when they see it. An individual of merit penetrates the outer defenses and begins to make his way toward the top. He wanders on, babbling about golf and giggling feebly, losing documents and forgetting names, and looking just like everyone else. Only when he has reached high rank does he suddenly throw off the mask and appear like the demon king among a crowd of pantomime fairies. With shrill screams of dismay the high executives find ability right there in the midst of them. It is too late by then to do anything about it. The damage has been done, the disease is in retreat, and full recovery is possible over the next ten years." C. Northcote Parkinson, *Parkinson's Law* (Boston: Houghton Mifflin Co., 1957), p. 82.

[5] Chester Barnard, in his classic study of the functions of the executive, for example, maintains that: "Organizations endure, . . . in proportion to the breadth of the morality by which they are governed. This is only to say that foresight, long purposes, high ideals, are the basis for the persistence of coöperation." Chester I. Barnard, *The Functions of the Executive* (Cambridge, Mass.: Harvard University Press, 1958), p. 282.

[6] Philip E. Jacob, "Values Measured for Local Leadership," *Wharton Quarterly*, Vol. III, No. 4 (Summer 1969), p. 31.

ethical connotations. The fundamental mission of the Fed is to promote the fullest sustained realization of the nation's economic potential. A similar goal, of course, is held by most individuals in American society. For better or worse, the typical American spends a great proportion of his working and "leisure" hours striving to "make it"— trying to put his talents and resources to the best possible use as he sees it. The fact that the Fed's objective is in close conformity with a basic value also held by society lends great strength to the Federal Reserve's position in society—its legitimacy, as Boulding would say.

A critical question for the future, however, is whether this materialistic view of human endeavor will continue to apply. From the time of the Greeks, philosophers have held out as the highest achievement of Man his self-realization, the fullest development of his potential. Even in this context, the Fed's basic value is in general conformity to society's; but, as and if society changes—perhaps as and if the "new generation" carries its less materialistic view of life with it into later years—it is possible that the relationship will become less strong.

This raises an obvious corollary to Proposition 1: namely, that **the Federal Reserve's values must change as society's values change.**

Barnard has made the point that an organization disintegrates if it fails to achieve its purposes; but it destroys itself if it does achieve them.[7] What it must do is constantly seek new goals. These, in the case of the Federal Reserve, should be new goals which society is seeking.

In the past, the Federal Reserve System has succeeded, and succeeded remarkably well in view of the narrow charge given it by Congress, in updating its objectives. Indeed, had the Fed been content with a literal interpretation of its original assignment to provide an elastic currency, etc., it would not be important enough to bother about today. Response to changing needs may not always have been as prompt, full, and voluntary as everyone might like, new objectives may not always have been achieved effectively, but on the whole I do believe the Fed has renewed itself over the years by broadening its objectives and values.

Two questions, however, arise about the future. One I have already suggested: if the public at large is shifting its emphasis from materialistic-economic concerns to humanistic-social concerns, how will the Fed respond? It is dangerous, of course, to extrapolate a short-run movement into a long-run trend, but it is clear that some such shift has

---

[7] *Op. cit.,* p. 91.

been in the making. The legitimacy of the Federal Reserve System may well hinge importantly on how its officials react.

Economic policies carried out by the Federal Reserve will have very great social impacts as they always have. Decisions in trading off unemployment against price increases do not simply involve statistics expressed in a Phillips curve, but impacts on human lives. The social costs of unemployment among Negro teenagers, for example, must be weighed against those of inflation for pensioners. Federal Reserve authorities know this—they are not bloodless computers—but they may have to give more consideration to this kind of calculation in the future than in the past. Moreover, the Fed traditionally has resisted pressures to deal with specific problems in specific parts of the economy. Would it be wise, for example, to devise some way of channeling Federal Reserve funds into the ghetto? The role which the Fed is to play in our society in the future may well depend on responses to and anticipation of pressures like this.

A second question for the future flows from this thought: how much weight will the Federal Reserve give to the value of freedom in trying to achieve new objectives? The very creation of the Federal Reserve System was an act of intervention, a departure from *laissez-faire* resisted by conservative elements at the time. Nevertheless, the philosophy under which the System has operated for the most part since has stressed freedom of the market place, and the tradition of minimum intervention in markets served the Fed well for many years.

Freedom, however, must be put in a relative context, relative to other values. This, in fact, is what society has been doing, especially since the 1930's. Society has tolerated, indeed demanded, increasing intervention by public authorities in markets in order to get greater security, justice, and other values. There is no evidence to indicate that this trend will not continue.

In this environment the Fed will find itself facing a dilemma: its stated philosophy is noninterventionist; its practice is increasingly interventionist. A review of history indicates that Federal Reserve authorities almost invariably resort to unorthodox "gimmicks" when crises arise and pressures become intense.[8] This behavior might be excused as necessary in rare and difficult circumstances, but I would

---

[8] Some of these devices include "direct action" in the late 1920's, margin requirements, moral suasion, Regulations W and X. "Operation Twist," the September 1, 1966, letter from the Federal Reserve to member banks. David P. Eastburn, "Uneven Impacts of Monetary Policy: What to Do About Them?" *Business Review* (Federal Reserve Bank of Philadelphia, January 1967), p. 21.

guess that the Fed will be confronted more often, not just in crises, with the need to innovate *via* special types of controls. Banks, much more innovative than ever before anyway, have been further stimulated by Regulation Q to explore new sources of funds. As the Fed, attempting to restrain the expansion of money and credit, closes one loophole after another, banks promptly discover new ones.

What to do about this schizophrenia? If my prediction is correct, the Federal Reserve will have to reconsider its philosophy of non-intervention in markets. This, I believe, would bring philosophy into conformity with practice and make possible a rational and consistent approach to regulation rather than one of *ad hoc* loophole plugging. And it would bring philosophy more nearly into the mainstream of what society now wants. The public demands an increasingly high performance of the economy and of public policymakers responsible for the economy. It is less tolerant of unemployment and alert to the slightest tendency toward recession. At the same time, it is increasingly concerned about inflation. It is more interested in how things are distributed—unemployment among disadvantaged groups, tax avoidance by the wealthy, the impact of tight money on housing.

All of this has greatly reduced margins of error for policymakers. Their response has been to try to "fine tune" the economy, not only by making small changes as promptly as possible to influence overall aggregates, but by dealing in specific ways with specific parts of the economy. The public at large has no interest in fine tuning *per se,* but the influence of its many growing and conflicting demands—and this, I believe, is an irreversible influence—is to force policymakers to fine tune.

Many experts believe that fine tuning is beyond our capability, and certainly much of the 1960's provides ample evidence to support this view. Therefore, they maintain attention should be directed to making markets more efficient by removing impediments to competition. For example, rather than imposing a ceiling on interest rates on time and savings deposits and devising special techniques for channeling funds into mortgage markets, efforts should be devoted to removing usury ceilings, liberalizing restrictions on competition among various kinds of institutions in various kinds of markets, and the like.

What economist, brought up in the competitive tradition, could argue against such a course? The only problem is that the likelihood of success is low. Vested interests are so entrenched that results are bound to be slow and incomplete. Much as we all would like markets to be free (at least in the abstract), the likelihood is that many serious impediments will remain. Meanwhile, the public continues to exert pressure which forces policymakers to fine tune.

It may be that public officials, including those at the Federal Reserve, cannot deliver what the public wants. Attempts to intervene in markets, efforts to fine tune, may fail because of human frailty. Perhaps the only evidence that can be brought to bear on this is history. I believe history shows that public policy can perform and has performed at ever-higher levels of competency. There is no reason to believe we have reached the ultimate. Today's fine tuning becomes tomorrow's orthodoxy.

The public, of course, should be made aware of the limited state of the art at any given time so that it does not demand the utterly impossible. This thought suggests a second corollary to Proposition 1: **the Federal Reserve's values should be clearly made known to and understood by society.**

Some kinds of institutions, like the church, may thrive for centuries on values which their constituents are asked to accept on faith. For most institutions, however, mystique, charisma, and ritual, although powerful forces for legitimacy over a short period, prove to be weak reeds in the end.[9] Federal Reserve authorities undoubtedly have yielded to the temptation to lean on them many times in the past, but chances of getting away with this are fast disappearing, if not already gone. The public is too sophisticated.

As the Fed confronts its sophisticated constituents, it may well find the going easier in some respects, more difficult in others. Up to a point, a more knowledgeable public should be more sympathetic with what the Federal Reserve is trying to do. Inflation is a good example. Proposition 1 should not be interpreted to mean that Federal Reserve authorities should supinely adopt inflation as an objective simply because society is ill-informed about its evils. The Fed must try to influence society's choice of values as well as adapt to them. The problem of overcoming inflation should be easier as the public becomes increasingly sophisticated.

In some respects, however, the Fed may find communications more difficult. It may not be so hard to enunciate and gain society's accept-

---

[9] Boulding suggests that legitimacy of central banks might be fostered ". . . by preserving a certain air of charismatic obscurity about their operations. Their officers might even take to wearing gowns and robes and their public pronouncements might be couched in even more mysterious and impressive language than they now use." *Op. cit.,* p. 20. He suggests, however, that in the long run an important source of legitimacy is payoff; an institution must provide good terms of trade with those who are related to it. (p. 3)

ance of the *basic* values governing the Fed's policies, but at a more technical level the criteria for action will be hard to explain and sell. Nor are prospects for success enhanced by history. The Federal Reserve all too frequently has tended to devise simplistic rationales for policy, develop a vested interest in them, and nurture them long past the period of whatever validity they may have had. The terms "productive credit," "pegs," "bills only," perhaps recall a few instances.

Confronted by an increasingly sophisticated public, the Fed may find the best course is to admit unashamedly that it has, as yet, no adequate theory of how monetary policy works. I say unashamedly because, although Federal Reserve economists should have been working much harder and longer on the problem than they have, no one else has an adequate theory either. If the Fed assumes a posture of humble agnosticism, it is likely to come out better in the long run. And it should feel perfectly at home with such a posture in today's relativist world distrustful of the old absolute values.

A third corollary which flows from this is that **the Federal Reserve must at all times be alert to society's changing values.**

Riesman, Glazer and Denney, in their influential study, *The Lonely Crowd,* drew the distinction between "inner-directed" and "other-directed" personalities. An inner-directed person is governed by absolute values and tradition. An other-directed person sees things in more relative terms and is influenced more by his peers.

If the Federal Reserve is to maintain values in conformity with those held by society, it will need to be more other-directed than in the past. This is not just a matter of information, but of attitude. Other-direction fosters an attitude of openness to change, of flexibility.

And it is a matter of involvement. As the economy becomes more and more complex, the Fed is increasingly tempted to withdraw into its specialty of monetary policy. Good arguments can be made for this course, but the institution will be stronger, I believe, if it is involved in other matters as well. Obviously, there must be limits. Not only could the Fed become over-committed and its efficiency impaired, but excessive involvement could produce severe conflicts of values and objectives, confusion, and a general weakening of purpose. On balance, however, the greater danger is that the Fed will become aloof. Such activities as bank supervision and truth in lending, troublesome though they may be, help to give it a sense of what is really going on, insights into the way other institutions really work, and how people are thinking.

A fourth corollary to Proposition 1 is that **the Federal Reserve**

should have confidence in its values, and its ability to establish them.[10]

In a recent convention of people concerned about social welfare, one speaker remarked on the attitude of young people toward theology.

> *If someone holding to the more traditional theology should attend an experimental liturgy on a campus, he would probably be horrified. The songs, the readings, dialogues, prayers, and homily would make as their chief emphasis: 1) how confident we can be that all of the barriers to true human life will be overcome, and 2) the awareness that God has given this task of breaking down barriers to us. The visitor would be sure that the students were guilty of colossal pride and that they had left Christianity far behind for a new humanism.*[11]

Today's young people are a remarkable lot, but in at least one important sense they are simply carrying on—in their own distinctive style, of course—what has been a trend over recent decades. In the realm of economics, at least, society has been less and less willing to subject itself to "economic laws" and "market forces" which appear to make the individual a helpless pawn. Not so long ago everyone believed that periodic recessions were inevitable; indeed, good for what ails us. But the Great Depression effectively destroyed the notion that widespread unemployment may be good medicine, and experience in the 1950's and 1960's has raised hopes that even mild recessions may not be inevitable. Society has been coming to believe it is master of its own destiny, and as the "new generation" takes over, this belief is likely to be intensified.

The Federal Reserve is not yet old enough to be preoccupied with its past heritage, but it is entering the dangerous age. Moreover, one can detect at times a latent persecution complex that, if permitted to develop, could prove debilitating. Sensitive to the fact that monetary policy must frequently frustrate people's plans and desires, Federal Reserve officials have been known to refer somewhat plaintively to their lack of popularity. They have said, for example, that the Fed is often in the position of the chaperone who removes the punchbowl just when the party is getting good. Also, in an understandable desire to have the public make a proper assessment of credit and blame for public policy, the Fed sometimes tends to underplay the extent of its powers.

---

[10] C. R. Whittlesey has argued elsewhere in this volume that for monetary policy to be effective it must be believed in. My point is complementary to his: the Federal Reserve must believe in its policy.

[11] Catherine L. Gunsalus, "A Theological and Campus Perspective on Changing Values," a talk given before the National Conference on Social Welfare, New York City, May 28, 1969, p. 6.

And, finally, there is the attrition in membership in the Federal Reserve System, a problem which makes no impression on many economists but which, I believe, is a cancer eating at the morale of the System. The problem is not—at least yet—one of a central bank losing control of the financial aggregates necessary to implement its policy, but one of an organization losing support of a major part of the community. The Federal Reserve does not exist to serve commercial banks, and a good economic case can be made that membership is unnecessary. Nevertheless, membership has been an important aspect of the System for over half a century, and its decline inevitably has a deteriorating effect within the Fed and on its image in the community—not the least of which is the political community. The Federal Reserve does, after all, live in a political world, and, like any public body, needs a strong, concerned, grass-roots support if it is itself to remain vital. The time is overdue to move vigorously and decisively to deal with the inequities created by present requirements for membership. Success in this effort would do much to increase the Fed's confidence in its ability to solve its problems.

A final corollary to Proposition 1 is that **the Federal Reserve must be responsive to the public through the political process.**

Officials of the Federal Reserve System are surrounded by certain safeguards designed to insulate them from the influence of party politics.[12] Yet it is clear that, as public servants, they must be involved in politics in the broad sense; they must respond to the wishes of the people as expressed through the political process. Mr. Dooley's comment that the Supreme Court watches the election returns, despite its note of cynicism, has real meaning for the Fed. The Federal Reserve is responsible to Congress which, in turn, is responsible to the people; and as the people express their wishes in elections, these wishes must influence Federal Reserve actions.

It is true that history demonstrates abundantly the abuses to which Government can subject money, and that the fathers of the Federal Reserve had this history clearly in mind when they made the Fed independent of the Executive Branch of Government. But they did not make the Federal Reserve independent of Government, and officials of the Federal Reserve System are very much aware of this.

---

[12] Albert L. Kraus has adopted Noam Chomsky's term, the New Mandarins, in describing Federal Reserve officials. Like the original governors of China, he says, they belong to a "secular priesthood" that is aloof from the people they serve. *New York Times*, April 9, 1969, p. 59.

They are less inclined to stress their "independence" than are many businessmen and bankers.

Nevertheless, the danger of becoming aloof is ever present.[13] It will be particularly important to guard against this tendency as the Federal Reserve becomes increasingly professionalized.

Professionalism

Proposition 2: **The Federal Reserve will be strong and effective in the long run to the extent that it fosters professionalism in its personnel.**

It is not enough for the Federal Reserve to want what society wants; it must have the technical competence to make good on those wants.

Congress long ago assigned to the Federal Reserve System various tasks of a highly technical nature which Congress felt it could not, and should not, undertake in detail itself. One of the advantages claimed for the regulatory commission approach always has been that it provides a means by which technical skill and expertise can be brought to bear on specific matters. The need for professional know-how is receiving even more attention today as the "knowledge explosion" grapples with the problems of an increasingly complex society.

The Federal Reserve demands professionals of many kinds in many fields—law, personnel, management, accounting, computer technique, to name only a few. In its conduct of monetary policy, it requires professionals in the field of economics, especially monetary economics. A number of years ago Fed personnel enjoyed outstanding reputations among professional economists; for a decade or so their standing seemed to deteriorate, but more recently it has improved. The Fed's research organizations have always been unsurpassed at intelligence gathering, but deficient at basic research. This gap is being slowly remedied. The greater number of economists among top decision-makers undoubtedly has contributed to the professionalization of the institution.

There are limits to professionalism, however, and this suggests a corollary to Proposition 2: **professionalism must be balanced with other values.**

---

[13] Bernstein concluded his study of independent regulatory commissions with this warning: ". . . the theory upon which the independence of the commission is based represents a serious danger to the growth of political democracy in the United States. The dogma of independence encourages support of the naive notion of escape from politics and substitution of the voice of the expert for the voice of the people." *Op. cit.,* p. 293.

Gardner indicates that one symptom of stagnation is that "how-to" becomes more important than "what to do"; technique supersedes purpose.[14] One can detect this symptom at times in the Federal Reserve. In open market operations, for example, technique in some respects becomes so sophisticated that there is danger of losing sight of the objective. Some critics have complained that the finesse of defensive operations gets in the way of an effective monetary policy.

This kind of thing happens because professionalism so often means specialization. The professional becomes intellectually involved in problems; he probes deeper and deeper, often passing the point of diminishing returns. Accordingly, any institution like the Fed must have its generalists, men with broad backgrounds who can see the big picture. If the professional can be both specialist and philosopher, so much the better, but this often is asking too much. This is one reason, undoubtedly, why Karl Bopp, himself an economist, has spoken of the need for some non-economists in top decisionmaking positions of the Federal Reserve organization. Another may be that the Fed must live and deal with many non-professionals. Reserve Banks must, for example, exist in their local communities. As their staffs become increasingly professional, as they pursue their interest in national monetary policy, there is a danger that they will lose touch, interest, and prestige in their communities.

If properly balanced, however, professionals can bring to the Fed the necessary characteristics for vitality—a creative attitude, a joy in playing with ideas regardless of the outcome—that lead to innovation. But an organization heavily composed of professionals must encourage freedom of thought, the heretical idea, and possess a decisionmaking machinery which gives a true sense of participation. This leads to my last proposition.

Decisionmaking

Proposition 3: **The Federal Reserve System will be strong and effective in the long run to the extent that decisions are made by a pluralistic process.**

John LeCarré, author of spy novels and former member of British intelligence, once made this revealing comment about espionage:

All our societies, even the American one, is administered by an extraordinarily lugubrious apparatus and the very development of events is controlled and paced by a pleasant human slowness and reluctance to take decisions, . . .

---

[14] *Op. cit.,* p. 47.

Now an efficient intelligence service moves at 20 times that pace and is frequently outrunning the decisive capacity of the people who should be controlling it. . . . frequently there is a short-time desirability to produce a revolution in a country X, but if it went through all the committee stages of bumbledom it is quite possible that one would reach a different decision.[15]

Only this, he says, prevents us moving from one international catastrophe to another.

It might be a backhanded compliment to the Federal Reserve System to say that only its complex decisionmaking machinery prevents it from moving from one monetary disaster to another. For there is no question that decisionmaking in the Fed—with the Reserve Banks and boards of directors, the Federal Open Market Committee, the Board of Governors, and staff all in the act in one way or another—is complex.

The dangers of multiple direction of an organization are fairly obvious. They include inconsistency of policy, delay, compromise, adherence to *status quo,* dissipation of enthusiasm and vitality, and general inefficiency.[16] It is not clear to me, however, that such results are inevitable. And even if there is a tendency in this direction, the disadvantages should be weighed against the advantages.

The main advantage of the pluralistic process is that decisions are more carefully considered. Each individual brings to bear on the common problem his own set of information, his own particular insights and interests.[17] As our society becomes increasingly complex, indeed, there is a serious question whether any other process will work.[18] Major decisions today require so much technical information, so many different kinds of expertise, that no one individual can be entrusted to make them. Finally, it often may be the case that the pluralistic process not only produces sounder decisions but more innovative ones.[19]

---

[15] *New York Times,* January 28, 1969, p. 46.

[16] Bernstein has observed all of these in regulatory agencies. *Op. cit.,* pp. 172-174.

[17] Charles E. Lindblom makes essentially this argument for what he calls "partisan mutual adjustment." *The Intelligence of Democracy* (New York: The Free Press, 1965).

[18] Philip E. Slater and Warren G. Bennis have concluded that because of growing complexity, "democracy is inevitable." *The Temporary Society* (New York: Harper & Row, 1968).

[19] John Gardner has written: "In an organization with many points of initiative and decision, an innovation stands a better chance of survival; it may be rejected by nine out of ten decision-makers and accepted by the tenth. If it then proves its worth, the nine may adopt it later." *Op. cit.,* p. 68.

All this suggests a corollary to Proposition 3: **the Federal Reserve should take maximum advantage of its federal structure.**

The fact that the Federal Reserve System resembles the United States Government in some important respects is no accident. The same fears of concentrated power induced the authors of both systems to build in a separation of powers and a federal structure. In both cases, however, the trend has been toward centralization, and a vital question for the future is how much further this trend can go without producing serious weakening.[20]

The Federal Reserve System has always been stronger for the fact that contributions to policy are made by many people from all parts of the country, not just in Washington. As formulation of monetary policy becomes increasingly difficult, as standards expected of the Fed become ever higher, as the System becomes involved in more and more activities of a complex nature outside of monetary policy *per se,* the Federal Reserve will need to rely increasingly on these contributions.

This is not just a matter of decentralization of work. The Board of Governors, for example, recently has passed on to the Reserve Banks some responsibilities in the field of bank supervision. More of this could be done. But a truly federal system requires that the sub-units contribute to the overall goal as a matter of right, not merely at the pleasure of the central unit. There is no real federalism unless " . . . local management derives its power and function from structural necessity, . . ."[21]

Not only does increasing complexity of the economy and the financial system enhance the unique role of the regional Reserve Banks as administrative units of the System and as centers of information, but it calls for continued participation of the Banks in the formulation of monetary policy. Because the Reserve Bank presidents serve on the

---

[20] Alexis de Tocqueville detected the weakness of centralization almost a century and a half ago: "Centralization imparts without difficulty an admirable regularity to the routine of business; provides skilfully for the details of the social police; represses small disorders and petty misdemeanors; maintains society in a *status quo* alike secure from improvement and decline; and perpetuates a drowsy regularity in the conduct of affairs, which the heads of the administration are wont to call good order and public tranquillity; in short, it excels in prevention, but not in action. Its force deserts it, when society is to be profoundly moved, or accelerated in its course; and if once the co-operation of private citizens is necessary to the furtherance of its measures, the secret of its impotence is disclosed." *Democracy in America* (New York: The New American Library, 1956), p. 67.

[21] Peter F. Drucker, *The New Society* (New York: Harper & Brothers, 1949), p. 275.

Open Market Committee as a matter of statutory responsibility, they are much more effective than if they were to participate simply as advisers to the Board of Governors.

*   *   *   *   *   *   *

As a prescription for a vigorous, long life, the foregoing propositions undoubtedly overlook many important ingredients; yet they are, I believe, the essential ones. Perhaps the most hopeful thing about them is that they require nothing radically new, but basically a continuation of what the Federal Reserve has been doing. The Fed *has* changed its values over the years. It *has* been developing an increasingly professional attitude toward its task. And it *does* follow a pluralistic approach in making decisions. What is needed is to be more prompt and sensitive in changing its values, to broaden and deepen its professionals' knowledge of the economic process, and to make even greater use of its federal structure.

All this, of course, is harder to do than it sounds. Many trade-offs must be made along the way. To become too professionalized runs a risk of losing touch with society's values. A decisionmaking apparatus that permits too-long deliberation over too many views cannot adapt promptly as these values change. But the path to the good life is strewn with hard choices. The Fed has made many wrong ones along the way, but if it can better its percentage of right ones, it can look forward to a long and useful existence.